CHECK-RAISING THE DEVIL

CHECK-RAISING
THE DEVIL

MIKE MATUSOW
with Amy Calistri and Tim Lavalli

CARDOZA PUBLISHING

FIRST EDITION
Third Printing

Copyright © 2009 by Mike Matusow
—All Rights Reserved—

Library of Congress Catalog No: 2008940741
ISBN 10: 1-58042-261-6
ISBN 13: 978-1-58042-261-1

Cover photo by Rob Gracie / GreasieWheels.com

Cardoza Publishing is the foremost gaming and gambling publisher in the world with a library of over 200 up-to-date and easy-to-read books and strategies. These authoritative works are written by the top experts in their fields and with more than 10 million books in print, represent the best-selling and most popular gaming books anywhere.

Visit www.cardozabooks.com for a full list of titles.

CARDOZA PUBLISHING
P.O. Box 98115, Las Vegas, NV 89193
Toll Free Phone (800) 577-WINS
email: cardozabooks@aol.com
www.cardozabooks.com

This book

is dedicated to

my Mom and Dad,

and all my real friends who helped me

through the rough times

Acknowledgements

Putting this book together wouldn't have been possible without a lot of people giving us their support and assistance. Mike wishes to acknowledge his parents, Bernie and Gloria Matusow, for everything they have given him throughout his life. We all want to thank Jessica Lee for her support and understanding. How many times did she come home to find someone with an audio recorder talking to Mike about yet another poker tournament. Rich Belsky has taken on a lot of the business necessities of bringing this book to your hands. Our literary agent, Sheree Bykofsky has ably ushered three new authors through the publishing terrain.

We also want to thank the "Poker Boyz" for their early, middle and late reads of the manuscript. Your suggestions, questions and laughter helped more than you know. Thanks to: Mike Englerth, Bill Moloney, Randy Glover, Joel Nease, Bill Curry, Dan Lavalli, Matt Garoian and Bob Close. Then there is the editorial team at Cardoza Publishing: Avery, Dana and Annie—not to worry I am sure we will all be back on speaking terms in a year or so.

We also want to strongly acknowledge the contribution of Michael Craig to both the successful beginning and the ultimate completion of this project.

Particularly for our non-poker addicted readers, we have added a short glossary. Poker and psychological terms in the text that may not be familiar to you have been defined in this section. We hope this will help you follow the very jargon-infused world of poker.

Finally, the names of most of the real-life characters have been changed to protect both the innocent and the guilty. Professional poker players and public figures were not changed, but all of Mike's girlfriends and other celebrants were. We would note that Sergeant Mike Gennaro and Mike Vento are unchanged names. (Purely by coincidence, the Mike Vento in this book has the identical name of a former poker manager in the Orleans and Palms poker rooms and is not to be confused with same.)

Table of Contents

Foreword: Mike the Mouth's Heart of Gold 9

1   Dead End Dreams 15

2   Drugs and Disorders 17

3   High on Poker 21

4   The Grind 27

5   Other People's Money 35

6   The Almost Bracelet 43

7   Hard Lessons at theFinal Table 49

8   On My Own 57

9   I Have a Dream 63

10   Out of the Shadow 71

11   Cards Make You, Egos Break You 79

12   The Day That ChangedMy Life 85

13   Main Event Meth 97

14   Without a Net 111

15   Stuey's Ghost 123

16   Up for Another Series 129

17   Last Tango in Paris 135

18   Judas Revealed 147

19   A Phone Call in the Alps 161

20   Playing on the Precipice 167

21   Island Payday 177

22   Six Months Flat 189

23   Last Dance at the Horseshoe 201

24 A Champion's Vindication 215
25 Bipolar Poker 229
26 My "Dark" Series 237
27 A Series of Changes 243
28 WSOP: A New View 251
29 Now I Know 257
Glossary 263

Foreword

By Phil Hellmuth, Jr.
1989 WSOP Champion and 11-Time Gold Bracelet Winner

Mike the Mouth's Heart of Gold

The first time I ever noticed Mike "The Mouth" Matusow was at the final table of the 1998 WSOP (World Series of Poker), when he was in the stands watching the man he had staked, Scotty Nguyen, try to take down the World Championship and the $1 million first-place prize. I was in the ESPN booth announcing play at the final table when I heard a great story through the grapevine: Mike and a partner had put Scotty into the tournament at the last minute, and now they stood to cash in a $667,000 ticket. The rest of the story is the stuff of legends: Scotty won it all after moving all in on a 9-8-8-9-8 board and telling his lone opponent, Kevin McBride, "You call this one and it's all over, baby!"

McBride called, Scotty showed him J-9 to claim the title, and Matusow suddenly had $333,000 in his pockets.

But what would Mike, the former poker dealer, do with $333,000? We all knew the answer to that question. He would blow it, of course! Nothing personal, regarding Matusow. It's simply a fact of life: money doesn't like people who get rich for the first time. But to everyone's surprise, three years later Mike had not only held onto that $333,000, he had built it up to over $800,000 in cash. In fact, he seemed like a poker genius as he mowed down the high-limit players while playing in mixed games like HOE (hold'em, Omaha 8-or-better, stud 8-or-better) that featured his game of choice: limit Omaha 8-or-better. There is no doubt in my mind that Matusow is the best all-around live limit Omaha 8-or-better player in the world these last ten years.

With tons of money, great results against the world's best poker players in the side games, and a seemingly bright future ahead, Matusow began playing in no-limit hold'em tournaments, where he played "his way" and became a force to be reckoned with. In fact, Matusow seemed to be the chip leader in almost every no-limit hold'em tournament that he entered, by using a super-aggressive strategy. If Mike felt weakness when you played a pot against him, he would raise you, reraise you, or move all in on you. A force he was, but as much as the top pros in the world admired the strong work he was putting in, Matusow simply wasn't putting any skins on the wall (no victories!) in no-limit hold'em tournaments. Eventually, Mike became a bit of a joke as he "blew up," time and time again. He would move all in, in a hopeless situation, and give away a couple of huge cornstalks of chips, for no apparent reason. ESPN commentator Norman Chad called it the "Matusow blow up," and the world watched as Mike accumulated mountains of chips and then gave them away in one spectacular, lightning-quick meltdown.

As poker grew in popularity, Mike became a bigger and bigger name, and not only because he provided great "When will Mike blow up?" entertainment. He also had a way of insulting players at the table, a hangover from his days playing side games. Back in the day, when any new player sat down at the table to play in a side game with Matusow, Mike would do two things. First, he would insult the new player who sat down, saying something like, "We've been waiting for a sucker like you to sit down at the table! Thank God you're here, now I can win an extra $20,000!" Second, he would insult the players who were already at the table. "Don't worry about it, buddy, as bad as you are, the other players at the table are all morons! You have moron number one who doesn't know how to play hold'em, moron number two who is a tournament player, and moron number three who is no-talent billionaire." But the more you played with Mike, the more you knew that his greetings were just a lot of bluster. Occasionally, though, he would rattle a few players and get them off of their "A game."

This abrupt way of insulting players when he greeted them did not hold Matusow in good stead in the poker world. But as the poker world got to know Mike better, we realized that he really did have a heart of gold. He felt empathy for players when they lost big or fell short of their goals, even going so far as to find players after they busted out of a final table, to give them a kind word of support. He also loaned out money and gave encouragement to guys who needed it. He was there for a ton of guys on the poker tour when they needed someone to talk to. And you could see the pain that he felt when he fell short of his own goals, or blew up one more time in a major tournament. Like when he would cry on ESPN because he was eliminated from the main event. As it became known that Matusow actually had a heart of gold, his insults began to lose their bite; the poker world had come to realize that Mike's insults were all bark and no bite. But when he went after Greg Raymer on ESPN (after bluffing him) in the 2004 WSOP, saying, "I have big cajones, you have little itty bitty cajones," while he held up his thumb and finger just a millimeter apart, he left quite an impression on the worldwide public.

I believe the public thought, "So, Mike really is 'The Mouth!' The Mouth is a serious trash talker!" What the world didn't see, or know, was that Raymer (now the 2004 World Champion) and Matusow became fast friends after that. Although Raymer felt some bite at the time, he later realized that with Mike, it was all bark.

In the early 2000s, I would talk about poker strategy with only a handful of players, and eventually I discussed strategy only with Matusow, because he was the only player who would consider throwing away pocket aces before the flop in a deep-stack no-limit hold'em tournament when another player moved all in. Both Mike and I knew that you could pick up gobs of chips "risk free" back then through skillful bluffing, so why would you settle for being a four-and-a-half-to-one favorite with pocket aces? Of course, we both reached the conclusion that we had to play pocket aces all in, but the fact that he was the only guy who would consider folding them preflop for an all in made me feel like I could talk strategy with him. Above all, Mike understood that winning no-limit hold'em tournaments was about picking up chips "risk free."

But in 2002, out of nowhere, Matusow's world suddenly came tumbling down! He was partying day and night. He was hanging out with strippers and doing drugs. He had found the seedy underbelly of Las Vegas, and he embraced it. He and a group of young poker players claimed that a drug nicknamed "crank" (methamphetamines) made them indestructible at the poker table. And crank did seem to make them indestructible, as they won millions of dollars in the side games in mere months. But then it ceased to work, and the next thing you knew these young guys were broke. Even worse, they were now addicted to crank. Matusow, too, had managed to go broke, he was now addicted to crank, and on top of that he began to talk about going to jail for dealing drugs! When Mike told me that he was pretty much innocent, I believed him. I was certainly convinced that Mike was no drug dealer. He was a top poker player, with means.

In any case, Matusow had now hit bottom, and perhaps a jail stretch in early 2005 was the healthiest thing that could have happened to him. He stopped partying, he did his time like a man, and he set his mind to making a huge comeback in the poker world. In 2001, I had been at the final table of the WSOP main event with Mike, so when I faced him at the final table of the 2005 Tournament of Champions, I knew the difference. In the Matusow of 2005 I saw a different player; he was a better, stronger, more disciplined, and more mature player. His rededication to poker, his avoidance of drugs and alcohol, and his all-around cleaner lifestyle paid off when he took down the 2005 Tournament of Champions title.

But Mike would relapse, though I don't mean to drugs and alcohol! He relapsed into negativity, and he seemed to be stuck there for a year or two. As he struggled to break even while playing more than a hundred hours a week of online poker, first at UltimateBet. com, but later at FullTiltPoker.com, he became famous for lines that focused on how much luck there is in poker. He had forgotten that he had once won 45 straight times in the side games. He had forgotten the power of the skill quotient in poker. Lines like, "I don't know why I bother, some idiot is going to suck out on me every time" and "Being good don't make no difference, a donkey can beat you with anything," became his theme. Then, in early 2008, I was there playing at the table of a filming of a *Poker after Dark* episode, where Gavin Smith told Matusow, "Of course you lost that pot! And the reason why is that you expect to lose those key pots!"

Just a few days later, while we shot another *Poker after Dark* episode, Matusow came out with a brand-new super-positive attitude, and the results were amazing! He won that episode, his first ever. He won $1 million playing online poker in one month at FullTiltPoker. com. He also won a $100,000 weight-loss bet against Ted Forrest, which required him to go from 240 pounds to 180 to collect. He won his third WSOP bracelet—in no-limit deuce-to-seven lowball. He beat nearly 6,800 players to reach the final three tables of the 2008 WSOP main event. And he won the hearts of poker fans everywhere with his new positive attitude and his comeback to the winner's circle. It was as if Mike lost money when he felt negative, and won money when he felt positive. But this is a subject for another book!

Check-Raising the Devil is Mike's up-and-down story of rock-star-like partying and excess, success at the highest levels of the poker world, a monstrous fall from the mountain, and a huge comeback all the way back to the top of the mountain. Today, most of you sincerely like Mike "The Mouth" Matusow—but love him or hate him, you will not be able to put this book down!

Chapter One

Dead End Dreams

My story starts in a trailer park out toward Boulder Highway, in a dead-end patch of Las Vegas where people never lived their dreams, if they even had any. There were old people living there, families with too many kids, and people who didn't seem to be going anywhere in life. People like me, hanging out and chilling, wondering what their next move would be. I'd hang out with my dog, that is, until he died, and watched TV until I fell asleep. My meals were generally junk food or pizza, or I'd grab something at the Showboat or Sam's Town, casinos where I tried to buy hope one quarter at a time.

I played video poker every night, pumping quarters into machines until I had no more to feed. I was twenty-three years old, living paycheck to paycheck, and dumping whatever money that didn't go to basic necessities into the machines. Every penny of it. Day after day, that was my life.

Five days a week, I worked at my parents' furniture store, always coming in late, always counting down the hours until I could get back to the machines. After the casino, I went back home, and waited until the next day rolled around. One day was not much different than another.

I didn't have much of a future. Fuck, I didn't have much of a present. Then one day, everything changed.

Chapter Two

Drugs and Disorders

I was living the life of a rock star: strippers and sex with lots of hot women, wild parties, jet-setting around the world, playing high-stakes poker with million-dollar wins, and throwing money around like it was confetti. I took drugs; lots of drugs. At times that lifestyle was great, like a fantasy come true. I can't deny it. That was one part of my world. The other part of my world, what the public didn't see, was much different. I'd be lying in bed in such despair that I'd be unable to move, so deeply depressed that even a trip from the bed to the kitchen seemed just too damn far. I was able to climb the poker celebrity ladder with "The Mouth" persona and win three World Series of Poker bracelets, but I will always be fucked up, thanks to drugs.

As a result of my drug abuse, I have Attention Deficit Hyperactivity Disorder (ADHD), which makes it difficult for me to concentrate. I didn't have this as a kid although that's when most people develop it. Kids with ADHD usually outgrow it when they get to be teenagers, but I developed this disorder as an adult, the direct result of drug use. I found out the hard way that drugs can cause brain damage. They can change the wiring in your brain. After you stop, some of that wiring changes back over time, but some of it never returns. Short-term memory and the ability to focus are things that don't usually come back.

I've done some really dumb things and made some really bad decisions in my life—the drugs, the wild parties, jail, and my ridiculous obsession with sports betting—but what I didn't know when I was holed up in my trailer was that I had a problem bigger than I could imagine.

I have bipolar disorder, which wasn't diagnosed until 2003. I've had it since early adulthood, which is when most people develop it. Bipolar disorder isn't a product of lifestyle, a brain injury, or anything I've done to myself. I was born with the genes to develop it. I didn't have any of the symptoms as a kid, and was never treated for any mental problems growing up. I was pretty normal back then, or so my family says.

When I first started playing with Daniel Negreanu in the '90s, he told me he had never seen anybody with higher highs and lower lows. It seemed like it had always been that way for me. I can't tell you the very first time I noticed the symptoms, but I can trace it back to some of my earliest days in poker. And it wasn't just that I was high after a win and low after a loss. Winning and losing didn't seem to have that much to do with it. I could have a huge winning session and be telling everybody at the table that I was the greatest player in the world. Hours later, I could be back in my trailer suffering a crippling depression, barely able to speak or move.

I knew something wasn't right; nobody could be that extreme emotionally, all the time. I just didn't know what to do about it.

They say that professional poker players always need to have control over their emotions whether they're winning or losing. But I never had real control. Other people talked about being happy, but I was never, ever happy—not in that "everything's going to be all right" kind of way. Even if I was okay at the time, I always felt that depression was lurking right around the corner. And when it snuck up on me, my only escape was to return to the tables. Poker was the only relief, the only therapy I knew and trusted.

Ending up on a mix of street drugs is pretty common for people with bipolar disorder. I know that now. But back then it was just a way to escape the depression.

But, of course, there would be a price to pay. Before the drugs, I was sharp. I didn't forget anything. I could sit down and play against someone and remember what and how he played eight months later. That's what made me one of the best in the world when I was on my game. Now I'm lucky if I can remember what happened yesterday. I can tell you the odds of any hand, but most days I can't find my shoes—and I might even forget that I'm looking for them three times before I actually find them. It sucks that I fucked up my brain like this, but it is what it is. I can't go back and change what I did.

Maybe things would have been different if I had gotten help back then, but I couldn't get help for a problem I didn't know I had. I'd have to hit absolute bottom before that help would come, and if things had played out slightly differently than they did, it might have been too late. There were long periods when my life seemed like a repeating series of depressing hours, days and weeks. Sometimes it got to the point where there seemed like only one way out of the darkness. I never actually tried to take my life—maybe I was too scared, or maybe I was simply too depressed to take action—but suicide hung around my life for way too many years.

I suppose if things had happened in a slightly different way, I wouldn't be writing this book. Someone else would, and he would have said it was a shame about Mike Matusow. Here was this sometimes brilliant but troubled poker player with tremendous potential who let himself get beaten down by drugs, like Stu Ungar who lost out to his own demons. I knew about Stuey, three-time World Champion of Poker, and I knew I didn't want to be like him, dying way before his time in a cheap motel room, penniless, and pumped full of drugs. But the similarities between his life and mine were getting too fucking close for comfort.

Today, I am ten times the fundamental player I was back then. Experience has taught me a lot about poker, but who knows how much better a player I would be today if I hadn't done all the drugs? There were times when I know the drugs made me a better player, but it didn't last. Then again, who knows what my life would have been without poker. Maybe I would be running my own furniture store. Or maybe I would have put a bullet in my head long ago after one more pathetic losing night at video poker. But I did drugs and fried my brain, that's all on me. You'll never catch me making an excuse for it. Of all the stupid things I've done in my life, and I've done a lot of stupid things, doing drugs was by far the stupidest.

Most stories that start in a trailer park end there. But one night I found poker, or poker found me. It's taken me on a wild ride.

Luckily, it's one that I'm still alive to tell you about.

Chapter Three

High on Poker

I moved out of my parents' house when I was eighteen and lived in an apartment with a couple of friends. In 1991, I moved into the trailer by myself, where I would live for the next seven years. I guess people will think it's weird that I was still living in a trailer once I started playing some of the bigger cash games in Vegas and even after my first final table at the World Series of Poker. But I was almost painfully shy, I didn't party, and I was uncomfortable around people, so living alone really worked for me.

When I worked for my parents, I was supposed to be at the store when it opened at nine a.m., which meant I usually got in around ten o'clock. I would sit in the office and wait for people to come in and try to sell them furniture or carpet. Sometimes I did the measurements for carpet installations, and when the regular help didn't show up, I'd also make furniture deliveries. Since the regular help was my brother, who made even me look like a hard worker, I went out on deliveries a lot. Deliveries really sucked because I wasn't very muscular. Even today, I'm just not a strong guy.

When we finished working for the day, my brother or sometimes my parents and I would hit a casino. Once in a while, we'd play bingo or go bowling. But mostly, we would walk across the street to the Showboat or drive over to Sam's Town, where I would play video poker. My results were always the same. I'd take the hundred bucks I'd made at the store and blow it on video poker at night. I always lost, but I couldn't stop playing. And I was always broke. Doing a little extra work at the store or getting an advance on my pay became a regular thing. I was almost always at least a couple of weeks ahead on my paycheck from my parents.

It was as depressing as it sounds. A couple of times, I actually went to Gamblers Anonymous. Thinking back on that now, I probably was in worse shape than even I thought. I mean, it takes a lot to get a twenty-one-year-old kid to show up at a G.A. meeting on his own. It did help me gain some control and perspective, but I eventually stopped going. After all, they wanted to cure my gambling and all I really wanted to cure was my depression. I was pretty sure they couldn't help me with that. I loved gambling—what I wanted to give up was losing. I guess that's how all degenerate gamblers think.

One night, I was slouched in my usual seat in front of a video poker machine at Sam's Town, cursing my luck, and well on my way to losing my nightly $100 when Phil Samaroff sat down at the next machine. I recognized Phil as one of the Sam's Town regulars and we started talking.

"How would you like to learn how to do something where you'll never have to work for the rest of your life?" he asked after a while.

Really sounds dumb, doesn't it? But that's exactly how he said it. I've never forgotten those words. *How would you like to learn to do something where you will never have to work again?*

I laughed. "Of course I'm interested!"

"Have you ever heard of the World Series of Poker?"

I was a big sports fan and watched ESPN a lot so I had seen poker on TV, but I hadn't really paid too much attention.

"Well, there's a game called Texas hold'em and I can teach you how to play," he said. "If you're any good at it, you'll never have to worry about money again."

Phil and I got up from those video poker machines and walked over to the Sam's Town poker room. He bought in for a rack of $1 chips and sat down at a table. I took a seat behind him and my poker education began.

I think about that sometimes, how things just happen. Maybe I would have tried poker when it got to be big time. Maybe someone would have told me about it or I would have stumbled into a poker room on my own. Whatever. But in 1991 Phil sat down next to me at a video poker machine and offered to show me how to play. And that's how I got started in poker.

By pure chance.

In our first session, Phil basically showed me his hole cards and answered my questions. I had plenty of questions. I knew hand rankings from playing video poker, but everything else was pretty foreign to me. Today, the average ten-year old knows more about poker than I did back then. As I watched Phil play, there was a lot to take in—the movement of the dealer button, how the blinds worked, and the whole concept of community cards. Just the rules were confusing to me. On a video poker machine, you play every hand all the way through to the end; you never fold. In this game, people folded. A few times, I saw Phil fold the same hand preflop that I'd seen him play earlier.

Phil explained a lot of the mechanics in that first session. But when it came to strategy, I didn't get many direct answers. In between hands, Phil talked a lot about starting hands and position. The same starting hand could be a keeper or a piece of crap, depending on where you played it from. While I had no clue about starting hands, I totally got the idea that hold'em was a game about strength and weakness. I was absorbed by the thought that timing, not just the cards you were dealt, mattered in this game. As I sat there and watched, it was like someone was showing me a jigsaw puzzle piece by piece. I had to learn more about the pieces, but I could already see the big picture.

Within the first hour, I was completely hooked.

It seemed like most of the guys at the table thought poker was about showing down the best hand on the river. It was so obvious to me, even then, that there was another level to this game. Until that night, I didn't even know Texas hold'em was played in the casinos, but as I watched, I started to feel that I had secretly known the game my whole life. Phil had a winning session, in spite of my asking about a thousand bonehead questions. For a shy and quiet guy, I couldn't shut up at the poker table.

After our first session, Phil told me to buy David Sklansky's *Hold'em Poker* and memorize the starting hands. To this day, that might be the only poker book I've ever read. Kids starting out today can read dozens of great books on hold'em and play thousands of free hands online before they commit a dime of their money to poker. And a lot of the younger players have a bunch of friends who started playing at the same time they did. As a group they live, breathe, read, post, IM, and talk about poker all day long. But when I was learning, not that many people played and there were only a few books about hold'em. I'd bet that other than Phil, there weren't that many players at Sam's Town, or anywhere else for that matter, who'd read even one poker book. People basically learned poker over a couple of hundred hands at a kitchen table before they found their way into a casino poker room. I was starting out with an edge; I had a book and I had Phil.

Sklansky's book gave me the basics, which meant that over the next couple of sessions, Phil got fewer questions about each hand he played. I still had a lot to learn, but after the third or fourth session watching Phil, I was itching to play on my own. Phil told me I should wait, but I wanted to get in the action. So I made up a starting hand cheat sheet, which told me which hands I should play and from which position.

After about a week of sitting behind Phil, I took my cheat sheet and sat down at my first poker table. It was really weird—I was a natural. In my whole life, I hadn't felt confident about anything. But on the very first day of playing poker, that changed. I had finally found something special that gave my life purpose, something that I was good at, something I was pumped up about. I just knew that my life was about to change.

I won my first session.

After a couple more sessions, I edited my cheat sheet down to a manageable size and played with it taped to the palm of my left hand. From the start, I made moves that a beginning poker player probably didn't make, especially back then. Maybe it was because I kept checking my cheat sheet, no one at the table gave me credit for bluffing or trapping. It probably drove players crazy to get beat by a kid. I had to look like the biggest fish at the table.

There were two parts of the game that were second nature to me. Reading other players seemed so simple. At the time, I didn't realize it was a special skill; I thought everyone had a good idea about what other players had. The other thing that came naturally to me was the idea of betting players off a hand. A chip wasn't money, it was a weapon. That seemed so obvious. In my first weeks, I could put a guy on A-K and bet him off the hand when he missed the flop. What could be easier?

I won my first week and I killed my first month. I was winning so much and so often, I began to wrap my whole life around poker. It was like a drug—actually, it was better than a drug. I say that in hindsight because, back then, I'd never done drugs; I barely took aspirin. But every part of me craved poker and every session gave me an unbelievable high. Before I knew it, I was playing poker six hours a day, seven days a week. I played in a $1/$4/$8/$8 game; I didn't know there were bigger games. I was so out of touch. I lived in Vegas and I didn't even know what high-stakes poker was. All I knew was the poker room at Sam's Town; that was my poker world.

From losing my $100 paycheck every day at video poker, I started winning every day. I was making about $500 a week playing poker. If you figure in the money I wasn't losing anymore, it was almost like having an extra grand a week. That was life-changing money for me; I was on top of the world. Of course, I had no idea what the world of poker was really like at the top

Phil had taught me the fundamentals of solid poker, now I worked on improving my game. Once I was playing the right hands in the right position, all I had to do was watch other players. I watched what they played and how they bet; it didn't take me long to get a read on them. I loved it. The more I played, the more I won. I started skipping work at the store, which pissed off my parents. I wouldn't show up half the time, because every hour at the store was an hour away from poker.

I lived to play poker. I played for the pure love of the game. It was like I was playing on a rush all the time. I loved to win. I loved to beat everybody.

For the first time in my life, I was better at something than other people. There are some great players that burn out or disappear from poker. It's hard to maintain the constant desire to win, and you need that to play poker at its highest levels. I think some people get bored or find they need more out of life.

But from that first time I sat down at a table, poker became my life.

Chapter Four

The Grind

Near the end of my first year in poker, I won my first tournament at Sam's Town for $10,000, a huge amount of money to me. That victory was an unbelievable high. It was a freeroll, so the casino put up the money for the prize pool. Sam's Town was my home poker room and most of the players in the tournament had played against me in cash games. At the time, they all thought I was the best player and was a lock to win the event. But even then, I knew that once the cards are in the air, reputation doesn't mean too much.

During that tournament, I was given my first nickname. I wasn't Mike "The Mouth" Matusow, the nickname I'm known by today. The players at Sam's Town started calling me "Primetime." This was when Deion Sanders, the real "Primetime," was playing football for the Atlanta Falcons and baseball for the Braves. While I never much cared for that nickname, I liked that I actually had one; it made me feel like a part of something.

Later, just before poker got big, Todd Brunson and Curtis Bibb started calling me Mike "Loud Mouth" Matusow. I definitely didn't like that nickname, which is exactly why they used it—Todd still calls me that today. My mouth opened the minute I walked into a poker room, and that was never going to change. But I was afraid that when television started to pick up on poker, the "Loud Mouth" nickname might catch on. So I managed to insert Mike "The Mouth" Matusow into a couple of conversations and thankfully everyone liked it.

It fit, right? Although I actually gave myself "The Mouth" nickname, I guess I'd have to give Todd and Curtis credit for the assist.

I still remember my "Primetime" tournament win at Sam's Town, not just because it was my first win, but because of how I won it. The tournament was half stud and half hold'em. In the middle of the event I was down to a single chip, which I had to put in as an ante for a stud hand; the blinds were 200/400 with a 25 ante. With that one lonely chip, I won the antes. On the next hand I put another ante in and bet the rest of my chips. I won again.

Then the tournament switched over to hold'em. On the very first hand, I was dealt a pocket pair, and flopped a set. I won and doubled my chip stack. The very next hand, I got another pocket pair, flopped another set and more than doubled up again against two players. On the third hand I got dealt my third straight pocket pair, flopped a third straight set and nearly doubled up again.

I went from a single chip to the chip leader of the tournament in five hands. Totally amazing.

From there I cruised to my first tournament victory and ten grand. It's one thing to walk away from a cash game with more chips than you started with, but it's a whole different monster high to be the only one left standing at the end of a tournament.

In my first few years, I played what I call great instinct poker and great laydown poker. I totally trusted my reads; I had such a good feel for what my opponents were holding. I just knew when I was beat and I made the laydown. When I had the best hand, I'd raise, reraise and reraise again. I punished my opponents. Poker players today call that "controlled aggression" and the best pros in poker play that way. But few players used that style when I first started playing, which probably made it even more effective. In his heyday, the great Stu Ungar was the master of controlled aggression. I didn't know about Stuey until I was able to watch him play in 1997, when he won the World Series of Poker Championship.

Eventually I started to use pot odds more in my game. Pot odds takes into account the cost of a bet compared to the amount of money already in the pot, and the percentages of winning the hand. I'm not a big fan of pot odds, although I use it and know the winning percentages like the back of my hand. But I swear I was probably a better player before I learned all that.

When I knew what everybody had and when I was beat, I made the laydown. And maybe that wasn't right if you consider the pot odds—but forget the pot odds. Say you're 4 to 1 to hit your card with one pull at the deck. Forget what's in the fucking pot! You gotta get lucky. My instincts told me that when you gotta get lucky with only one more chance to catch your card, you're supposed to fold. You're not supposed to give away that extra bet, and that's how I played. I think nowadays, too many players rely strictly on pot odds and percentages. And that hurts their game. They begin to trust the numbers more than they trust their reads. Poker is about maximizing the pot when you have the best hand and releasing when you're beat. You earn a lot of money in limit cash games by not losing that extra bet. When I was a great limit hold'em player, I never gave away that extra bet.

They say if you fold once and you're wrong, you gotta be right maybe twenty times to make up for it. But if you start calling all the time because you're worried about being wrong, you'll find yourself paying off all the time. When I first started, I made some of the sickest laydowns, and I was always right.

Now I have to give away the extra bet because I'm not sure of myself. I really don't know what anybody has anymore, not like I used to. I like to blame it on pot odds and getting away from my instincts, but it could just be that the game has changed so much since I first started playing. Daniel Negreanu says the players today are harder to read because they play so many hands. Maybe they're better now. Or maybe they're just tougher to read because they're a bunch of idiots who don't know what they are doing. Nobody folds now. They think every raise is a bluff.

When the World Series drew over 250 players for the first time in 1994, Johnny Moss, a poker legend from Texas and the first winner of the WSOP championship, told me, "Kid, it's getting so big, whoever catches a card is going to win." His words are even truer today. More than it ever was, winning is getting to be about who catches cards at the right time. I guess any way you look at it, the game has changed.

In those first couple of years, I continued to play and beat the limit cash games, but eventually the grind set in. It was becoming harder to make money, mostly because I wasn't enjoying it as much and my attention at the tables would wander. Everyone, and I mean everyone, who tries to make a living playing cash games, eventually hits the wall. Poker becomes one long grind, day after day. For me, it was starting to be a struggle to make that $500 each week.

Poker had become a job.

Just when I was having my first problems grinding out a profit at poker, I got whacked out of the blue by a relationship. I had a horrible break-up. Julie and I had been dating for about six months and I was completely in love with her. When the relationship started, my poker playing was going great. I had more money then I'd ever had before. We were having a great time together; at least I thought we were. Then with no warning and no explanation, she dumped me. I felt like someone had slammed me in the head with a two by four. I had no clue why it ended and she wouldn't talk to me. My whole world had shattered.

That was the beginning of maybe eight years where I just didn't date. I didn't want to get hurt like that again. I always had problems with low self-esteem and that break-up pushed it down even lower. Eight years sounds like a long time to get over a girl, but with me, emotionally, it's always been all or nothing. When I commit to something or someone, I'm all in. It's the same reason why, after playing poker for more than fifteen years, you'll still see me cry sometimes when I bust out of a tournament. When I put everything I've got into something, I'm devastated when I have to walk away empty.

After the break-up, I tried to refocus all my energy into poker, but the painful grind continued. My earnings started to drop. I'd been playing and earning for nearly two years, but I didn't think I could rely on just playing poker much longer. And I certainly wasn't going back to the store.

My friend, Glenn Denno, offered to teach me how to deal poker. Poker dealers had always been sitting right there in front of me and I knew a lot of them, but I had never thought of dealing myself. I was too wrapped up in playing the game. Dealing was a way to back away from the grind, but still be involved with the game I loved. Glenn was a dealer at Sam's Town, which had the best poker-dealing jobs in town. Before all the locals-friendly casinos opened away from the Las Vegas Strip, Sam's Town was the place where all the locals played. You made good tips and it was an easy $800 a week job.

I could grind out $400 to $500 a week playing poker or I could be around poker and earn twice as much a week, dealing.

The decision was a no-brainer.

The poker room manager at Sam's Town let me train there late at night, during the graveyard shift when nobody was around. Glenn would teach me an hour or two a night. I already had a good head start because I knew the game, but he taught me stuff like how to box shuffle and pitch the cards. I wanted to work at Sam's Town, but I needed to get experience somewhere else first, so they sent me off to the Gold Coast to audition. The Gold Coast was the only place that ran regular tournaments in 1993 and it was a good low-limit house. I was a nervous wreck during the audition, but I got the job on my first try. Like most of the casinos, there was a three month probation period.

I started off by dealing tournaments and some cash games five days a week. The poker room shift manager didn't like me much, mostly because I talked a lot in the box and my voice carried. Just before my three months were up, I walked in for my regular shift and he fired me. I learned that they did that all the time: You'd get fired just before the end of the probation period so they wouldn't have to pay your insurance. I got my next job at Palace Station and the same thing happened: I got fired right before the end of my probation. In fact, I got fired the day after I asked for Rosh Hashanah off. My boss gave me a hard time about not being able to work on the Jewish holiday and at one point I thought I overheard him call me a derogatory name. But when he fired me, I didn't push the issue, I let it go. I didn't want to work with people like that anyway.

I talked a lot at the Gold Coast and they had warned me about my big mouth, but I didn't feel like I did anything wrong to lose the Palace Station job. So, I talked with the poker room manager at Sam's Town. He was also concerned that I'd talk too much in the box and that I might annoy the regulars, but he took a chance and hired me. I promised him I would watch my mouth and it ended up working out fine. I used to play with those people all the time, so they already knew me and they liked me. It became more of a family situation. People would actually play at my table to talk and hang out with our group of regulars. After getting canned at my first two dealing jobs, the whole experience of being accepted at Sam's Town helped build my self-esteem. I really liked being there and the first three months were great.

After about six months on the job, the urge to play started to outweigh the desire to deal. I heard they were spreading $10/$20 and $20/$40 games downtown at Binion's Horseshoe. I'd never played higher than $1/$4/$8/$8 limit hold'em, but one day I decided to make the move. I took $1,000 to the 'Shoe, a lot of money to me at the time, and sat down in the $10/$20 limit game. I was petrified. To me, that was the biggest game in the world. I was dealing for a little more than $100 a day, and suddenly I was playing for $100 a hand. It was a monster jump.

I wasn't sure I was ready, but there was only one way to find out.

I played for about nine hours that first session and lost $470. I didn't win a hand. Not one. But I thought I played good and I didn't give my money away. I just didn't catch any cards and I knew it. I wasn't discouraged and I didn't think my shot at moving up was over. The next two or three sessions, I ended up winning a decent amount. I started to realize that the game wasn't that tough. For one thing, a lot of players were using the $10/$20 game to move up in limits and they played tight and scared. I must have won 90 percent of my sessions those first few months.

It became much harder to deal for a hundred-dollar bill each day once I started playing $10/$20. Just like it had been hard to go to work at the family store when I could make more at the $1/$4/$8/$8 table, it was really difficult to deal for a daily wage that was the size of a single small pot in the $10/$20 game.

And there was an even bigger game. I remember the first time I jumped to $20/$40 at Binion's; it was the biggest game in the world, or at least in Vegas, back then. Minh Ly, who now plays $4,000/$8,000 at the Bellagio, and I were the two new hotshots in the game. We played all the time and even got to play with Johnny Moss for about six months before he died. Johnny was really a nice guy when I knew him, but he was not the great player he once had been. He was in his eighties, he could barely see his cards and his desire to dominate the game had pretty much vanished. He was giving his money away at the end.

I found myself playing $10/$20 or $20/$40 every day, sometimes for twenty-four hours straight. It was brutal to finish a session like that and then have to deal poker. Fortunately, we had something called the designated player at Sam's Town. The "DP" was basically the house prop player, an employee who played with his own money and sat in games to keep them going or helped start up a new game. I was always so tired from playing the $20/$40 game at Binion's. It was much easier to be the designated player than it was to deal, so I took the DP slot whenever I could. The dealer has to run the game, keep track of the pots, and deal every hand. The DP just has to play tight, which means folding most hands. When the poker room got busy, the DP would be pulled back into the dealer's box.

When I'd played a long session at the Horseshoe, I would go to work thinking, "Oh please, God, don't let them be busy today. I don't know if I can deal." After those all-nighters at Binion's, I would spend the next eight hours dozing in my seat as the DP at Sam's Town. I actually fell asleep in the box one time in the middle of a hand, I was so exhausted.

We'd get a list every day with our dealing assignments on it. The person at the bottom of the list was first up to deal. The person at the top of the list was the first to be the DP. Most dealers had families and wanted to work and make money, so they would try to substitute their DP slot for a dealing assignment. Luckily most people on my shift wanted to deal and I wanted to be DP. Once in awhile, I actually paid someone $100 to deal for me. Even though I was playing for $1,000 a night, I still kept dealing. It was a secure job, with medical insurance and $800 a week, and that was a good living in those days.

Once I started winning regularly at the bigger cash games, I found myself starting to live the high life. Unfortunately, having a lot of spare cash for the first time in my life led me to make a couple of mistakes. First, I was getting pretty smug about my winnings and I was flashing my bankroll around at Sam's Town. Sometimes I'd have $40,000 after a few big days at Binion's. One night as I was walking to my trailer after work, I heard a voice behind me say:

"Hi Mike, is that you buddy?"

I turned around and even though I didn't recognize the guy, I said hello.

"Hey, can I ask you a question?" he said.

I said sure and he pulled a gun on me. Everything happened so fast after that. I pushed him and fell on him, smashing him down to the ground. He went down pretty hard. I kicked him a couple of times and ran away. When I looked back he was running in the other direction. Yeah, I know money isn't worth getting shot over, but it's not like I thought about that as it was happening. I had my first big bankroll ever and that bastard wasn't going to get it. And he didn't.

My second mistake was sports betting. When I first started dealing, I was making roughly $100 a day and I only had $300 in monthly expenses, so I made a pretty comfortable living. I always liked betting on sports and made $100 bets without really thinking about it. But once I started making so much money playing poker, I began betting $200, $300 and up to $1,000 a game. I didn't really care if I lost money on sports because I'd become so good at poker I figured it wouldn't take me long to make it back.

But it got out of hand.

I was quickly reverting back to the same kid who used to blow all his money on video poker, only on a much bigger scale. I became the king of blowing $10,000 poker bankrolls, losing it all on one weekend of NFL football. Then I'd have to get in the dealer's box, dead broke, and deal eight hours for $100. I'd work until I had $600 in my pocket, then buy into the $10/$20 game, and eventually the $20/$40 game. In about a month's time, I'd build up to $10,000, or even $20,000, and then I'd blow it again.

During this time, I learned how good a poker player I had become. I walked around with confidence. I knew poker was my game; I knew it that very first day when I sat behind Phil at the poker table. I had the desire to be the best, the hunger to win. A lot of these young kids that win big tournaments today have the hunger. They are out to prove something to themselves and maybe the world. But once the hunger fades, it's hard to stay on top.

I had worked through the grind and found the hunger to win again. I thought I was on top of the poker world. But I had no idea how big that world was—or how much bigger it would become.

Chapter Five

Other People's Money

I'd come a long way since Phil had first found me at that video poker machine in 1991. By 1996, I'd been playing poker for five years. I'd gone from selling furniture in the family business to dealing poker at Sam's Town. I was still living in the same trailer, but I had become a monster winning poker player. No one at Binion's really wanted to see me in their game. A couple of other pros and I did what high-stakes players are supposed to do: We chopped up the fish who came in to try their game against the best players in the world—or at least against the best players at Binion's Horseshoe in downtown Las Vegas.

Playing and dealing for five years had turned me into a great player. Maybe it sounds like bragging coming from a guy who was only playing $20/$40, but that was a huge game back then and I owned it.

I had the best of both worlds, a secure job with benefits, and a killer game with a five-figure bankroll.

I still got a rush from poker, but once I was back at work and the adrenaline high from playing was gone, I was exhausted. I barely slept. While I was sure that I could make a living just playing poker, my ridiculous obsession with sports betting meant that I always needed the job to fall back on. It was a cycle I needed to break, but

I just kept doing what I was doing, hoping that something would change.

And it did. Just like that fateful night when Phil Samaroff told me about a game where I'd never have to work again, someone else came along and changed my life one more time.

At Sam's Town, I knew all the local players. I'd been dealing their games for years and when I was the Designated Player, I played against them. The cardroom had a loyal following, so everyone pretty much knew everybody else. One of the regulars was an older guy named Neil Rose, who played poker almost every day.

"I really like your game, Mike," Neil told me one night.

We talked about it a few times. I just thought it was basic friendly table talk. He was also at the table plenty of times when I talked about my degenerate sports betting habit and my busted, then flush, then busted rollercoaster ride with my bankroll. One day after I had finished telling yet another story about blowing off yet another bankroll betting on football games, Neil said he wanted to talk to me.

On my coffee break, he asked me a question I never expected.

"Are you interested in having me stake you in the $20/$40 games? I'd want you playing full time, so it would mean giving up your job."

Sure, I was interested, although at that point I had never even considered a backer. There are pros and cons to having someone put up your bankroll for a piece of the action.

"I need to think it over," I told him.

"Sure you do," he said. "Take your time and get back to me."

Playing poker full time was a real dream for me. Even though I had been playing a lot the last few years, I always had the dealing job for security, health insurance, and as a way to refill my bankroll when I blew it betting sports. Giving up the job completely seemed like a huge risk. What if it didn't work out? What if I couldn't get my job back at Sam's Town? I didn't like the idea that I might end up dealing at some crappy, second-rate poker room. I'd rather put a bullet in my head than go through all that probation bullshit again. And besides, I knew my mom would kill me if I quit my job.

But then again, for a poker player, this was one of those lifetime opportunities.

I talked about Neil's offer with my boss at Sam's Town. He said I'd be crazy to quit my job because if it didn't work out, I would have to start all over on probation as a new dealer. But he also told me that I could take a leave of absence for a month, and that he could probably arrange to extend that for up to three months and still hold my job for me.

Perfect! That was what I needed to hear. I really wanted to see how I would do playing full time without having to work or worrying about losing my day job. I called Neil.

"I can't quit my job completely, but I can take a leave of absence for a month," I explained when we met that night.

"That's fine with me," he said, "but I have one more condition. You'll have to promise that you won't bet on sports as long as I'm backing you." Neil wasn't stupid. He knew that without that condition, I would be a bad risk.

"All right," I agreed, "but I have a condition too. I want you to put up $100,000 to back me. I don't want to have to worry about a bankroll while I'm playing."

I figured if I got off to a rough start or went through a few weeks of losing sessions, I wouldn't be pressured to give it up too early with that kind of bankroll behind me. I didn't want to sweat losing $1,000 or $2,000 a day for ten straight days. If I was going to play poker every day, the bankroll pressures had to be completely removed.

Neil agreed to put up the $100,000 and I agreed to stop all sports betting. On November 26, 1996, I took a leave of absence from my job at Sam's Town.

More than anything else, I wanted to be able to play poker and think only about poker. When you play the higher limits right at the edge of your bankroll, you put a lot of pressure on yourself and it can start to affect your game. In poker, it's called playing with scared money. You don't always raise when you should and you start to second guess your calls and bluffs. When you play without bankroll pressure, you can play pure, fearless, poker. One of the big advantages is the freedom you have to move on a hand when you need to, knowing that you have money behind you.

Neil started our deal by handing me $10,000. It would be a long time before he had to go into his pocket again. In the first two weeks, I won $11,200; I remember that number exactly. That's an average of over twenty-five big bets every day for ten days. That's an amazing amount of money to win in a ten day period playing $20/$40 hold'em.

"Oh, man, you're better than the stock market!" Neil said.

"Neil, I'm playing great, but I'm running great too," I said. I was pumped too, but I remember telling him, "You're a poker player, you know how it goes. It's just not this easy."

I continued to win over the next few weeks. I wasn't winning at that same ridiculous rate, but I was still winning and Neil was still way too happy about it. Sometime in early January of 1997, Neil heard about a $40/$80 game at the Crystal Park Casino, which had just opened in Los Angeles.

"Wanna give the big game in L.A. a try?" he asked.

"Yeah," I said, "Let's go!" I mean, if I was crushing the $20/$40 game in Vegas, maybe we could double our profits in the $40/$80 game.

On January 5, 1997, right before we left for L.A., I gave up my dealing job at Sam's Town. After six pretty spectacular weeks of playing and a much fatter bankroll, I decided to devote myself full time to poker. I didn't want to leave the folks at Sam's Town hanging when I knew I had already made my decision. Of course, my mother told me it was the biggest mistake of my life.

"You're stupid to give up a steady job with benefits," she said, just like I expected.

But hey, any guy who tells his family he's giving up a job to play poker for a living isn't going to get a lot of encouragement.

My mom doesn't think it was such a bad decision now.

Neil and I packed our bags and moved into the Crystal Park Hotel. When I say we moved in, we literally moved in. The casino comped us for everything—room and board—and I played $40/$80 limit hold'em every day. It was still six years before the poker boom, and the $40/$80 game was the biggest regular game in California. There might have been higher games on the weekends in some casinos or during a tournament, but this game ran like clockwork, seven days a week.

The first two weeks playing $40/$80 were an unbelievably difficult adjustment for me. The jumps from $1/$4/$8/$8 to $10/$20 and then up to $20/$40 were no big deal. But I was playing with a different caliber of player in this game. The game was ultra-aggressive; it definitely wasn't the weak-passive $20/$40 game I had been able to run over in Vegas. Things didn't start out very well. In my first couple of weeks playing $40/$80, we were down about $16,000 and I still hadn't made the adjustment. I wanted to quit and go back to playing $20/$40, but Neil wouldn't let me.

"I know you can do it, Mike, I know you can win," Neil reassured me. "You just gotta figure it out."

He was right, but it took me awhile before I finally realized what I was missing. It was the extra bet. In most of the games I had played, there would be a bet and a raise in a round of play. But in this game, they would three-bet. They would bet, raise, and then reraise in a round. They did it way more than I was used to, but once I picked up on it, everything else clicked. I figured out when to three-bet and when to release my hand, and my reads became a lot clearer. I could see when my opponents had better hands than me and when they didn't. It was like shifting into a different gear.

I ended up winning $63,000 straight over the next six weeks. It felt pretty damn good to book an average weekly win rate of $10,000, especially after giving money away for the first two weeks.

Of course, Neil thought I was the god of all poker gods. I kept telling him that I was playing great, but that I was also running really good and it couldn't always be this good. But he wasn't listening, not with all that money rolling in. Neil was a smart guy about some things, like making me promise not to bet on sports, but he refused to see a hot streak for what it was. He needed a reality check, and I knew that at some point he would get one.

The idea that the biggest running game was a $40/$80 limit game seems almost ridiculous today. Any day of the week, games that size are being dealt in card rooms around the country. And online you can find a game ten times that limit at any time, day or night. I was probably lucky that the limits were gradually creeping up in some cash games back then, because it gave me a chance to slowly move up and adjust to higher and higher stakes. Even so, this Crystal Park game was a ball buster and attracted some of the best players in the world.

One night I found myself sitting next to Huck Seed. Less than a year earlier, Huck had scored a million bucks for his win in the 1996 World Series of Poker main event. Up to that point, I had played with some really good players, but I can't say that I had played with a lot of great players. Huck was in a different category; I was shocked at how good he actually was. That game had some of the best players around and he was simply better than anyone else at that table.

Huck was about my age, but unlike me, he had played against all the greats, guys like Johnny Chan, T.J. Cloutier, Billy Baxter, Berry Johnston and Freddy Deeb. This was long before I even knew who most of them were. Huck had already won two WSOP bracelets and had made it to eight WSOP final tables. He had made two of those final tables while I was still throwing quarters into a video poker machine!

We talked a lot at the table. Yeah, it's true that I always talk at the table, but I was pretty pumped up to talk about poker with someone my own age and with his experience. A couple of times, Huck told me that I was one of the best new players he had ever played with. Here's the world champion of poker, a guy whose game I totally respected, telling me that I was good enough to be in the game. That meant as much to me as all the money I won at Crystal Park.

Tournaments always attracted good cash games, Huck told me, and he was going to move his play to the Commerce Casino once the Los Angeles Poker Classic started over there. The LAPC was a three-week series of tournaments in February with twenty-one events. Eight of the tournaments, including the championship, were limit hold'em. The tournaments and the cash games were still dominated by limit games at that time. Neil and I gave the Commerce a try once the LAPC started, and the cash games were as good as Huck had promised. For the next three weeks, I split my time between Crystal Park and the Commerce. I played a couple of the limit tournaments and made one final table. But I was basically a cash game player, not a tournament player.

I was in L.A. to grind out wins in the biggest and softest cash games I could find.

One day I was playing at the Commerce with a guy that I'd played once or twice at the $40/$80 game at Crystal Park. But at the Commerce, my reads on him were off. He was jumpy and hyper-aggressive, not at all like the calm, solid player I'd played a month earlier. He was playing way more hands and nearly every time he lost a big pot, he walked away from the table. I couldn't figure out how or why his game had changed so much in such a short time. The table was taking him apart, but I couldn't get him nailed down. He wasn't the same player he had been at Crystal Park. He was the monster fish in our game and I wasn't winning a dime from him.

Just as the guy got up to take another walk after losing another big pot by making a really dumbass call on the river, I saw Huck come into the room. I pointed the guy out to him and started telling him what was happening when a big grin spread across Huck's face.

"Mike, this is L.A., man!" he said, putting his finger to the side of his nose and snorting.

Shit, how dumb was I? Of course, the guy was doing coke.

I couldn't get a new read on him because it never occurred to me that someone who could play solid poker would bring his bankroll to a tough poker game while he was doing drugs. What an idiot he was. What a bigger idiot I was. It was hard to tell whether he was losing his bankroll faster at the table or up his nose in the bathroom, but the combination ensured he was going to lose it all. And after my talk with Huck, I won a piece of it before he disappeared. I probably should have forgotten all about that cokehead at the Commerce. It's not like I never again played poker against someone on drugs. Far from it. I mean, what's one more druggy in L.A.?

Instead, I thought about that poor bastard a lot. Mostly because a few years later, I became that guy—sitting at a Commerce poker table, out of my mind on drugs, losing all my money, unable to break out of a downward suicidal spiral.

Chapter Six

The Almost Bracelet

In 1997, I was riding high after beating up on the games in L.A. I'd already made something of a name for myself and was recognized in Vegas as one of the best young limit hold'em players. But I hadn't played against the best players in the world. I was about to get my chance because all of them were coming into town for the World Series of Poker. Not as many of the great tournament players lived in Vegas in the 90s as they do today.

At this point I was as much a fan as a player, looking forward to seeing the greats like Doyle Brunson and Johnny Chan. But more than anything, I wanted to play against these guys, I wanted to test my game. I wanted to prove to myself and to the poker world that I belonged there. Looking back on that April, I can't think of a time in my life when I was more anxious to play poker, more excited for the World Series to get started. It represented the ultimate challenge.

I was a great limit hold'em player, but I didn't really know anything about the other poker games like Omaha and no-limit. It's strange, because today I am known for those other games and I'm basically a horrendous limit hold'em player. By 1997, limit hold'em had become like breathing to me. I had put in so many hours to master it and had such a great feel for the game.

In my very first WSOP tournament, I came up empty. I played about four or five hours into the $2,000 Limit Hold'em tournament and never picked up a good hand. Strangely enough, it was a hand that I folded that kept me from being discouraged about my final result.

During the tournament, I played at the same table as Phil Hellmuth who, in 1989, had become the youngest player ever to win the WSOP Championship. Going into the 1997 Series, he already had won five bracelets. It was our first time at a table together and I was definitely watching how he played. At one point, I laid down top pair with a nut flush draw to Hellmuth after he bet the turn. He looked annoyed that I was folding, so I showed my cards. He had me beat; he had me out-kicked and he was pissed that he didn't get more chips from me. He couldn't believe I gave up the hand.

"How could you lay that hand down? How could you lay that down?" he kept saying over and over.

I'd never met Phil and didn't know about his reputation for outbursts. But when I folded my cards face up, he went nuts. If you've seen Phil on television, you know how emotional he gets. He thought I should have given him at least two or three more bets with that hand. I think he was trying to get under my skin, but the more he bitched, the better I felt.

Even though I didn't make money in the tournament, that hand convinced me I could compete against great players. Most people get pumped when they take down a big hand against a pro, but it was a hand that I didn't win that gave me confidence. Somewhere in between all Phil's whining, I got the confirmation I needed that I could play with the big boys.

A couple of days later, I took a break from my cash game grind and decided to play some satellites. The line was really long for the hold'em satellites, but they had one open seat at an Omaha high-low table. Why not? I only had a vague idea of how to play Omaha and I was a little unsure of how the low side of the game worked. But a friend of mine that I played limit hold'em with, Mark Gregorich, played Omaha a lot.

He was standing there and told me, "Oh, just play ace-deuce, ace-deuce-three and ace-three-four. Then use your poker instincts to play the rest."

I bought into the satellite for a hundred bucks or something, I don't remember exactly, and I won. I had a great time. I thought, "Wow! I've never played this game before and I won the satellite. Man, I must really be a great poker player!" It was like when these Internet kids take down their first online tournament; you feel like you're the best ever.

"What do you want me to do with this satellite chip?" I asked Neil later that night. "Should I play the Omaha high-low tournament or just buy into another limit hold'em event?" I was sure he'd tell me to play what I knew best.

"Well, maybe it's meant to be. Play the Omaha," he answered.

"But I don't even know what I'm doing."

"You won the satellite, you gotta know something."

I talked to Mark a little bit more about Omaha. He warned me that the biggest problem people have in split games like Omaha high-low is that they play too many hands and they try to make too many things happen. He told me to just play really tight and to use my hold'em instincts to occasionally bluff. But mostly, I should just play snug.

Thirteen hours into the $2,000 Omaha high-low event, I was the fucking chip leader! We had 215 starters in the tournament and we were down to just twelve players at about one o'clock in the morning. I had done what Mark told me to do and played tight. And just like he said, I watched lots of players fire away at too many pots and walk away busted. This was a different game than hold'em and clearly, tight was right in Omaha. Mark had given me great advice, but was it really that simple? I was damn close to a WSOP final table and it started to hit me. Was it really happening? How was this possible?

It got trickier when we were down to twelve players. Rock solid, tight play would have gotten me to the final table, but not with a huge stack of chips. The players who already had short stacks knew they had to fight hard to make it, so they were mixing it up. And the big stacks, like me, wanted to go to the final table well armed. So there was a lot of play the last hour or two on that first day.

But I made it.

I was pretty ecstatic. It had been one really long day of play, and I knew I needed to get some sleep for the final table the next day. But I just lay in bed, wide awake, thinking about the possibility of a big money score. Most veteran players spend the night thinking about their shot to win a WSOP bracelet, but I was focused on the cash.

I didn't know what a bracelet meant back then. It really didn't mean shit to me—the bracelet never even entered my mind. The only thing I was focused on was finding a way to finish first or second and boosting the bankroll by six figures, which would really, really take the pressure off me. I was second in chips and thought I had a real shot. A win of $156,000 back then was like millions to me today. With that kind of hit, I wouldn't have to win for a year—my living expenses would be covered, and Neil would be happy. He'd definitely stick around and back me for at least another year.

Since this was my first year playing the WSOP and my first Omaha high-low tournament ever, I didn't know the other players at the final table as well as they all knew each other. I was the new kid on the block. I got to know these players much better in the years to come, and some of them are still household names in poker today.

The chip leader was Dan Heimiller with 81,500 in chips. This was the eighth event at the '97 Series but it was already Dan's second final table of the year. He went on to cash six times in '97, which is sort of amazing since there were only twenty events that year. Subtracting two events that he couldn't play because he was still playing in the previous day's tournament, and the ladies-only event, the most events he could have played was seventeen. He actually cashed better than one-out-of-three times *if* he had played all the other events. By 2008, Dan had racked up thirty-two cashes at the WSOP, including his Mixed Hold'em/Stud bracelet in 2002.

Second in chips was the new kid, Mike Matusow, with 76,000, playing in his first Omaha high-low tournament. "Watch out for this guy. He'll be a famous poker player one day!" I wanted to tell everybody.

Lindy Chambers was third with 69,500, playing his second final table of the '97 Series and the third of his career. Ted Forrest, one of the best all-around poker players in the world, was next with 67,000 chips. In 1993, Ted had won three WSOP bracelets, and was making his second final-table appearance in '97. By 2009, his resume included five WSOP bracelets, a World Poker Tour victory, and an NBC Heads-Up Championship.

Volker Beyer had 39,500 chips. Volker had already cashed in one event in '97 and he would make it to another final table just two days after this one. Jack Culp was next with 38,500 chips. This was Jack's first cash in '97, but it was his fifth final table appearance in a World Series event.

Brent Carter had 26,500 chips coming in. This was Brent's twelfth World Series final table. And like Ted Forrest, Brent was coming in with some hardware; he had won a WSOP no-limit hold'em bracelet in '91 and a limit Omaha bracelet in '94.

Scotty Nguyen was one of the two short stacks with 16,500 chips. This was Scotty's first World Series final table, but he had played in the WSOP the previous two years and had made money finishes in both '95 and '96. The other short stack was Joel Kreps with $15,500. Kreps had made his first final table in '96 and this was his second.

I had the least World Series experience at the table. And sure as shit, I had the least Omaha high-low experience. In fact, it had all come from exactly one satellite and about fourteen hours of tournament play the day before. But I really liked this game and thought that I had learned to play it really well. About halfway through the first day, I wouldn't say I was the best player in the field, but I didn't think I was outclassed by anyone either.

Even though I didn't have the experience that some of these players had, I wasn't worried about my play going into the final day. I had very good instincts for the game. But as it turned out, that would be the least of my problems. There's a lot more to poker than cards, chips and pots. I didn't know it then, but I was about to learn one of the most important lessons of my poker career.

Like most of the lessons I've learned in my life, I would learn this one the hard way.

Chapter Seven

Hard Lessons at the Final Table

As predicted, the shortest stack, Joel Kreps, went out first. But Scotty Nguyen, the other short stack, gained some breathing room by doubling up twice in the early going. Brent Carter was the next player to be eliminated, finishing in eighth place. I wasn't sorry to see a two-time bracelet holder leave the table. After Brent went out, the play really loosened up.

When you're the big stack at the table, you can really push the other players around. But sometimes that strategy backfires. Sometimes the sheriff takes a bullet, and that's what happened to Dan Heimiller. He started the day first in chips and busted out in seventh place. So within the first hour of play, we lost three players and I had taken over the chip lead.

Volker and Scotty's chip stacks were all over the place in the next hour, bouncing back and forth from nearly out to average stacks. Jack Culp and Lindy Chambers made solid attempts to chip up, but neither one could gain any traction and both went out pretty early into the second level. With just four of us left (Scotty, Ted, Volker and me) I had a huge lead with almost 225,000 chips. At that point, Scotty was short-stacked again with around 15,000 chips. Ted and Volker were hovering at just under 100,000 each.

I was still following the "tight is right" advice I had received before the tournament began; maybe that's why I was able to get and hold onto the chip lead for most of the day. The other players were mixing it up and playing a lot of pots. It was the craziest thing. It didn't make a difference to them when I came into a pot after folding ten or twelve hands in a row. No one slowed down and I kept picking up chips with my tight play. By the time we took our break at the end of the second hour, Scotty had gotten himself back to over 100,000 while Volker was down to less than two big blinds.

Shortly after the break, Volker went out in fourth place and Scotty and Ted suggested we take another break to talk about a deal. At the time, tournament reporter Tom Sims asked sixth-place finisher Jack Culp about the potential deal. Jack said, "If I were Mike, I wouldn't even talk deal; I'd keep the other guys on the ropes."

He was absolutely right, but I was new to all of this. I had no idea what winning a World Series bracelet meant; all I could see was the money. When it came to poker skill, I was as good as these other guys, but I was a rank amateur and an idiot when it came to any other kind of poker wisdom. And I proved it by making the worst decision of my poker career.

When we stepped away from the table to talk about a deal, I had a ridiculous chip advantage; I had 280,000 in chips to Scotty's 90,000 and Ted's 60,000. Just like today, the payout structure was pretty steep. The third-place finisher would receive $40,850. Second place got $81,700, while first place got almost twice that with $156,950.

My mind was racing. I was down to the final three at a World Series final table. I had the chip lead, but I was up against Scotty Nguyen and Ted Forrest. Scotty was short-stacked, but it wasn't like I could count on him to stay that way. He had been short-stacked at least a dozen times during the final table and had bounced back every time. He just wouldn't fucking die. Ted was the shortest stack, but he was a three-time bracelet winner and I was sure that if there was a way to fight back, he'd find it.

Also, there were a lot of people watching us play and that was a whole new thing for me. Granted, it wasn't like today, where hundreds of people line up to watch. There wasn't a lot of media back then; even ESPN didn't come in until the main event. But some of the players' family and friends were there. And a lot of the other World Series players, the big guys, were watching.

"Man, am I really this good? Can I actually win this?" I started asking myself.

Ted and Scotty took me aside and offered me most of the first place prize money while we were still three-handed. I was shocked, which shows you just how naive I was. Of course, they had to offer me most of the first-place money; I had a monster lead on them. All I had wanted was the money, and that's what they offered me. Maybe I should have thought more about it. Deal making was pretty common at final tables and there were plenty of people I could have asked for advice. But at that moment, all I saw was enough cash to play for a full year without worrying about money. The money would be guaranteed to me no matter what happened in the rest of the tournament. We'd still play down to a winner, because the World Series had to have an actual bracelet winner. But whatever happened, I would get the lion's share.

So Scotty, Ted and I made the deal—I would get a guaranteed $126,000, Ted and Scotty chopped up an additional $20,000, and we set aside $10,000 for the eventual winner.

Did Scotty and Ted take advantage of me? I don't see it that way. Did they make great deals for themselves? Well, financially, Ted sure did. And since Scotty would eventually walk away with the bracelet, I think he made a great deal from a professional standpoint. But the real question is: Did they know just how much my game would change once they let me lock up a big chunk of cash? Both Scotty and Ted are very smart poker players and they had watched me, the new kid, play for two days. Knowing my mouth, they also knew this was my first Omaha high-low event and my first WSOP final table. I'm also guessing they thought there was a good chance I would lose my focus once the money was settled.

I should have thought about how many hands Ted would need to win before he was back in the running. I should have thought about the fact that even if Scotty took out Ted quickly, I'd still have over a 100,000 chip lead on him going into heads-up play. But I wanted the security of the guaranteed money and I just couldn't see beyond it. To me I was getting a guaranteed $126,000 when the most I could win was $156,000. I knew that anything could happen in poker; a lead can disappear in a matter of a few hands. I was honestly surprised they offered me such a good deal.

Financially, I understand why I took the deal on that day in 1997. But it didn't take me long to realize what I had potentially given up. I'd never take that deal today, and Ted, Scotty or any other pro wouldn't even waste their breath offering me a deal like that.

Just after the deal, Scotty got hit over the head by the deck. He caught some pretty sweet cards and it took him about fifteen hands to take Ted out in third place. I'm not even sure how I played those early hands, I was still so stoked from making the deal. Then suddenly, Ted was gone and Scotty and I were heads-up. I still had a good chip lead with 260,000 chips, but Ted's chips had helped Scotty narrow the gap; he had about 150,000.

It took just twenty-one hands of heads-up play for Scotty to beat me. I won only five of those hands. And in two of those five hands, Scotty laid down to my preflop raises, so I didn't win many chips. We played only three split pots heads-up, and Scotty won thirteen of twenty-one hands outright. Was he getting some cards? Yes, he was. But if I had maintained my focus, I would have folded a lot of those thirteen hands and Scotty's hot streak would have had a chance to burn itself out. He probably would have been ahead after those first twenty-one hands, but I still would have had at least 100,000 chips and we still would have had a match.

In the final hand, I held A-Q-4-2 and Scotty had K-9-6-4. We were all in before the flop and I was about a 2 to 1 favorite to scoop the whole pot. But the board ran out K-9-2-J-7. There was no low hand and Scotty made two pair for the high hand. It was over.

I still feel that if I had kept my head down, there was no way I could have lost that tournament, in spite of Scotty's run. But once I made the deal, the pressure to play my best game disappeared. All I thought about was taking home $126,000. Winning more than a hundred grand seemed like such a miracle to me. When I finally got beat, I was happy. I didn't care; I got the money.

Everybody will look back on that '97 Omaha tournament and say Scotty won it, but anybody who was there knows that I got all the money. But it cost me more than money to give that bracelet away. I know what a bracelet is worth now; it's like an Olympic gold medal. It shows people that in that event, on those days, no one in the world could beat you. They don't give the Wheaties box cover to the guy who comes in second.

I might have had four bracelets today. And even though the WSOP gives away something like fifty-five bracelets each year now instead of the twenty or so back then, there are still only about thirty people in the world who have four bracelets. Four is just a different category than three, a whole new level.

"You can't overcome the luck of the cards, but I'm so completely ecstatic to get so far," I was quoted in an interview after the tournament ended. "Until one week ago I'd never played any high-low poker in my life. I'll be back. I'll win one of these tournaments."

And I was ecstatic. I had just made the biggest score in my life and on top of that, it was my twenty-ninth birthday. It's almost funny now to think about it, but the media made a big deal about how young our final table was.

"The average age for the final four competitors was just over thirty," one reporter wrote, "almost certainly setting a World Series of Poker youth record."

Imagine that? In 1997 you were young if you made a WSOP final table at thirty. Now they measure the youngest bracelet winner by how many days over twenty-one he is.

"How do you want your $126,000, sir?"

I just loved being asked that question by the cashier.

"Give me cash!"

I settled up with Neil the next day, but for a short time I had fun with my $100,000 brick of cash. All the way home I tossed it back and forth with my friends in the back of a limo. I remember thinking it was the biggest, most incredible, thing that had ever happened to me. And maybe it was. In my second WSOP tournament, I had finished second and won a big brick of cash.

I played two more limit hold'em tournaments at the Series that year and didn't cash in either. But I crushed the $75/$150 cash games, winning around $35,000. While my tournament score was in Omaha high-low and I came up empty in the limit hold'em tournaments, no one beat me in a limit hold'em cash game. I had that game locked up.

Today, I tell people how much I suck as a limit hold'em player and they just say that I'm being hard on myself, I can't be that bad. But I know that I'm not what I was. Limit hold'em is a game of feel. If I played the game every day for a couple of months straight, I could get good again. But could I ever get back to my prior level?

No, impossible. I used to be hungry to play limit poker, but hunger isn't something you can just turn on and off.

I didn't play the main event in '97. For one thing, I had never played no-limit hold'em. I know that sounds strange now, but casinos didn't spread no-limit cash games back then. Only three of the events at the World Series were no-limit hold'em tournaments, including the main event. But I knew that if I was going to be a professional, I had to learn how to play no-limit hold'em. So I watched the main event from beginning to end as a learning experience. I followed every detail of the entire tournament, who was still in and who had chips. I tried to learn about the guys I hadn't seen play before. And like a detective, I tracked the players I did know.

That, of course, was the year that Stu Ungar came back to win his third main event. It was also the year that Binion's moved the final table outside onto Fremont Street to get more media attention. Even in late spring, playing outside was a bad idea for Vegas. It turned out to be a 100-plus degree day and every once in awhile a breeze would blow through and flip the cards on the outdoor table.

If you take a look at the television footage of that final table, you'll see me sitting right there in the front row. I watched Stuey play the last two days and I can tell you that the final table went down differently from what the media reported. They made it sound as though he had made moves all day long, muscling the table. But that's not what I saw.

Stuey was not ultra-aggressive like you hear people say today. He was actually pretty conservative and tight, but he picked his spots when he had hands. He was methodical, thoughtful, and took his time with each decision. No one at that final table played fast like the game is played today, not even Stuey. He also made some great laydowns. He didn't win because he was aggressive and the other players weren't. He won that event because the other players knew how well he was playing; they just didn't want to put their chips into a pot with Stuey. He controlled the final table from beginning to end. There's no doubt Stu Ungar was a great no-limit hold'em player, maybe the best ever. He knew how to play poker against any opponent and that's what he did at the final table.

The whole time I sat in that ridiculous heat watching Stuey play, my heart was pumping while I thought, "That's going to be me one day." I wanted it to be me; I wanted it so bad. Right out there on Fremont

Street I set my goal to win my way to the WSOP Championship final table. Right then, I just knew I was going to make it happen; my heart was set on it. I knew that had to be something I did in my lifetime.

Watching Stuey play was a great experience—for a lot of different reasons. For the first time, maybe in my life, I had a goal, one that wasn't measured by winning sessions or big bets. What I didn't know, what I couldn't have known, is that Stuey would have a much bigger influence on my life in another way, a way that was so much more important than a poker game.

But I never saw that coming as I watched what would become Stu Ungar's last victory.

Chapter Eight

On My Own

For years, the big games in Vegas were downtown at Binion's Horseshoe. Since so many of the big players didn't live in Vegas, there were also plenty of big games in California, Texas and a few other places like New York. But in Vegas, the big game was at Binion's. Of course, one reason was that the World Series came to Binion's every spring and Jack and Benny Binion treated poker players like royalty. Another reason was that there just weren't that many poker rooms back then, even at the big Strip casinos. The Stardust had a great room but it didn't have many big limit games. So once players moved up in limits, they pretty much played at the Horseshoe.

The Mirage opened one of the first big new rooms in 1989, but it took awhile for it to catch on and initially the bigger games stayed at the older rooms. But the Mirage offered a tempting benefit that most of the old rooms didn't have — the casino attracted a lot of tourists. Tourists who played poker wanted to play on the Strip and the newest, cleanest, fanciest poker room was at the Mirage. Slowly, the regular players began to move there just to pick them off.

Initially, it was hard to count on getting a good high stakes game going every day at the Mirage. Not every player showed up every day and some players just didn't like the idea of fighting the Strip traffic. But when Johnny Moss passed away in December of 1995, the game at Binion's died with him.

By 1996, the big game at the Mirage was $40/$80, but that would change pretty quickly over the next couple of years.

It was during that period that the new young players really got to know each other because we played together every day. Minh Ly and I had known each other from Binion's where we were known as the "youngsters." But once the game shifted to the Mirage, we played with people like Jennifer Harman, Todd Brunson, Curtis Bibb and a lot of other younger players, many who eventually dropped out of poker somewhere along the line. Jennifer and Todd were very good limit players, but, of course, I thought I was a bit better than them. Daniel Negreanu also played the Mirage, but during that time he was generally in the smaller games—people sometimes forget that Daniel is younger than the rest of us. Many of the older players had earned their chops years earlier and didn't have to constantly work on their games or need to grind it out like us young guns did. But the game did get top players like David Sklansky, Berry Johnston and Roy Cook popping in from time to time.

After the Series in 1997, I probably played at the Mirage seven days a week, sixteen hours a day. And sometimes the game was so good that I played around the clock. There were stretches where it seemed like we never went home. The big game was the highest limit hold'em game we could keep going, which was always $40/$80 and sometimes $100/$200. I remember days of sitting at a table with Jennifer and Todd and one or two others, trying to get the $100/$200 game going. It was literally the four or five best young limit hold'em players in the world playing against each other waiting for the fish to arrive.

Of course, it was the tourists who made the game. As full time professional poker players, we were basically "going to the office" every day and playing poker while we waited for the tourists to contribute. But that did a lot for all of our games too. Poker is about winning, but to do that you have to learn about, and from, better players. And if you were already playing at a high level, the Mirage was probably the best place to get your continuing education. If your game wasn't at that level, then the Mirage was where you donated to our education fund. We always made sure that the big game at the

Mirage was a fun table to play. Smart pros never, ever scare the fish away.

In early '98, I was splitting my time between the Mirage in Las Vegas and trips to the Commerce Casino in Los Angeles. I also started playing a lot more Omaha high-low and even some stud high-low split at the highest limits I could find to learn all the games better. I wanted to become a complete poker player. Looking ahead to the '98 WSOP, I wanted to be prepared to play more tournaments, especially the no-limit hold'em main event. The problem was that the casinos still weren't offering any no-limit cash games, so there was no game to learn in. It was hard enough to keep even the bigger limit games full, let alone a game where players could lose their bankrolls in a single bet.

After my big score at the '97 Series, I felt like I had both the time and the money to develop my skills in the other games. But not everyone saw it that way.

My backing arrangement with Neil had a lot to do with how the 1998 World Series turned out for me, and for everyone else too, right down to the champion. The only real conditions of our deal were that I would stop sports betting and Neil would put $100,000 behind me. We didn't have an attorney write that up or anything—it doesn't work like that in poker. This was two guys shaking hands and we just had to trust each other. How deep would Neil have gone into the promised $100,000 stake if, say, I had lost $30,000 right out of the gate or $50,000 over half a year? I knew he probably wouldn't just keep shelling out his cash if we were going straight down the crapper. But that never happened. I was a winner from the moment I sat down at Binion's Horseshoe on the very first day he backed me.

Neil was a poker player, which was important. You really can't have a backer who doesn't know the game. You need somebody that understands the ups and downs of poker. When I played in a high limit game, Neil was usually in the same room playing the $4/$8 game. It helped to have someone right there to give me advice about game selection and to talk with about strategy. When we first got to Crystal Park in L.A. in '96, I was an immediate loser; I couldn't get a handle on that game. But it was Neil who talked me into staying in the game, assuring me I would figure it out. And I did.

Neil liked to win and I was a winning player for him. Even though he sometimes had unrealistic expectations, that hadn't been a problem and our arrangement worked pretty well. But to some extent, it hadn't really been tested either. Before the '97 Series we drew down $120,000 from the bankroll. So from November of '96 to April of '97 we each pocketed $60,000, which was a pretty fantastic earn rate. Neil was happy, I was happy. I bought my first new car. After the '97 World Series and my almost bracelet in the Omaha high-low tournament, we chopped out another big chunk of money for each of us. I had won money in the side games and there was the $126,000 from the tournament deal. So far, our handshake arrangement had been good for both of us.

When the Series ended, I wanted to branch out and learn all the other games. Neil wanted me to stick with limit hold'em. I could see his point; I had been a pretty reliable limit hold'em cash machine. But I'd seen poker from the perspective of the World Series and I wanted to become a better all-around player. I knew that the learning curve for new games would naturally result in a lower win rate in the early going. And the non-hold'em games were played at lower limits, so when I did win, I won less. But those were things I was willing to ride out.

For about six months after the '97 Series, I went on an extended streak of break-even play. It wasn't that my losses in Omaha high-low and stud 8-or-better were balancing my hold'em wins or anything like that; I just wasn't having a particularly good streak. I was still breaking even; it wasn't even a losing streak. Maybe the most we were ever down was around $15,000.

But Neil wasn't happy. He wanted me to play the games he picked. And for the first time, I felt like I had a boss telling me what to do. The backing deal started to hit a rough patch.

Limit hold'em was beginning to be a grind again, even at the higher limits, but Neil thought that shouldn't matter. "You just need to suck it up and fight through it," is something he told me more than once. It was all about the results, and at that moment, the results were flat. Neil wasn't used to that. Suddenly I was no longer a poker god. Of course, I never had been one, but no matter how many times I had told Neil that, he hadn't listened while we were winning.

Now that we were break-even, he listened to me even less.

Another source of friction was that Neil had started backing another player, Eddy, one of my best friends. I had no problem with that and I was glad that Eddy had found a backer. But he was not nearly the player I was and from the beginning, Eddy was a net loser for Neil. I was basically breaking even, and maybe losing a little bit now and then, and Eddy had him stuck around $100,000. To Neil it was all the same money, coming out of the same pocket. So, almost everything Neil had won with me was gone and he was digging into his pocket again. In Neil's mind, it was my job to make up for his losses, even if those losses came from his decision to back a losing player. As a result, our relationship began to deteriorate. He started getting worked up about my game selection and was put off anytime I didn't play exactly what and when he wanted me to play.

"Mike doesn't listen to me," I heard him complain more than once. "Mike plays whatever he wants."

All the while he was losing money staking Eddy, not me. To my way of thinking, we had a backing deal and I had made him nearly $140,000 in a year. I thought that should count for something.

Neil and I were already on some pretty rocky ground in the fall of '97 when we went back to L.A. to play at the Commerce Casino. We had traveled together to play poker, but the friction about who would decide on game selection was constant. All the big games at the Commerce were held in the same section of the card room, so you always knew what high limit games were being spread. There was a big $150/$300 cash game going on. When I say big, I mean more than just the stakes. The game was being played fast, with a lot of capped betting and aggressive, even loose, play. There was a lot of money on the table. I sometimes took a break from my $75/$150 game nearby just to watch the play there.

Neil wanted me in that $150/$300 game. I explained to him that it wasn't an easy table and that it really wasn't a game I thought I could beat big. I don't know if it was the money or an ego thing, but he really wanted his horse in the big game. I'd watched the game enough times to know that I really didn't want to risk it.

"Neil, this is a really big game. We could drop $20,000 or $30,000 very fast," I warned him.

"I'm sure you'll figure out how to beat it," he insisted, "just like you did in the $40/$80."

Neil eventually won the argument and I sat down to play. Almost immediately, I started losing. Instead of recognizing that I shouldn't be in the game, Neil pushed me to hang in. He told me I always figured out the game. It's true that I had eventually cracked the $40/$80 game, but it had taken me a couple of weeks to do it and we had the bankroll to ride out the learning curve. This game was more than three times the stakes, and time and money weren't on our side. I told Neil that just because it was the biggest game in town, didn't mean we should be in it. He just kept saying he was sure I'd figure it out.

I didn't. I lost $22,000 that night, our biggest single session loss ever. The next day Neil went berserk. He had never lost it like that, at least not with me.

"I don't want to stake you no more," he yelled. "You're costing me money. I can't afford to just let you do what you want to do."

He started going off on me for all his losses.

"It's not my fault you got no money to stake me anymore," I shouted back at him. "You're the one that staked other people and blew off all the money I won for you."

It was pretty upsetting. In my mind, I was still a winning player. I'd only lost about $30,000, at most, of the nearly $140,000 Neil won with me and he acted like the world was coming to an end. I still had most of my net earnings, while Neil had lost his half staking Eddy. For some reason, Neil was going to cut me loose, blaming all his losses on me. The really crazy thing was, he kept staking Eddy—and Eddy kept losing. I don't know even today what was going on with Neil, but he wasn't making good business decisions. I felt bad that Neil and I had a falling out after we had such a good start.

I guess the real lesson is that deals, whether they're made with a handshake or a legal contract, are only good as long as things run good. When things don't run good, you're on your own.

I was on my own again.

Chapter Nine

I Have a Dream

I had about $60,000 to $70,000 of my bankroll left when Neil and I parted ways, a good chunk of money. I continued to play mostly break-even poker, bouncing between L.A. and Vegas, playing high limit hold'em along with some lower limit mixed games on my own. Earlier, that would be fine, but the money I'd been winning had changed my lifestyle a lot. And with Neil gone, the deal was gone, and so was my promise not to bet on sports. I had no problem betting a couple of thousand dollars on weekends. I was living pretty large; between eating out, picking up the tab for my friends once in awhile, and sports betting, I was probably spending more than $5,000 a month, even while I was still living in my trailer.

In February of '98, I went back to Los Angeles for the L.A. Poker Classic. I made a couple of tournament final tables there, one in Omaha high-low and another in limit hold'em. But that amounted to only about $5,000 in winnings and I was down about that much in the cash games. After about five more months of playing break-even poker, my bankroll had shrunk to about $35,000. Neil and I were still on the outs and it was looking like I had a tough year ahead of me. With the '98 World Series right around the corner, I realized that I wasn't going to have the bankroll I needed to play. After the big highs from the '97 Series, I started to worry that I might not even be able to play the few tournaments I wanted to enter. In fact, I wasn't sure I'd even have enough money to play in the higher limit cash games.

I talked to Eddy, who was still working for Neil. I told him that I really wanted Neil to stake me in the cash games at the Series. I knew I could make money for him. Eddy worked out a meeting, and Neil and I got together at the beginning of March. We had calmed down a lot from our big blowout in L.A., which I think made us both feel better. Neil offered to stake me in both the cash games and the tournaments. About this time I heard that Neil was also staking Scotty Nguyen for the Series. It was Neil's money and Scotty was a great player, but I wondered how thin he was spreading himself. I was a little worried that if just one horse got off the track, it would increase the chance that Neil would have another blow up.

A couple of days before the Series began in April, I went to Neil's house to pick up money.

"I've changed my mind," he told me the minute I walked in the front door. "I've decided not to stake you."

What? The World Series started in two fucking days, and I only had $28,000 to my name. I was devastated.

If I had had a little more time, I might have found another backer. I had become a pretty respected name in poker and I knew a lot of people who could probably hook me up. I definitely wanted to work out something before the Series began; I didn't want to be hustling cash at the Horseshoe. It's one thing to have a backing deal—it's another thing to have to beg outside the tournament room at Binion's.

That night I went to my parents' house and told them about the mess I was in. They knew I was really upset. The next day, without my asking her for it, my mom gave me a $20,000 cashier's check. I'll never forget it. I knew she was still mad at me for quitting my job to play poker, and I never would have asked her for that money. I didn't think she even paid that much attention to what I did in poker, at least not back then, so I was completely blown away when she gave me that check. I put it in my safety deposit box at the Horseshoe, and I'm happy to say that I never had to use it. But it was great having that safety net behind me. It was like having a $50,000 bankroll for the World Series, which I thought would be enough to play the $75/$150 cash games and maybe a couple of tournaments.

The night before the Series was about to start, Neil called and said, "I can't stake you in the cash games but I will stake you in the tournaments." Apparently, Eddy had gone to bat for me again once he heard that Neil had withdrawn his backing offer. Eddy, who proved what a great friend he was, told Neil that if he didn't have enough money to stake us both, he should stake me and not him. So I had Neil backing me for the tournaments and my own $50,000 bankroll for the cash games in a deal that was worked out the night before the World Series began.

Neil backed me in a few tournaments, but I didn't score in any of them. I did, however, crush the cash games. Not only didn't I have to cash my mom's check but I added another $32,000 to my bankroll. And although I was a net loser for Neil, he more than made up for it by backing Scotty Nguyen in the tournaments. Scotty cashed three times, including two final tables in the preliminary events. Those three cashes netted them each about $35,000. As far as I could tell, that meant Neil was up overall for the Series going into the main event.

After watching Stuey play in '97, I was so sure I was going to play the main event in 1998 that I probably would have bet all the money I had on it. But once again, my life didn't quite go according to plan. For one thing, Neil wasn't going to back me for another ten grand. But also, I still hadn't really played any no-limit hold'em. While I wasn't quite ready to play the main event in '98, Scotty was more than ready to play. He was tournament hot and was anxious to make a run at the "Big One." At the '97 World Series, I had lost out on a bracelet to Scotty, but I also had forged a friendship with him that would last for years.

As it turned out, Scotty and I crossed paths again big time in 1998, just not in any way I ever could have imagined

Without warning and just two days before the main event, Neil changed his mind about backing Scotty for the championship. And just as suddenly, he stopped returning phone calls from all of his players. None of us could reach him. It could have been his bankroll or nearly anything else, I really don't know. Neil never spoke to any of his players about his personal finances.

Scotty was counting on Neil to stake him in the main event. And unfortunately, Scotty had lost almost everything he had won in tournaments playing $50/$100 pot-limit Omaha cash games. It made sense for Neil not to back me for the $10,000 to enter the main event, but Scotty had won $35,000 for him and he was clearly playing well. Scotty was a great horse to back in the main event, but Neil was nowhere to be found.

Then something strange happened: I had a dream.

I've never had a dream as vivid and real. I was sitting in the front row of the bleachers at Binion's and Scotty Nguyen was standing in front of the poker table with Jack Binion. Jack was putting the championship bracelet on Scotty's wrist. The dream was so powerful that I woke up in the middle of the night and just sat there, stunned. The next day at Binion's, I couldn't stop thinking about that dream. It was the day before the main event and I knew that Scotty hadn't registered for the tournament yet. But to me, it was like it had already happened: I had seen him win the World Series of Poker championship. In reality, Scotty and all of us were still trying to contact Neil, but he hadn't returned any calls.

Finally, I took Scotty aside.

"Screw it, Scotty. I got some money and I had this dream you were going to win the World Series of Poker. I want to put you in satellites to try and win you into this tournament."

"That's right, baby. You know the dream. I can win it, baby. I just gotta get in."

I put up $1,000 for Scotty in a single table satellite that paid one winner for one seat in the championship. He lost. Did I mention it was a really powerful dream? So I put Scotty into another $1,000 single table satellite and he lost again. This was going to be a long day for Scotty, but what the hell: I had this dream. I put him into two super satellites with rebuys and he never got close. But he was Scotty and nothing fazed him.

"Just one more baby, I can do it. Just one more, Mikey."

"Scotty, I'm already in for 10 percent of my bankroll. I have no backer and I am out of a job now. If I go broke, I don't know what I am going to do. So I guess my dream is wrong, I can't put you in any more satellites."

"Come on, Mikey. One more, one more. I tell you I am going to win this one."

"Scotty, I'm already in for almost $5,000, my bankroll can't take anymore."

"Just one more baby. First place is a million dollars!"

I gave in.

"Okay, Scotty. I'll put up $500, but you gotta find two other guys to put up $250 each."

Scotty got one of the cash game players to put up $250; no one seems to remember the guy's name. Then Scotty ran into Jesse Jones in the men's room and told him he was looking for a final $250. It was almost midnight and they were getting ready to run the last couple of satellites for the night. Jesse wasn't backing anyone at that time and had decided to stay away from backing deals completely, but there was something about Scotty that told him to make the deal.

So Scotty had his $1,000 for the final satellite before the main event.

On the very first hand, Scotty was dealt two aces, another player got two kings and a third player had two queens. Scotty tripled up and cruised to victory in the final satellite of the final day before the World Series of Poker's "Big One" began. We agreed that Scotty would get one-third, I would get one-third, and Jesse and the mystery player would receive one-sixth each of whatever Scotty won in the main event.

On the first day of the tournament, I went to see my mom because she was worried about me.

"What are you going to do?" she asked. "Neil's not staking you. You're low on money."

"There's nothing to worry about," I assured her. "Scotty's gonna win the World Series."

I kept repeating it so that she would stop worrying, but it just made her worry more.

"Listen to me," she begged. "You've got to stop living this pipe dream that Scotty's going to win the title. You sound crazy."

"But Mom, I had this dream. It was so clear," I kept saying.

She thought I'd lost it. She was certain that I would come to my senses the minute Scotty busted out of the tournament.

I went to Binion's to watch Day One of the main event and play some cash games. The main event drew 350 players and Scotty was off to a pretty good start. I took breaks from my cash game and checked on him every couple of hours, although there was really no need. There would be plenty of time to watch Scotty; the main event lasted five days. He survived Day One and started the second day in pretty decent chip position. And then he began to pick up steam. Before I knew it, he was one of the top ten chip leaders.

Seeing Scotty near the top of the leader board on the start of Day Three was really weird. It wasn't like I was holding my breath, "Oh

God, what am I going to do? I think Scotty is going to win." Not at all. I knew he was going to win. I had never been so sure of anything in my life. With two days to go in the tournament and 100 players left, I was counting my third of a million dollars. I was that sure of what was coming. To this day, it is the most incredible feeling I've ever had.

When it got to the last nine players, my mom even came down to watch the final table with me. Don't get me wrong; she still thought I was crazy, but that didn't mean Scotty wasn't going to win it all either. Watching it unfold was amazing. It was like watching a final table on television once you've figured out who's going to win the tournament: The poker is still interesting but there's no suspense. I mean, it's 10:58 p.m. and the two final players are all in; you know the show is over at eleven, so what can possibly happen? Except that this was live.

Scotty Nguyen won the 1998 WSOP Championship!

I really didn't know that Scotty was going to win, yet I did. What a strange feeling. Of course, it was a feeling that came with $333,333.33, my share of the $1 million. I was almost in tears. And yeah, I was pretty ecstatic. You can see me in all the press photos and the video-tape smiling and jumping around.

That win catapulted Scotty to amazing heights in the poker world, and it did a lot for me too. All the players knew that I had put Scotty in; they knew I'd backed the right horse. I had told a lot of people about the dream, but I don't think many of them believed me. They just thought I was a guy with a good eye for talent, not some idiot who put up ten percent of his bankroll on a dream.

Right after the championship, Neil suddenly reappeared. He called and said that since he had backed Scotty and me in the earlier tournaments, he should get a piece of Scotty in the main event. I was stunned. That wasn't the deal. In fact, there was no deal. He was the one that made the decision not to back Scotty in the main event. Where was he when we were all calling him and when Scotty needed the $10,000 buy-in? Neil wanted about $100,000 of my $333,000 and I think he wanted the same piece of Scotty's share.

I honestly thought that Neil didn't deserve anything. But to be sure, I asked a bunch of players about the situation. They all told me the same thing. Three guys took the financial risk to back Scotty and they were the ones that should get paid according to their prearranged deal. Neil wasn't even in the equation. I thought maybe I should give him something because, even as ugly as things had gotten between us, he still was my first backer. I finally offered him $5,000. He was totally insulted. But if it had been up to Neil, Scotty wouldn't have even played the main event. He basically got what he deserved, which was nothing.

I was the talk of poker for a long, long time because I staked Scotty in that tournament. I'm sure I'm a net loser staking people by now. But in 1998, I was ahead in the backing game, and my score came at a perfect time. I needed the money.

I found myself with a nice little bankroll. I bought a house, where I still live today. I put $100,000 down while it was under construction. It was my first house so I had no idea how many extra costs there were. By the time I was done with the blinds, the furniture, upgrades for the kitchen and flooring, I was into the house for another $125,000. So I found myself putting $225,000 into the house out of my $400,000 bankroll. But there was still plenty left over.

I was set on never going broke, so I never played higher than $100/$200, avoiding the $200/$400 and $300/$600 games, even though I knew I could beat them. I just didn't want to put myself in a position where something bad could happen really fast. I liked being the only person making decisions about what games I played and which ones I passed on. I finally started to enjoy the freedom of being on my own.

Anyone who knows me now won't believe that I had phenomenal bankroll discipline back then. For the first time ever, I had financial security and did everything I could not to piss it away. After the Series, I was back playing the cash games at the Mirage nearly seven days a week, sixteen hours a day. Like most young professional poker players, I had to spend a good part of my life doing nothing but playing poker. seeing hundreds and hundreds of hands at many different tables under various game circumstances. And that meant spending weeks on end at the tables.

Of course, playing online poker now, you can see thousands of hand in a day. This is just one reason why so many Internet players are as good as they are at a young age; they go through the learning curve so much faster. But whether you play at a casino or online, to be a professional you have to go through the grind and rack up experience.

I was picking my games carefully and was running good again. I didn't win huge, but I was getting the job done. I grew my bankroll to about $400,000 and kept it there for a whole year, while paying all my bills. I was pretty happy.

Was I as happy or content as I could or should have been? Probably not, but I was okay. By that time, depression had become a daily part of my life. I figured that was just the way it was. I didn't know anything about bipolar disorder or that there might be a way to medically treat the way I felt. But I was worried about money less and that helped. I had a new house and a nice car, and things looked and felt better in my world. I sure wasn't missing the trailer park.

In October of 1998, the Bellagio opened with an amazing poker room. Bobby Baldwin, who won the WSOP main event in 1978, moved over from heading up the Mirage to heading up the Bellagio. He was going to be sure that the Bellagio had the best poker room anywhere and had the world's best poker players playing in that room. The move of the big games from the Mirage to the Bellagio was fast. It had taken years for everyone to slowly move to the Mirage after it opened, but the shift of the big games to the Bellagio took less than a week.

By January of 1999, if you were looking for a big game, you just went to the Bellagio. You could pick up all the poker news and gossip at the tables there. You found out who was on a winning streak, or more likely, who had gone bust and was trying to raise a stake. You heard about every drug problem, drinking problem, marriage problem or backer problem. Stories about the old players were told and retold and new stories were constantly being put together.

But my story was taking a twist that I didn't like at all. I was beating the games at the Bellagio on a regular basis, but instead of being known for my game, I'd become "Mike Matusow, the guy who backed Scotty Nguyen when Scotty won the World Series."

I was a phenomenal hold'em player. I had probably become one of the best, if not the best, Omaha high-low players in the world. But I felt like I wasn't getting any respect for my game. I started telling people that I was sick of being known as "the guy that backed Scotty." I was on a mission to prove something. Anyone who knows me knows that when I have to prove something, I can play some amazing poker.

There was really only one way to do it: I was going to have to win a World Series of Poker tournament. All through the spring of '99, while I was playing the cash games at the Bellagio, I was thinking about the Series coming in April and how I was going to win a WSOP bracelet and get out from under Scotty's shadow.

Chapter Ten

Out of the Shadow

One of my missions going into the 1999 World Series of Poker was to play no-limit hold'em. It wasn't just about me wanting to play in the championship event. I knew that to truly become a world-class player, I simply had to play all the games well. I started to realize that each game developed certain strengths and skills that you could use in all the others. Some games are all about position and starting hands; others are games of outs and draws, and still others require you to have a precise read on your opponents. Learning each new game and playing that game at a professional level improves your overall poker game.

In 1999, the WSOP had fifteen open tournaments, a few less than in 1998. Every event, except the championship, was scheduled as a one-day tournament. You started at noon and played until someone won a bracelet. But since the fields were getting bigger and bigger, the tournament director would sometimes make the decision to add a second day. If it was getting very late, they could stop play when the event got down to the final table and continue play the next day.

I was planning to play six or seven events, depending on how deep I got the day before or if I made it to a Day Two final table. My plan, of course, was to be at one or more final tables. I liked the fact that I was playing on my own bankroll without a backer or anyone else telling me what to play. And I would sure as shit guarantee that no one talked me into making a deal at any final table I made. I wouldn't screw myself out of a win again. More than anything, I wanted the other players to see Mike "the guy who backed Scotty" Matusow with a bracelet on his wrist.

In the first ten days of the Series, I played the limit hold'em tournaments and one Omaha high-low event, but I didn't cash. Even though I was playing well, I just wasn't getting any traction. In the cash games, however, I was ahead by a nice chunk of change. So while the Series was going okay for my bankroll, it just wasn't doing much good for my empty wrist.

The $3,500 No-limit Hold'em tournament, one of the bigger buy-in events, was coming up next on the schedule. This was a real chance to get no-limit experience in preparation for the main event. No-limit hold'em cash games were still non-existent in '99 and most of the tournaments were limit hold'em or other games. I decided to play despite the fact that the big buy-in would attract some of the world's best players. While I didn't have any no-limit experience, I had thought a lot about no-limit strategy. Bits and pieces of it were floating around in my head: "Okay, Mike, don't go broke with one pair in an unraised pot. Look for weakness. Don't be messing with the other big stacks…"

The strategy everyone calls "small ball" today was the game plan I was setting for myself in this no-limit event. I knew that, overall, I wanted to make lots of small bets and win a lot of small pots. Mostly though, I was just going to draw on my poker instincts. I figured I'd have to develop a strategy as I played. I knew I shouldn't just "play my game," because that was a limit hold'em game. And no matter what anyone tells you, no-limit hold'em and limit hold'em are not the same game. They're as different from each other as piss and water.

Within the first few hours in the tournament, I found situations where I could pick up chips and I started to figure out people's habits. There was a bigger range of betting patterns in no-limit than in limit, so I watched when players limped, when they raised, how they raised, and how much they raised. It didn't take me long to figure out the difference between a weak raise and a strong raise. I just took it all in: "That guy's weak, so I'll just move in here and pick it up." When I saw weakness, I attacked it.

There were 205 players in the event, so we knew we'd be playing late and probably coming back the next day for the final table. After about eight hours into the tournament, I was in great chip position, well above average. I had played really well and was shocked at how many chips I had been able to steal. I'd been able to attack weakness over and over again. I was able to keep the pot small when I wasn't sure, and play bigger pots when I had a hand. This strategy seemed to work for me. That's how I developed my no-limit game, playing in my first WSOP no limit event.

There really weren't any fish in this event. This was practically the highest no-limit buy-in tournament ever run, other than the main event. No amateurs were walking in off the streets to plunk $3,500 on the table. There weren't any Internet qualifiers and even the players who bought in through satellites were experienced pros. There just wasn't a lot of dead money in the starting field. Today, you might see over 3,000 players in a $1,500 no-limit event. While a lot of fierce, experienced players will be in the mix, there also will be a pretty large number of players who don't have a clue. In the '90s, the top professionals still had an edge, but the average skill level of players was much higher than today. You didn't run across too many players donking off their chips.

No-limit Texas hold'em was also a very different game in 1999. Yeah, players bluffed, but not every hand. Mostly, players put their chips in good and played for the showdown. It was probably easier to learn back then because there weren't a lot of different strategies that you had to defend against. The small ball strategy that I was trying to play wasn't used by many players like it is today, which made it easier for me to win big pots and make laydowns in small pots.

As the night wore on and the field got smaller and smaller, my strategy continued to keep me near the top of the chip count. Around midnight there was a break as they reseated the remaining eighteen players at two tables. I was one of the top three chip leaders and we had a strong lead on the rest of the field.

At my new table, I raised the first pot after the break and they all folded to me. I shifted my plan and raised pot after pot. I kept building my stack. If someone played back at me, I figured I could slow down and fold my cards if I needed to. But I had the monster stack at my table and players just weren't willing to go up against me.

One of my pre-tournament strategies was, "Don't mess with the big stack." Now I was the big stack and they weren't messing with me.

The play was fast and it didn't take us long to get from eighteen players down to the final nine. Most of the bust outs were coming from the other table, which made me think that some big stacks were building over there. But when the night ended, I was the chip leader. As we were bagging our chips, it hit me. Wow! I had just made my second final table at the World Series in another game I hadn't really played before. But this time there wasn't going to be any deal making. I could finish fifth or ninth or second, but I was playing this one out for the bracelet.

The lineup for this final table, like nearly all WSOP final tables back then, was loaded. Really, until about 2003, you almost never saw a WSOP final table with more than one final table virgin. It was unusual when Scotty Nguyen and I both ended up playing at our first one in the Omaha high-low event in '97. But hell, this whole fucking tournament field was filled with quality players who really knew what they were doing. I expected this was going to be a long and tough final. All the players had been around the block and there was only one guy on a short stack. But strange things can happen in poker.

Noel Furlong might not be a name that all the players knew when he sat down to play on Day Two, but two weeks later when he went on to win the WSOP Championship, that would change. Alex Brenes, Humberto Brenes' brother was there, but he's a really good player in his own right and he was going to be my nemesis at this table. Hilbert Shirey had three bracelets coming into this event, including the two that he'd won in 1995. He had made the final table of the 1991 WSOP main event, so I was pretty sure he knew the game. Ken Goldstein cashed three times at the '99 Series including this tournament and he would make another final table just two days later. This was Dewey Weum's sixth WSOP final table, all in no-limit hold'em, including his fourth place finish in the '98 main event one year earlier.

All three remaining players had final table experience: Jamie Ligator was heading into his second WSOP final table and Michael Davis his third in three years. And while Pascal Perrault from France was pretty new to the poker scene, this was already his second final table. Of course, now he has a track record a mile long with tournament cashes from every corner of the globe, including a European Poker Tour championship.

Then there was me. Even with my first final table appearance two years earlier, I was still the player with the least number of hours played at the Series. While I was trying to get experience to play in the main event, most of these guys had already been there, done that.

On the very first hand, Ken Goldstein got into it with Hilbert Shirey. All their chips went in preflop with Ken's Q-10 dominated by Hilbert's A-10. To seal the deal, an ace flopped, and Hilbert moved up from a medium stack to fourth place behind the three big stacks. And just like that—one hand, one bust-out—we were down to eight players. A couple of hands later, Jamie Ligator raised all in with K-J and I called him with A-5. The board ran out K-10-7-10 giving him a pair of kings, but an ace hit the river. I busted him and increased my chip lead. On the very next hand I got pocket aces and raised, but no one called. I showed the aces before mucking them.

Two hands later, I moved in on a big pot with pocket kings and Hilbert laid it down to me. Yeah, I showed the kings. There was something going on here and I wanted them all to know that I was on a big rush. I thought I could pick up some easy pots with next to nothing if they felt threatened by my hot streak. But as it turned out, I didn't exactly have next to nothing on the next hand. Noel Furlong raised and I looked down at pocket kings again! Now the question was, would Noel believe that I was still on a great card rush if I re-raised, or would he think I was just trying to push him around?

I was good at signaling weakness when I was strong and Noel, who is an aggressive player, took the bait. He moved all in and when I called, he showed pocket deuces. Another king fell on the board—not that I needed it—and Noel went out in seventh place. I had an even bigger chip lead and had separated myself from the pack. I was getting pretty damned excited and I'm sure the other players were wondering when my sick run was going to stop. Four hands later, I was dealt pocket sevens, just good enough to eliminate Pascal Perrault in sixth place. In that first hour, we'd lost four out of nine players, and I'd taken out three of them. There were 717,500 in chips on the table and at this point I had about 440,000 of them.

A couple of hands later, I moved Shirey all in with J-8 to my Q-J. But a low board with an 8 gave him the pot. I guess I wasn't invincible after all, but I didn't take that as a signal to become conservative. I had the big stack and I kept raising preflop, just like I had the night before. I sure wasn't going into a shell with a monster chip lead, although the next two eliminations came in hands that I had folded.

And we were suddenly down to three—me, Alex Brenes and Dewey Weum.

I had a chance to put it away. On a hand against Alex Brenes, I flopped two pair, jacks and nines, against his pocket kings. I got all of his chips in, but the board paired sevens on the river and his bigger two pair took down the pot, keeping him alive in the tournament. If I'd won that hand, I would've been heads up with Dewey Weum with about a 6 to 1 chip advantage. But instead, Alex took his big stack up against Dewey, who raised all-in with pocket queens and was in good shape against Alex's A-9. But Alex flopped two pair, turned a full house, and just like that we were heads-up for the bracelet.

I slowed down a little once we got heads-up because I wanted to see if Alex would change his style when we were playing one-on-one. But I lost a big hand early when Alex rivered a pair. Without that river card, I would've won the bracelet right then and there. Now Alex had the lead with about a 15,000 chip advantage over me.

I had gotten to the final table with aggression and I decided I was going to win the bracelet with aggression. I started moving all in to push him into a defensive game and he kept folding. I got the lead back and just kept the pedal to the metal. He was going to have to play back at me at some point, and until then I was going to apply pressure. When Brenes had his brief lead, he led 365,000 to 350,000. When I started pushing and taking down the blinds, hand after hand, the numbers turned around pretty quickly. I won one medium sized pot we played to the river. After a couple more laydowns to my all-in bets, it was time. He was down to just over 50,000 and I knew a confrontation had to happen soon.

Alex raised preflop to 16,000 and I moved all in again. He snap-called me and showed pocket fours. I had A-10. A small pair against two overcards was probably the best he could have hoped for at that point. The board fell K-8-7-J but with just one more card to come, I had a lot of outs. Any queen or 9 gave me the straight and any ace or 10 gave me a bigger pair.

The 10 hit the river and boom! It was over. I won my first WSOP bracelet.

They gave me the WSOP bracelet and $265,000. No matter how much you think about it, plan for it, and dream about it, you just can't imagine the feeling. I was on top of the world. I had proved myself where it counted, at the World Series of Poker. And I proved myself in the game that counted.

A couple of days later I made another final table in an Omaha high-low event and finished fifth, which just added to my already bursting self-confidence.

I played in the main event, but I was card dead and didn't survive the first day. By then, it really didn't matter: I was young and there were plenty of WSOP main events in front of me. I'd make that final table at some point. Hell, I was too good not to!

Before the '99 World Series, I truly believed that there wasn't anybody better than I was at reading people in limit hold'em. With two final tables in Omaha high-low, I felt I was starting to own that game. Now that I had a bracelet in no-limit, there was really no limit to my ego. If you think I'm full of myself now, it's nothing compared to what I was like after the '99 Series.

You have to know just how high I was on my poker game to understand the next six months of my life.

Chapter Eleven

Cards Make You,
Egos Break You

One way to not lose your bankroll is to put it into something you can't spend. I'd bought my house with the money I'd won backing Scotty. After the '99 win, I added a pool and spa. I think they call that investing. I wish I had put money away every time I hit it big, but at least on those two scores I did. Even after living expenses and the new pool, my bankroll was up to a half million by the summer of '99. I was just killing the cash games with no end in sight.

After the Series, I had headed back to the Bellagio and the high limit cash games. Bellagio had become a very hot room, and the limit hold'em games were getting up to $200/$400 on the weekends and the $100/$200 was going every day. The Omaha high-low was up to $75/$150 and there were plenty of games and players, making for a good selection of tables and limits. At the poker tables, I was feeling great. I was bulletproof. When I walked into the Bellagio, no one wanted me to sit down at their table. I was playing the biggest game they were spreading and I was crushing it day after day. It wasn't *if* I was going to win that day, it was *how much*. That much success and consistency plays with your head and my head was already huge from the WSOP win.

I changed from being the ultra-hungry kid with something to prove. I became a poker player with a dangerously big ego.

I had reason to be proud of my game. But after the Series, I completely lost my discipline. Hell, I didn't think I needed any. I was crushing every game I played. People think that when you're losing, you're at your most vulnerable, but I don't agree. It's when you're running hot that you have to watch out. I was good; lots of players get that good at some point. But eventually you hit the wall, you suffer a losing streak, you lose your focus, or you spring major leaks in your game. Some players develop leaks like sports betting, craps, drugs or women. It was right about this time that I almost got trapped into what easily could have become a big "life" leak.

I had a really hot girlfriend, who was psychotic. I mean, really psychotic. Even her name, Castiana, was phony. My mom thought there was something wrong with her and wanted her out of my life. So she hired a private investigator to check her out. It turned out this girl, a runaway from Oregon, was a complete fucking whack job. She was a prostitute who had been in jail for hooking and for passing bad checks. The woman I thought I was dating actually didn't exist. When I found out, I broke it off with her immediately, but she wouldn't go away. She would just show up at my door. One time she showed up at the Bellagio when I was in a big game. She attacked me once at my house. She was so nuts and out of control, I just ran out of the house and left. I certainly wouldn't hit her back, and she was strong enough and crazy enough to really do some damage. Getting her out of my life was tough, but she finally disappeared with the next fool.

As it turns out, the leak in my poker game was something much simpler—I thought I would never lose.

Now, you might say, "Well, Mike, you knew that wasn't true. You told Neil when he was backing you that there were no poker gods, that you were only running good. You knew better, Mikey."

I did. But I didn't.

I forgot my own words. I thought I could live my life any way I wanted because I couldn't be beat. Why should I think anything else? I was at the Bellagio every day playing the best players in the world, in the best poker room in the world, and I won every single day. With my bankroll growing and the limits at the Bellagio going up, I stepped up from the $200/$400 games to $300/$600.

I was one of the best poker players in the world. Why shouldn't I play higher and higher?

Then it started. I went on a minor losing streak. I played on Rosh Hashanah, a big Jewish holiday, even though I knew better. I don't know what I was thinking. Probably I wasn't thinking; my big ego had taken over and nothing else mattered. I couldn't lose at poker—until I did. I dropped maybe $70,000 over a month or so. It was a hit, but I knew I was a winner and could get it back. So I did what I tell every poker player not to do: I stepped up in limits. I started playing the biggest game in the room, the $400/$800 mixed game. I'd be pissed when the game wasn't being spread and I had to step back down to the $300/$600 game. I hated going as low as $200/$400.

I went on an eight or nine day losing streak. I never backed off or slowed down. I never refused a seat at the biggest game or took one minute to consider what I was doing. In eight or nine days, I lost $400,000. In less than two weeks, I lost the bankroll I had grown and protected for three years. It was gone, all of it.

I couldn't cope with what had happened. I didn't know what I was going to do; I didn't have any money. I didn't have anyone to back me. I was a walking time bomb. I had it all and I flushed it all away. I knew what I was supposed to do when I hit a losing streak. I knew I wasn't a poker god. I knew the run would stop. But when it happened I pushed all the wrong buttons. I played longer sessions. I moved up in limits. I pressed and I pressed until there was nothing left.

For six months I had walked around with the biggest ego in town, thinking that I could just show up and win. When I finally ran bad, I didn't know what hit me. I didn't know how to react to adversity because I had never really had that kind of setback. I really had no way to cope with it. After nearly a week of rage and tears and more rage, I sat down and decided I had to find a way out.

I went to the bank and borrowed $100,000 against my house. The new pool and spa in a booming real estate market meant that I had over $200,000 equity in the house and I took out a loan for half of it. I knew I had to be careful. I had to play smart. I went back to the Bellagio and sat down in the $200/$400 game, never looking at the high limit games. I told myself that I would take two $10,000 shots at this limit and if I lost, I would play $100/$200. But even playing at $200/$400, I felt like I was playing small. It's really hard to step down in limits once you've played higher. It's tough psychologically. All those players I had lost all that money to were sitting in the same room, playing in those higher limit games. I couldn't help thinking about the fact that they were playing with my money.

I had the money from the home loan and that was it. If I lost it I was broke. If I had to play lower I would, but I knew that would kill me. When you have been up there at one level, it is so damn hard to imagine being way down again. I was used to winning or losing $10,000 or $15,000 a day and it was hard to focus with less money on the line. But I tried not to think about all that as I sat down at that first $200/$400 table, starting on what I hoped would be my road back.

As 1999 was coming to a close, I started my comeback. Fortunately, I was able to reach down and find my game. I won about $180,000 over the next six weeks. I immediately paid back the loan on the house and within a few more weeks, I had built my bankroll to over $200,000. It surely wasn't where I started from, but I didn't owe anyone any money and I wasn't in danger of going broke. That is, of course, if I kept my ego under control. And that's hard to do in poker.

You need some ego in poker, almost like a person needs to eat. It keeps you going, it fuels you. But if it gets out of control, you can't just shut off your ego any more than a person can stop eating food. But I had my bankroll again. It wasn't as big, but I could build it back up. I knew how not to go broke. I knew it meant living with, and controlling, my ego. Once I started winning and winning again, I still wasn't sure how I would keep it from going to my head. When it comes to my head, control wasn't—and still isn't—my strongest suit.

The truth is I won all the money playing great. I lost all the money thinking I was great. I got it all back knowing I had to play great.

I dropped about $40,000 at the poker tables over the next few months. That hit, added to my normal living expenses, had me a little worried about my bankroll heading into the 2000 Series. I wasn't short, but I was getting there. No one wants the pressure of going into the Series short.

By that time, I was used to my own cycle of emotional highs and lows. I had lived with it for years. I'm sure that blowing my bankroll and having to borrow money on the house took a mental toll. I started to struggle more mentally. During my comeback, I was depressed a lot and started to feel like I was getting closer to some emotional edge. This would have been a good time to get some help; it was probably another missed opportunity to identify my bipolar disorder. But that isn't uncommon. Bipolar can creep up on people in early adulthood and a lot of people are slow in getting help.

Besides, if people had asked me to talk about my depression or to see someone, I probably would have blown them off and headed for the poker table.

Chapter Twelve

The Day That Changed
My Life

Professional poker players plan their entire year around the World Series of Poker. The WSOP was not just a big bunch of tournaments in one place at one time. The World Series was bigger than all the other tournaments put together. Anybody who was anybody in poker was at Binion's Horseshoe every spring. If you didn't show up, you were either broke or dead. If you were broke you showed up anyway and begged or borrowed a stake.

The cycle started with building up a bankroll before the WSOP, working the tournaments like hell for five weeks straight at Binion's, and then taking a much needed vacation after the main event. Poker players don't make New Year's resolutions. We make New Series' resolutions. In the first few days of the tournaments you hear them all:

"I'm going to play tighter this year."

"I'm only going to play five events, no matter how I do."

"I blew too much money in the cash games last year, so I'm only going to play tournaments this year."

The WSOP still is the monster event today, but poker players have been given a lot more opportunities in just the last five years. The World Poker Tour hands out millions of dollars at every tournament. The European Poker Tour is a big player today, Aussie Millions is a great event with a big prize pool, and the Asian and Latin America Tours are just beginning to produce big events. Today, you actually have to choose between major tournaments sometimes. You might have to miss the Borgata or Foxwoods to play the European Poker Tour events in London and Barcelona, especially if your girlfriend wants that European vacation you've been promising her.

But in 2000, players were still telling their daughters that spring weddings were out of the question if they wanted daddy to walk them down the aisle. No one made any commitments until the World Series schedule was announced. Everyone in poker got psyched for it. You got your bankroll in place. Maybe you even took some time off right before the Series to rest up for it. Some players got so pumped for the Series that a bad Series, or a really bad beat at a final table, could send them into a career-threatening tailspin. But you can't let your highs and lows rely on the turn of a single card, even if it's in the main event of the WSOP. You do that and you will eventually make yourself crazy.

In each of the past three Series, I'd walked out of Binion's with six figures more than I walked in with. That was the way every World Series had been for me and that was the way it was always going to be. Binion's was a place where only good things happened. In 1997, I made that unbelievable run in my first Omaha high-low tournament. Then in 1998, I killed the cash games and backed Scotty to his main event win. I won my first bracelet in 1999. In 2000, I was ready for another monster Series.

Even though I had two big tournament scores in '97 and '99, I had spent most of my WSOP time in the side games. For 2000, I was planning to play a lot more tournaments. The open tournament schedule was up to twenty-five events with a really good selection of mixed games. Three years earlier, I had been a limit hold'em specialist, but I'd been playing and winning a lot more in mixed cash games over the last year and I could compete in almost any game.

My plan was to play in all the Omaha high-low events, maybe one stud 8-or-better tournament, and as many of the limit and no-limit hold'em events as I could manage. In 2000, all of the tournaments except the main event were scheduled to play down to the final table in one day with the final table scheduled for the following day. So I was hoping to play in more than a dozen events, factoring in possible—and in my mind, likely—final table appearances.

Going into the 2000 World Series of Poker, I had only one resolution—kick some serious ass. I was totally psyched for the tournaments to begin.

Before the first week of the Series was over, I had made a final table in the $1,500 Omaha high-low tournament. I had worked my way through the starting field of 290 players, surviving on patience and tight play. A huge part of the success of any tournament player is survival. You can't catch a big run of cards late in the day if you donk off all your chips early in the tournament. I wasn't crushing the game—I never had the cards or the right table mix to make too many moves—but I still had chips when it got down to the last nine players. Brent Carter, Vince Burgio and Mark Gregorich also made it into the next day. There was a lot of Omaha experience at this final table and the pros knew enough not to let strong players with short stacks get back into the game.

At the start of the final table, I had 29,000 in chips and the blinds were starting at 2,000/4,000. Along with Robert Turner and Young Pak, I was one of the short stacks; we each had less than eight big bets to work with. Even though I came out firing with some good starting hands, I couldn't close. I wasn't alone. All the early action went to the big stacks and the rest of us never managed to find chips. My final hand was a short-stack move with A-K-Q-10 after a flop of J-10-3. I had the wrap on a nut straight draw and a low pair, but Brent Carter held two aces and I didn't improve. I was out quickly in ninth place, with Pak and Turner finishing right behind me.

My payday was $7,000, hardly the cash I was looking for from the event. Still, I felt really good. I had my first final table under my belt. I liked my reads and my play. My expectations were already high for the Series, and this just kicked them into overdrive. I was ready to move on to the next tournament and take a serious shot at a bracelet.

One afternoon when I wasn't playing a tournament, I went to the Horseshoe to check out the side games. None of the cash games looked all that juicy yet, so I stuck my name on a $200/$400 Omaha high-low "interest" list, hoping that enough players would show up so a game could start. Then I wandered upstairs to the tournament room. The $2000 Pot-Limit Hold'em final table was in progress and, even from across the room, I could hear Phil Hellmuth going off about something. In 2000, Phil and I were poker acquaintances. He respected my game, I respected his, but we weren't the friends we are today. One of the things I have always liked about Phil is that sometimes he can make me look almost normal. I could tell this was going to be one of those times.

As I got near the final table I ran into Andy Glazer, the ace reporter who was covering the event. Andy told me that the floor had just made a ruling about a marked card that had set Phil off. I didn't need to be told that Phil was "off" because he was doing the "Hellmuth talking to himself" thing at full volume. Andy added that he sensed the Hellmuth volcano was about to erupt. Phil had been playing a short stack since the final table began and David Colclough had been coming over the top of Phil all afternoon. Phil had already laid down at least half a dozen hands to David and he was pretty steamed about it.

While Andy and I were talking, Phil doubled up. Some unsuspecting player must have thought Phil was on tilt and tried to take advantage of him. One thing I've learned about Phil is to never assume he's on tilt, no matter how much he spouts off at the table. His mouth may be working, but he is almost always in the zone. Phil had some chips now, but he was still talking. I grabbed a ringside seat to wait for more fireworks. It didn't take long.

Phil got into a hand cheap with 2-4 offsuit. He couldn't shake David Colclough off the pot with a bet on the 4-5-8 flop. Hellmuth hit a deuce on the turn for two pair and fired out a huge bet. David stared Phil down for a long time, but eventually made the call. Hellmuth announced to the crowd that he thought Colclough had an overpair. The chips went all in when a 9 hit on the river.

Phil was right, but unlucky. Yes, Colclough had an overpair—pocket nines! David had made a set of nines on the river, and busted Phil from the tournament. Phil instantly went ballistic.

"How could you not fold on the turn? You knew I had you beat when I made that bet! You called when you knew you were dead to two outs."

Actually, Colclough had more than two cards that would improve his hand to a winner, but no one was going to interrupt Phil in full rant mode. It was a classic Hellmuth bust out. He calmed down quickly and walked back to the table to shake David's hand. David totally dissed him and left Phil standing there empty handed. Glazer called it a 3.5 on the Hellmuth/Richter scale. But you have to understand that the losing moment in any poker tournament totally sucks. Anyone who tells you any different is a liar. To be a great player, you have to play with passion. With Phil and me, that passion sometimes boils over on a river suckout.

It's not an act. You play with passion, you lose with passion.

The next day, I played in the $2,500 Seven-Card Stud high-low event and kicked ass, cruising to the final table the following day. I'll always remember that tournament because it changed my life forever—just not in the way I imagined.

When I sat down at my second World Series final table in less than a week, I didn't just think I had a shot at a bracelet, I thought it was as good as mine. I had played Day One well and was confident in my stud game. In my earlier Omaha high-low event, I knew I didn't have a real shot at the bracelet, since I was starting the final table from such a big chip disadvantage. In this event, I was going into Day Two in excellent chip position.

Half of the players had cashed in the Omaha high-low tournament the week before; Mark Gregorich had finished sixth, Andreas Krause had finished twenty-fourth, I had finished ninth, and Nat Koe had won it. Oddly enough, we were all together again for this seven-card stud high-low final table.

I started out with 57,500 chips, which put me solidly in second place. Other than the chip leader, there was only one other player, Joe Wynn, who was above 40,000. With the limits at 3,000/6,000 and a 300 ante, the two shortest stacks, Ray Miller at 10,000 and Gino DiPeppe at 15,500, were only going to get to play one hand for all their chips. Even chip leader Nat Koe with his 82,000 chips only had around fourteen big bets. With the antes at 300 and no other forced bets, players had time to find a hand. Committing to a second-best hand early, however, could cripple the bigger stacks and end the day for the short and medium stacks. Everyone expected that we were going to lose two or three players early and then settle in for some real poker with the remaining big stacks.

We lost Ray Miller on the second hand of the day. On the very next hand I was dealt A-2-3; you can't ask for a better starting hand in seven-card stud high-low. As the hand played out, I ended up with A-2-3-4-6 for low and two pair, aces up. This was a great hand: the second best possible low hand and a very good high hand. I knew I'd get half the pot for the low hand and thought that my two pair could hold on for high and scoop the pot. It wasn't until Andreas Krause raised me on the river that I thought I was going to have to settle for a split pot. I was dumbstruck when he scooped the pot, showing down the wheel (A-2-3-4-5) for the best possible low hand and a straight for the high end.

Before Andreas had even finished stacking my chips, I looked down at my next hand and found A-A-5. On this hand, I again made a 6-low with aces up for high. I ran into another wheel, this time held by Joe Wynn, the eventual bracelet winner. Unfuckingbelievable! I had made two big hands with second best lows and aces up in each for high, and they both got ironed out by wheels.

My chip stack was decimated. I felt like someone had stuck a knife in my gut and left it there. Two hands later, I went out in seventh place.

Devastated doesn't even begin to cover how I felt. I knew I was going to win that bracelet and instead I finished seventh out of eight players. How could this happen to me? In the first ten minutes of the final table, how could I pick up a 6-low and two pairs in back-to-back hands and run into a wheel both times? The cocktail waitress hadn't even had time to deliver my fucking Mountain Dew. I won about $10,000, but compared to the $129,000 for first place, it seemed like nothing. I was living large back then and my bills were almost $10,000 a month. My poker bankroll was down to around $80,000, so I was feeling really tight. I had wanted to win this tournament, but more importantly, I needed to win it. I started hyperventilating and feeling anxious. I didn't want to have to borrow money again. Getting the loan on the house had been a headache and I didn't want to have to go through that process again.

I started this final table thinking I was bulletproof. I ended it feeling that everything in my life was broken. I cried the rest of the night. I couldn't get those two hands out of my mind. Why had that happened to me? How could I have picked up back-to-back hands like that? How could I have finished seventh? How could I have been so fucking unlucky?

The World Series had always been my ticket to financial security. Now all I could think about was how I'd be hurting for money. I knew what depression was, but this aching, helpless feeling was way beyond anything I had ever experienced. This was just blank, dark emptiness and it scared me. I could barely breathe and I was shaking. It scared me a lot and there was absolutely nothing I could do to make this horrible darkness go away.

I went out drinking with two of my best friends, Jeanie and Mark, that night. We were meeting a group of friends at Club Rio. I tried to beg out of it, but they told me I shouldn't be alone. And to be honest, I was afraid to be alone. I don't remember much about the club that night. With every drink I had, all I kept thinking was, "How could I lose those hands back-to-back." Eventually we wound up at the VooDoo Lounge, the exclusive bar at the top of the Rio with a balcony that overlooks the entire Las Vegas Strip.

Jeanie and Mark were trying to cheer me up, trying to help me, but I was inconsolable. They told me I should try doing this drug called Ecstasy, showing me this little pill as they each took one. Ecstasy would fix everything. It would make me happy. They promised. Mark and Jeanie both knew I didn't do drugs. I know people might find it almost funny now, but back then I was like the poster boy for the anti-drug movement. I had never done an illegal or recreational drug in my life. I didn't even like to take aspirin. It was difficult for me to be around anyone who did drugs, or anything illegal for that matter. Mike Matusow was one hundred percent straight.

Jeanie and Mark kept pushing. Over and over they told me, "Take this. It will make you happy!"

I couldn't really blame them. It's not like "The Mouth" goes silent when I'm depressed. They had been listening to me go on and on about my troubles like a broken record.

"How could I be so unlucky….back-to-back wheels…..6-lows and aces up…."

I don't think it was just a case of them wanting me to shut the fuck up. They really thought they had my best interests at heart. They could see how far and fast I had fallen, and they were trying to give me a way out. And I wanted out. I was the guy who always walked away when drugs were mentioned, but I was still there, listening. I wanted to believe it. I wanted something to take that pain away. Something. Anything.

I remember walking around the VooDoo Lounge tapping people on the shoulder and asking, "Hey, did you ever try Ecstasy before?" "Hey, have you ever done this before?"

"Yeah, man. Try it."

"It's great, you're gonna love it."

At least twenty people told me to try it and not one—I mean, not one—told me not to. Maybe I should have thought a little bit more about who I was asking. Think about where I was; these people were all Vegas drinkers and partiers. I guess it shouldn't have been a total surprise when pretty much every one of them said the same thing.

It was like asking a room full of poker players if they liked to gamble.

I had been knocked out of the tournament early that afternoon before my seat was barely warm, and it seemed like my depression would never end. It was only midnight and I had been crying for hours. I was in a crowded Vegas bar, but I felt completely alone. It was dark, music was playing, and everyone around me was having a great time. But I felt defeated.

"Mike, it won't hurt you; it's just a little pill. It will make you happy."

It was past two in the morning before I finally came to a decision. Maybe my friends were right. I was convinced that anything was better than this crushing depression. I started shaking again, but now I was shaking because I was thinking about taking the pill. I had never taken a drug in my life and I was scared shitless.

Finally, I swallowed my first little Ecstasy pill and for the better part of an hour, all I could say or think about was, "Please God, don't let me die!"

I didn't know what to expect or exactly what "It'll make you happy" even meant. Happy, whatever that meant, seemed like a whole lot better place to be than where I was. About an hour or so after I took the pill, I was even more bummed out than before. I was still depressed. I still had lost the tournament. I still wasn't happy. I didn't feel anything, except guilty that I'd taken drugs. We decided it was time to call it a night. After we left the VooDoo lounge, we figured we'd stock up on supplies and made our way to the supermarket.

Driving down Tropicana Boulevard, the Ecstasy hit me. I'll never forget what it felt like. One minute I was the most miserable person on the planet and in the next minute I was the happiest person the world had ever known. It was crazy, but crazy good. I had an immediate sensation of euphoria and confidence. After hours of crushing depression like I had never felt before, it was an incredible release, a complete and unbelievable reversal. I remember walking around in the parking lot talking to Mark for what seemed like hours. We just walked around Smith's Food King parking lot and everything was perfect.

When I woke up the next day and walked outside, the world was a different place. The sky looked bluer, the mountains looked clearer, and the air felt cleaner. My life had fundamentally changed. I know a lot of people have an Ecstasy hangover; in fact, most people have a bad day after using X. Maybe I was still high, but my "day after" rocked.

Some first time Ecstasy users say they have a life changing experience—put me in that category. X was like a magic key that unlocked the world. I could see the air, taste the breeze, the mountains had moved and changed shape. All I wanted to do was drive around in my Mitsubishi with the top down and enjoy life. I hopped in the car, cranked up the music, smiled at everyone I saw, and cruised around Vegas all day. It was crazy, but it was a much better crazy than it had ever been before.

I couldn't stop thinking about this pill. It was the most amazing thing I had felt in my whole life. All I could think was, "This is wonderful!" and "Where do I get some more of these pills?"

Whatever else changed in my life, poker was always a constant. I might have found a new world, but it still definitely included poker and especially the World Series. I took Sunday off to enjoy my new happy world, but on Monday I was back in my seat playing another Omaha high-low event at the Horseshoe. As a poker player, unless you're bleeding from your eyes or broke with no backers, you are in a chair at noon playing for another bracelet during the Series.

I thought about that little pill and how it had made me feel. I thought about it all week. I also made sure there would be more available for the next weekend.

I was always at home and confident at a poker table, but that was the only place I felt that way. In any other social situation, I was uncomfortable and had zero self-esteem. So much of the world had seemed closed off to me because of my insecurity and low self-esteem. It had gotten to the point where I avoided going out. People see that loud boisterous guy on television and he looks like the most outgoing dude in the world, but that was only because I was at the poker table. The whole lack of self esteem thing got even worse if you threw women into the mix. I had a hard time saying anything to them. Everything I did say was wrong. I made high school nerds look like Hugh Hefner.

That next Saturday night I took Ecstasy and went partying at Studio 54 with Mark. The club at the MGM Grand played to the young California crowd and drew an incredible number of hot L.A. babes. The club's four dance floors were packed with gorgeous, fun women who were looking to enjoy life. Of the three or four clubs in town, Studio 54 was the hottest. We were rolling on X and having the greatest time. In just one week and two pills, I'd gone from a quiet person who rarely drank and hated clubs, to someone who couldn't wait to pop a pill and party.

When I talked to girls, whatever came out of my mouth was the right thing. I felt confident. People actually thought I was fun to be around. And in Vegas, being a successful high-stakes poker player didn't hurt either. This was a level of attention and social success that I'd never experienced in my life. The poker world used to be the only place I had any confidence. Now, the whole world was like that for me.

I looked at my new self and wondered, "Who is this guy and where has he been all my life?"

I played the main event of the Series and didn't cash. But that wasn't so important anymore; my life had changed. The next couple of weekends I was back on the club scene. My new X world was great. I was the star and I was loving it.

Mark and I had booked a cruise that sailed out of New Orleans a couple of weeks after the World Series main event. We figured there was no reason not to continue our partying ways on the high seas. My X connection supplied me with a bottle of fifty pills for the cruise. I didn't know anything about the danger in taking multiple pills. Hell, I had just overcome the fear of taking just one. I figured Mark and I would take a pill a day for the weeklong cruise, so we had about three dozen extra pills.

It's amazing how many friends you can make when you have extra Ecstasy. I had no idea how many people were into it. When everyone around you is doing something, it makes it seem normal and safe somehow. Our entire little singles corner of the ship was constantly high on Ecstasy. It was one of the most unbelievably outrageous times I've ever had. We drank at the bars on the ship and in every port. We'd pop a pill and just keep rolling on Ecstasy. I was walking around on cloud nine and I had lots of company. It seemed like every girl was sleeping with every guy and every guy was sleeping with every girl. All these single people were doing each other and staying up all night and all day.

Sex will definitely make you happy, but it wasn't just the sex and X. I liked living in a world where I didn't fear anything. I was a different person and people liked the fun, spontaneous Mike Matusow. I liked him too.

On the first night of the cruise I hooked up with Deborah. We were all hanging out in one of the lounges and I was just coming on to my first Ecstasy high of the cruise. She was from somewhere, I was from Las Vegas. She worked for some company, I played poker. I liked X, she liked X. I gave her a pill. We went for a walk and ended up in her stateroom or my stateroom or somebody's room. Soon, we were naked. You don't sleep while you're rolling on X, so an hour later we found ourselves back in another bar, hanging out with more of the singles group.

I had just had sex with a hot woman an hour after we met. That was how it was in my new X world.

It had been a long time since I had that much sex. I hadn't completely recovered from falling for Julie and getting totally crushed. I wanted a girlfriend, but I couldn't get past the fear—the fear of being hurt and the fear of being rejected; in short, my inability to get past my low self-esteem. Fear had been the biggest stumbling block in my life but now it was gone, thanks to that magic pill.

On one of the islands, a bunch of us decided to take a dune buggy tour up the coast, stopping at some beautiful isolated beaches. At one point toward the end of the tour, a gorgeous blond named Emily ended up in my lap. She was five foot ten and stunningly full figured. Earlier, I hadn't thought much about the bumpy ride, but now I was totally digging it. She was cool, and like all the rest of us, was having a great time. She asked me for some X when we reached our next stop. Back on the ship that night, they announced the first dinner seating. At that moment, Emily appeared in a brilliant yellow and orange sundress that almost contained her breasts. Almost.

She asked if I was hungry, but before I could answer she ran her hand up my thigh and whispered, "I'm starved."

She took my hand and led me down a couple of flights of stairs into her room. The entryway to her room was narrow and had a handrail just as you walked in. I had seen handrails all over the ship and I guessed they were there in case the sea got rough and you needed something to grab onto. Emily took my hand that she still had firmly in hers and placed it on one of those rails. Then she was on her knees. She wasn't lying. She was hungry. Really, really hungry. I can't tell you how long this scene lasted; maybe three minutes, maybe ten, but I know I didn't last much longer.

"Now I really am hungry," Emily said.

We met up with the whole Ecstasy gang for dinner, with Emily still wearing that great yellow and orange dress, me wearing a big dumb grin on my face.

In seven days, we might have had twenty hours of sleep. This was a whole new experience for me, a world without stress, anxiety or insecurity. Only three weeks earlier, I had been the totally anti-drug guy, the guy walking around the VooDoo Lounge praying to God not to let him die from taking one Ecstasy pill. But I wasn't that person anymore. I was the guy people liked to be around, the guy women loved, the guy who thought the world was one fucking great place.

That little pill had changed my life.

On the plane trip home to Las Vegas, I remember saying to Mark, "Man, I'm not going to party when we get back. I'm not going to do anything for a week but sleep."

That resolution didn't even make it out of the airport. We met some girls who told us about this big party at the SRO Club that night.

"It's going to be great, everyone will be there. You guys should come."

So what did we do? We slept for an hour, took a shower, popped some more pills, and headed to SRO for a great party. The next night we went to another, even better, party. I would show up at one party and someone would invite me to the next one. That's the way it went in my new X life.

We ended up popping pills for ten straight days. Starting with the cruise, and continuing with the parties that began the minute we got home, I was in full rolling mode. The lifestyle had me hooked. Even when I took a day or two off from X, I wanted to go out and pop more. I wasn't addicted to the pills, but I was definitely addicted to a lifestyle I'd never had. I was meeting women and enjoying the social life that I thought only other people had.

From the ages of twenty-three to thirty-one, I didn't go out. I didn't try to meet girls. Suddenly, that all changed. I couldn't imagine a reason to ever leave this new wonderful world. For the next six months, I rolled on X three or four days a week. Did I stop playing poker? Absolutely not. In fact, I went on a huge winning streak over the next few months. I was killing the cash games.

I remember thinking, "I've got it all."

I had money. I had a different woman or two interested in me every time I went out. I had a beautiful home. I was considered one of the top poker players in world. My game was at the point where, when I sat down at the table, nobody played me shorthanded. Nobody. I was doing this drug that made me love life every single day. I felt like nothing could go bad in my new world.

I was so wrong.

Chapter Thirteen

Main Event Meth

The depression that had haunted me for the past nine or ten years seemed to be on the back burner. For the first time in my life, I had a social life with lots of friends and I was enjoying the time I spent away from the poker table. Sure, it was because of the parties and the drugs.

I knew that, but so what?

I was having a great time. I guess if I had known just how common it is for people with bipolar disorder to self medicate with street drugs like X, I'd have had one more clue that I needed professional help. There were a lot of signs I had a treatable disorder, but I had no idea how to read them.

After I took my very first hit of X, I did a lot of online research. There was some stuff that mentioned people having trouble remembering things that happened to them while they were on Ecstasy. I didn't know it then, but eventually I learned that it could permanently damage your short-term memory, even after you were off it. Taking X didn't really change my view of drugs. I was still as afraid of them as I'd always been. It's just that I didn't see Ecstasy as a real drug. I found out that a lot of poker players were doing X, and a whole group of us really got hooked on it for awhile.

I spent the last half of 2000 on my "Party and Poker" schedule. I woke up, headed to the Bellagio to play poker, and then hit a club. If the game was really juicy I might give up a night of clubbing. But for those six months, I was partying about three or four times a week. My wins at the tables covered my living expenses, which had taken another bump up with the added entertainment costs, so my new schedule was pretty much a break-even lifestyle.

About three months into my new life, on Labor Day weekend, I met Teri. She and her roommate were in Las Vegas with my friend Scott, who I had met at a club a few months before. She was in town from Phoenix for the weekend and we hooked up at one of the clubs. We hit it off right away. Once she was back in Arizona, we talked on the phone almost every day. She came to Vegas almost every weekend to see me and I went to Phoenix a couple of times to spend time with her. In December, she went to the United State Poker Championships in Atlantic City with me. We had a great time and I took first in a no-limit hold'em event for $46,000.

By the end of that month, Teri had moved in with me in Las Vegas. On some levels, it was great. It had been far too long since I had a real girlfriend. But I shouldn't have just jumped into a live-in relationship and I kind of knew it at the time. Everything became way too involved, way too fast. I loved Teri as a person, but I wasn't sure whether I was in love with her. I also probably should've realized that the X made any connection seem more intense and significant. I mean, you love everybody on X. I had just started with the whole Las Vegas party scene, something I had never done before in my life. I liked being part of the singles crowd. All the club girls wanted to be with me. Having a relationship with Teri was cool, but living with someone takes a whole different level of commitment, and I don't think either one of us had thought about that.

Things were pretty good for me at the start of 2001. I had a hot girlfriend and was playing poker well enough that I didn't have any real money pressures. Teri and I cut the clubbing back to weekends and I went to work four days a week at the Bellagio. Teri treated me well, she really cared for me, and life around the house was pretty great. Sometime before the 2001 World Series, I remember joking about "Black Tuesdays." After a weekend of partying, with Monday as a day of recovery, the first day back at the Bellagio was always hard. Paying attention for a full day of poker was pretty difficult and Black Tuesdays were becoming a drain on my bankroll.

I started to lose. It wasn't so much that I lost a lot of money, but just playing break-even poker meant that my bankroll was shrinking by the amount of my monthly bills. When I was actually losing, even just a little, the drain on my bankroll was just that much faster. Concentration had never been an issue for me, but my lack of focus had spread past being just a Black Tuesday thing. My game was based on instinct and an ability to read opponents, but I was losing that critical part of my game. I couldn't maintain my focus and I knew my poker game was in big trouble. I got worried that my new cool life was starting to unravel, beginning at the poker table.

The six plus months of using Ecstasy was starting to take its toll. The bouts of depression that had disappeared when I first starting taking X returned. And it always seemed worse during the days when I wasn't doing X, which of course was when I was playing poker. My focus was shot and I talked about it all the time. Teri understood that I was getting depressed and agitated. She also had to think that it wouldn't help our relationship any if I continued to struggle at poker.

My game got worse. I found myself playing poker for the first time in my life without knowing where I was in a hand. It was scary. I remember feeling completely lost. I didn't know what to do. To me, it was unimaginable to show up at a poker game that I'd owned, a game where I could read everybody, and suddenly not know what cards anybody had. I didn't know how to bet or what to bet. I was totally freaked out.

At my lowest point, Teri said, "Why don't you take a little sniff of this? It's crystal meth."

"What's that?"

Other than X, which I thought of as just a party thing, I still really didn't know anything about street drugs.

"Well, it's like speed, it's going to wake you up and make you more focused. It'll make you a lot sharper when you're struggling."

"Will it hurt me?"

"Oh no, it's just to wake you up."

I was an idiot. I took a little bit of the meth, and boom—everything was back to normal. Actually, everything was above normal. At the tables, I knew what everybody had. I started playing at a ridiculously high level. In the next five months I won over $1 million in live poker action. Let me say that again real slow: *In less than five months, I won over $1 million in the cash games.* I was a fucking money machine!

I didn't have to do a lot of "ice," the street lingo for meth, to get where I needed to be. I would take the smallest amount I could, just for the incredible focus it gave me. With a tiny line of crystal I could play at an amazingly high level and take everybody's money. I had found the greatest thing ever created, the answer to my focus issues, my exhaustion, and my game. I didn't read about meth or do any research on it; I really didn't want to know. All I needed to know was that if I snorted a little line of ice about a quarter of an inch long, nobody could beat me. I had no idea that people used it to get high.

Right after I started taking meth, I bumped into my good friend Roy at the Bellagio. He immediately asked me what I was on. He knew I was taking something. I told him it was crystal meth.

"That stuff will destroy your life, Mike. You need to stop it now."

"Don't worry, I know what I'm doing, I'll be fine."

"Listen, Mike, you gotta stop this right now and never touch it again," he pulled me aside, really upset. "I know what I'm talking about."

I knew that Roy was hooked on some kind of drug. And I knew he was trying to save me from going through the same hell he was experiencing. But I had already decided this was the greatest thing I'd ever found and I wasn't giving it up. I blew him off with a story about trusting him and telling him I would quit.

Speed makes you feel invincible. You fear no one at the poker table. You make plays without ever thinking about losing—hell, you can't lose with meth in your body!

How could I give that up?

I continued taking meth right into the 2001 World Series of Poker. I played a few preliminary tournaments, but it was hard to take all that time away from the side games. With my new drug, I barely noticed the tournaments, the cash games were so juicy. My bankroll was bigger than it had ever been.

The main event drew 613 players, and I tore it up! I played at a level so high that I knew it was just a matter of time before it would be me and only eight other players still left with chips. I was fucking flying on crystal meth. For the first five days of the main event, I was speeding my brains out and playing the best poker of my life. The amateurs might as well as have been playing with their cards turned face up. The wonder drug had turned me into a phenomenal player. The more meth I did, the deeper my focus got. The deeper my focus got, the better I played. Meth gave me unbelievable confidence.

As I expected, I made the final table! And it was loaded with talent, including Phil Hellmuth, Carlos Mortensen, Dewey Tomko, and Phil Gordon. Only one WSOP tournament was televised back then, the championship event. We had to get there a little early so that they could clip microphones to our shirts and hook transmitters on our belts. As they did our sound checks, one by one, I remember looking around the table.

"This is going to be a very tough table, but I'm going to win," I said to myself.

Of course, I believed it—the meth wouldn't let me think anything else.

At the first break, a friend and I went up to his hotel room in Binion's to do a line. I talked about how the meth was giving me such great focus and how it was the wonder drug of all wonder drugs and how I hoped nobody else would discover it. Speed makes you talk a lot, which wasn't exactly an area where I needed any help. That's why it was so easy for me to cover up my meth use; I had always talked so much that no one noticed the difference.

When we got back down to the tournament room, one of the sound techs came over and said, "You know, Mike, there's an off switch on that microphone."

"Oh, shit! You didn't hear all that, did you?" I asked.

"Don't worry, Mike, we can keep that to ourselves," he said.

I looked over and saw the entire television crew smiling at me; they knew everything. I was lucky those guys were roadies. I don't really know what I'd have done if they hadn't been so cool about it. It's not as though I would have listened if anyone had given me the anti-drug lecture anyway. Why should I? I was at the final table of the championship event of the World Series of Poker.

I'd wanted to be at this table ever since I had seen Stu Ungar win his third championship out there on Fremont Street four years earlier. And now I had made it.

It didn't matter to me that I had made it the same way Stuey had—on drugs.

The final table action was fairly slow in the early rounds. We only lost one player, John Inashima, who had started the day as the short stack. Henry Nowakowski had maintained the chip lead in the early going. Then he got into a big pot with me in which he had pocket jacks and called my all-in bet. I had pocket kings and took down 950,000. A couple of hands later, Carlos Mortensen called Steve Reihle who also had a pair of jacks; Carlos made a flush with an A-K offsuit and we were down to seven players. The pace started to pick up.

Then I played a hand that totally got away from me. Henry Nowakowski had been limping a lot and Carlos had been raising him off those pots preflop. The next time that happened, I was going to take the pot away from Carlos. Nowakowski limped in and Carlos made it 80,000 to go. I raised another 200,000 but Nowakowski moved all in and, just as I expected, Carlos folded. The all-in bet was only another 65,000 to me and with over 850,000 already in the pot, I was calling with any two cards. The problem was that I had exactly any two cards—7-2 offsuit, the very worst hand in hold'em. I played the hand to pick off another Carlos bluff and I ran into Nowakowski's pocket kings.

Crap! I guess I should have considered that he would eventually limp with a big hand to trap Carlos—instead he trapped me, or I trapped myself.

"Mike, this is the final table of the main event of the World Series of Poker and you just shipped it with seven-deuce offsuit," I remember Phil Hellmuth saying as the dealer counted out the pot. "You've got a lot of heart, kid. If you come back and win this thing, you'll be a legend after that move."

The whole crowd busted out laughing. That hand knocked me down to under 400,000, but I was nowhere near ready to give it up. I decided to do some talking of my own.

"I knew you had nothing, Carlos," I spouted off. "We're here to play poker, boys. Back to work. Now you guys are never going to know what I have when I move in. All I have to do is get a few chips back, and we can have a little party."

I was playing with no fear. I knew I could get those chips back. Two hands later, I made it 60,000 to go, they all folded, and I picked up the blinds and antes. Two hands later, I did it again and they all folded again. The third time I tried that move, Phil Gordon popped me back another 200,000. Phil had a huge tell back then when he was holding a big hand. He hadn't given that tell on this hand, so I moved all in. It wasn't much of a raise, so Phil made the call with A-7 suited. I showed A-10. The flop came A-10-2, giving me two pair. The turn was another 10 and I had a full boat, doubling my stack.

"I told you boys, it's time to have some fun!"

Just four hands later, I limped in. Dewy Tomko completed from the small blind and Phil Gordon checked his option in the big blind. Dewey checked the K-K-Q flop, Phil bet 40,000, I called, and Dewey folded. We both checked the 10 on the turn. When a 6 hit the river, Phil bet out 200,000. I raised another 200,000, knowing that Phil would think I was trying a cheap steal. He called and I showed my K-J for trip kings. He mucked his cards.

I was the chip leader of the main event!

"I told you not to let me have chips again," I boasted. "You made a big mistake here, boys!"

Soon after that, we lost Nowakowski in seventh place. Then "The Hand" came down—the hand between Carlos and I that changed the entire tournament for both of us.

You need to understand that I had tells on two players at this table; one on Phil Gordon and another on Carlos Mortensen. Dewey Tomko and Stan Schrier were playing tight. Phil Hellmuth was playing his normal game and I knew he wasn't going to trap me. I had a stone cold, locked plan for this table. I was going to take chips from Phil Gordon if I got the chance, but my big target was Carlos.

When "The Hand" began, I raised to 60,000 and Carlos raised 150,000 more from the small blind. I knew he had nothing and I was ready to ship all my chips to the center. And if I had, Carlos would have folded.

But one thing stopped me. I'd had a conversation with Chris Ferguson, the reigning world champion, the night before that made me stop and think about moving all in. Chris told me that I didn't have to put my whole stack at risk when I came over the top of a player. He said that a big reraise would be enough to get the laydowns I was after. He said that if, by some chance, my read was wrong and the other player actually had a hand, I could still lay it down and not bust out.

That's what was going through my mind as I looked at Carlos' 150,000 raise. My game would have been to push all in and watch him fold, but I was thinking about what Chris had told me. At the last second, I reraised another 350,000 and Carlos moved all in. I went into the tank. His tell had me totally convinced he had nothing, but I was only holding A-2 of hearts. I finally folded.

Carlos tabled Q-8 offsuit to show that he had successfully bluffed me.

I shot out of my chair like a bullet, I was so angry. I wasn't mad at Carlos; I was angry with myself. I had the read cold. I knew he had nothing. I basically committed more than half of my stack to that read and like an idiot, I had laid it down. I had no one to blame but myself. I had the perfect tell on Carlos. I just couldn't pull the final trigger. Sure, I was only 60/40 to win the hand. If I had lost, I would have been out in sixth. I guess I thought that even with a short stack I could come back. But if I had pushed all in, Carlos would've folded the Q-8 and I would have been the chip leader by over 400,000.

I wish I'd never had that conversation with Chris the night before. But to be fair, Carlos had four-bet me all in, so he must have had some kind of read on me too. In the end, I actually made the fold because I didn't want to be the laughing stock of poker for calling all my chips with ace-deuce. I didn't trust my read and it cost me. In my mind, that hand cost me the championship.

A few hands later I tangled with Dewey Tomko, who was even shorter than me. I had pocket tens and Dewey had pocket kings. Dewey doubled up, and now I was super short. Two hands later, I moved my last 200,000 in with pocket eights. Phil Hellmuth had the pocket kings this time and I busted out of the main event in sixth place.

At first, I walked out of the room without doing the exit interview. I eventually came back to give them what they wanted.

"I can play great poker for the next twenty years and I still might never get back to the final table of this tournament. It's that hard to get here," I said. "That's why it's so painful to go out when you get so close. This might have been my only chance for my entire lifetime and I couldn't get it done."

I should have made that call against Carlos. Instead, I hung around another twenty minutes with a short stack and finished sixth anyway. That hand haunted me. That hand still haunts me.

After I got knocked out of that tournament, I was almost unable to live with myself. When Carlos went all in, I knew he didn't have anything. I felt that if I had followed through, I would have won the championship. I folded my cards when I knew I had Carlos beat. I couldn't cope with it.

For the next month, I never left the house. I sat home, cried, and felt sorry for myself. At least I thought that's what was happening. But I was also coming down off the crystal meth. I didn't realize that when you come off meth, you get as depressed as you can possibly be, every single day. I couldn't tell you how much of my depression was just because I didn't win the World Series, or how much was actually drug withdrawal. I really have no idea. All I know is that I was devastated.

It took me six months to stop talking about that hand. Can you imagine being around me for those six months? The same hand, over and over. Once you have that goal to win the World Series, and it's finally within your grasp, there is no greater pain than walking away without the bracelet. Winning the main event was a dream planted in my head the very first time I sat behind Phil Samaroff in a poker room. I could still hear him ask, "Have you ever heard of the World Series of Poker?" Now I had to live with the nightmare of losing it the way I did.

I won almost $240,000 for my sixth place finish. But that's how cruel poker is: You can win almost a quarter of a million dollars and feel like you lost everything. Carlos won the championship and $1.5 million, but it had almost nothing to do with the money. It had everything to do with being the last one standing in the main event, claiming the championship in a world class field. Some of the world's greatest players have played for years and never made it to a main event final table. You can count the number on your fingers that have played two main event final tables in their lifetimes. I could have been the chip leader at the final table and instead I played the hand wrong. I knew the odds against making another main event final table. I had my shot and it was over.

I started to ramp up my drug use because when I wasn't on them, I was depressed. I went back to Ecstasy and meth. I tried cocaine, but it didn't do much for me, so I did very little of it. I did what kept me happy. By the middle of 2001, I was doing a lot of drugs. Was I an addict? I don't know. I did drugs because I hated the pain when I was off them. I couldn't bear the thought that I would have to live with that pain all the time. I didn't know that a lot of what I felt when I was off the drugs were the symptoms of meth withdrawal.

After about three months, I got back to the tables, but it wasn't like it had been before. I was doing meth and X, but the euphoria and clarity that first drew me to those drugs had faded. When I had first started doing Ecstasy, the world looked different and I was the happiest human alive. When I first did crystal meth, I had unbelievable focus and nobody could beat me in poker.

But now it was just like Roy said it would be: One day you think you're controlling meth, and suddenly the tables turn.

From just after the 2001 main event to February 2002, I lost over $700,000. I couldn't win. I would sit at a table for two or three days at a time, unable to leave, unable to sleep. I could still play well for 10 to 15 hours, but I couldn't get up and leave the table. I played hand after mindless hand. It was like an out of body experience: I was watching myself sitting at the table, throwing my money away, but I couldn't stop.

Years later, people told me, "Mike, when you were on that shit, you just gave it away."

They were more than willing to play me back then. Initially, I had won all their money, but on meth, I gave it all back.

Now when people ask me about my experience on meth, I tell them all the same thing: "The good thing about crystal meth was that I never had to get up from the table. The bad thing about crystal meth was that after awhile, I couldn't get up from the table."

I proceeded to pretty much lose everything. I'd sit at the tables for days at a time, sleep for twelve hours and go back and do it all over again. My relationship with Teri was a mess. I was edgy and agitated all the time. Meth can turn you into a real monster. You start to hate yourself and everyone around you. I lost a lot of weight. I hardly ate. I was miserable.

Emotionally and physically, I was deteriorating at breakneck speed.

By early 2002 Teri was ready to leave me. We'd had a couple of really horrible weeks and said some cruel things to each other. But that was nothing compared to the ugly scene that marked the end of it all. I was in L.A at the Commerce Casino. It had already been a bad trip for me. I'd lost about $85,000 in a session that was into its second day. I was trying to cut back on the meth and I was totally crashing. I only knew that the worst of all my depressions had come back to haunt me and I was suicidal.

At one point I took a break from the cash games to call Teri, who I thought was in Vegas. It was Valentines Day and I wanted to check in with her and apologize for how things had gone down between us. If she needed any revenge, she got it in that call. She wasn't in Vegas or Phoenix, she was right there at the Commerce. She told me she was with Roy, my meth-using poker-playing friend. She made it perfectly clear that she and I were over and that she and her "new boyfriend" were together in their room.

After she hung up, I went back to my cash game, just sitting there at the table, continuing to give away my money and thinking about what "my girlfriend" was doing upstairs with "my friend."

It was harsh. I knew I had wanted to end things with her at some point, but it's like wanting to quit a job. You hate going to work every day and you look for any excuse to leave. But just before you get ready to quit, they fire you. Instead of being happy, all you can think is, "I got fired. Those bastards!" It makes no sense. But I was withdrawing from that damn drug and there was nothing in my life that made sense at that point. Sitting there in that game while she was upstairs with him was total agony. That may have been the lowest point in my life. I had been through a lot of shit and the future would bring more lower-than-low moments. But right there, sitting at that poker table at the Commerce Casino, was the lowest. I deserved it, but it didn't make it any less brutal.

I'd been trying to figure out how to break up with Teri without hurting her any further. When it came to hurt in our relationship, I played small ball. Teri pushed all in, threw it all at me in one big hand, and dragged a giant pot.

I left the Commerce that night, dead broke. I didn't have anything. I couldn't cope with anything. I was devastated. I called my very best friend Melinda. She and her boyfriend drove down to L.A. and picked me up. She drove me home to Las Vegas and her boyfriend drove my car back.

Once we got back to Vegas, Melinda stepped in and kind of took over my life for the next couple of weeks. Teri had a bunch of my stuff, including an uncashed check from one of my poker wins, and some of her things were at my house. I just couldn't deal with it. Melinda got on the phone and had a couple of long and nasty calls with Teri and arranged for an exchange. It was ugly, but with Melinda's help, it all got settled. The break up with Teri had been hard, but knowing she was with another guy just about ripped my heart out.

With just more than two months before the World Series, I wasn't in any shape to play at that level. I knew I had to get clean. I had to stop using meth completely. So I did.

I fought off the initial depression and fatigue by making myself work out at the gym everyday. I started running thirty minutes a day and eventually built it up to an hour. I watched what I ate, which meant I stopped living on pizza and wings. I lost about twenty pounds of fat and gained a lot of muscle. I was probably in the best physical shape of my life. Slowly I got over Teri and came to a place where I was okay with her being gone from my life. I was ready to find another girlfriend. I was going to be happy. I was on my way to being drug free and I was certain that my game would get back to a high level. Everything was going to be good again.

Heading into the 2002 World Series of Poker, I had been drug-free for almost two and a half months. I felt good, mentally and physically, and I wanted to play again. The problem was that no matter how I felt, I hadn't played much poker in the last couple of months. And it had been a lot longer than that since I had played good poker. From the minute the Series started, I found myself struggling. I didn't have the focus and it was killing me. Two weeks into it, I had done absolutely nothing. I just couldn't score, not even in the cash games. I thought back to the last time I had struggled like this and Teri had given me speed for the first time; it was the year before when I had won $1 million straight in the cash games and made the final table at the championship. Had it really only been one year? I'd worked so hard to get myself off meth, but here I was at the World Series and my poker game was gone. My play totally sucked and I didn't know what to do.

I've done a lot of dumbass things in my life, but this may have been the dumbest — I bought some meth. "I'm gonna be really careful," I told myself. "I won't take a lot of it. I won't play for days at a time. I'll just take a little at a time and space it out like I used to when I made all that money."

And boom! I won. I was back in the zone again, crushing the side games, growing my bankroll by over $120,000 in a matter of days. I had the wonder drug back. I had my game back and I was able to control the meth.

Why had I ever been worried? I could do this.

But just as suddenly, the meth took control of me again. I found myself playing for more than thirty hours straight and losing big. I went from being a huge winner to struggling for a bankroll. I wasn't broke, but I had dropped everything I'd just won. I couldn't believe I had put myself back into this nightmare—back on meth and right in the middle of the WSOP. I was disgusted with myself. It wasn't a question of thinking that I was an idiot, I knew I was. I'd fought so hard to get past whatever physical addiction I might have had. I'd been clean for over two months, but here I was again. The real danger of this drug was that I had come to believe that I couldn't perform without it.

People say that when you kick drugs you have to hit bottom or that you have this sudden frightening realization. Some of that came in the middle of the 2002 Series when I realized that I couldn't do this drug "a little bit." There was no way I could control meth, even for a short time. It could never be Mike using meth anymore; it was always going to be meth using Mike. I knew I had to quit again, right then and there.

I stopped cold, just two days before the $5,000 Omaha high-low event. This was the tournament I had been gearing up for. I had made three WSOP Omaha high-low final tables in the past four years. I knew that on a good day, I could do it again.

But what were my chances of having a good day? I was coming off speed and was totally depressed.

Chapter Fourteen

Without a Net

I went ballistic. I called the floor man every name under the sun. Security had to forcibly remove me from the Horseshoe, but before they did I walked back over to the table and yelled at them.

"Listen, you motherfuckers, I'm going to win this Omaha tournament tomorrow for what you did to me. You can mark it down. I'm the best Omaha player in the world. Nobody can beat me at this game. Fuck you all, I'm going home. You're all going to get what you deserve."

I don't think I've ever been so angry about a floor ruling, but I already was an emotional wreck that day. The night before, I had quit meth again and I was a total basket case when I got up that afternoon. But I still made myself go down to Binion's to play the cash games. Maybe that's fucked up, but I play poker, that's what I do.

In all the poker books you read stuff like, "Don't play unless you can bring your 'A' game." Or, "You have to leave your emotions at the door."

All of these things are good advice, but when you play poker for a living, it doesn't always work that way. Your life can be up, down, or totally fucked, but if the game is good, you still show up and play. With just a week left before the 2002 championship event, the side games had gotten even juicer. So, I showed up to play.

The $400/$800 Omaha high-low cash game had two monster fish in it. The wait list was nearly six hours long, and I was on it. In fact, every professional Omaha player who was in the building was either on that list or already in the game. After almost five hours, I finally got called for my seat while I was killing time in a $500 satellite. The $500 didn't mean anything compared to that big game, so I was just going to walk away from the satellite. I bought my chips for the game and put them at my seat at the Omaha table. The cash game players told me to go ahead and finish the satellite; someone would play over me until I came back. No one at the table had any problem with that and I went back to finish up the satellite.

Shawn "Sheiky" Sheikhan was next on the Omaha wait list. To get my seat, he complained to the floorman, claiming that I was holding the seat without playing a hand. Shawn could be a real prick back then. What am I saying? Shawn can still be a real prick today. The floorman picked up my chips without telling me and moved me out of the game, which was a ridiculous ruling. To make a fair ruling, all he had to do was walk across the room and tell me that I either had to take my Omaha seat or stay in the satellite. I would have left the satellite immediately as the Omaha game was almost too good to be true. With those two fish in the game, that seat could have easily been worth thirty-five or forty thousand dollars.

I was escorted to my car by security and steamed all the way home. I was still wound up when I walked in the door, so I popped a sleeping pill. I had to get some rest before the tournament I had just proclaimed that I was going to win. The $5,000 buy-in tournament was like the Omaha high-low championship of the world. It was the most important event of the Series for me, even more so than the main event. Omaha was my game, but I wasn't in any shape to play and it was my own damn fault.

As I lay in bed staring at the ceiling, I relived the last few months of my life. What a fucking rollercoaster.

How the hell was I going to play the tournament? If I was lucky, maybe I'd feel better in the morning. Who was I kidding? I knew the depression would be back. I knew the second day after I quit was always the worst. Instead of playing the most important tournament of my Series, I wondered if I shouldn't just stay in bed.

I woke up the next morning in the middle of one of those dreams that's part dream and part real life. In the dream some crazy guy was screaming in the Binion's Horseshoe poker room and telling everyone in the place that he was going to win the World Series event the next day. Then I was fully awake. It was the next day and I was that crazy guy.

Oh shit, did I really do that?

I forced myself to get up and drive back to Binion's for the tournament. From the second I sat down at the table, I desperately wanted to do a line of speed. Every five minutes I had to tell myself, "No, no, no. You're not going to do it. You're not going to do it." I had the meth in my pocket; it was there all day, just waiting for me to give in. This wasn't like ex-heroin addicts, who keep a syringe to remind them of their bad times. I had the real thing in my pocket, just in case.

It was an absolutely crazy way to play poker. There was no chance I was getting any reads on the other players. I was doing all I could just to stay upright in my chair. I should've been in rehab or at home in bed with someone watching out for me. But no, I was sitting in a World Series of Poker tournament. I was playing only the cards and trying to focus on where I was in a hand. I've talked about playing instinct poker, but this was more like survival poker, one hand at a time. Actually, I think my survival poker is probably better than most people's "A" game, but I felt like I was fighting my way through every hand and the dealer just kept the cards coming.

All afternoon and into the night, I pounded down Mountain Dews for the caffeine. At first it worked pretty well and I was able to play with just enough focus to stay alive. But as night started to fall, I started to lose it. I began to get jittery. I started to hallucinate at the table and actually believed I was going to die. I tried to keep myself focused on the game, trying to resist the hallucinations and mind tricks. I don't know how I kept playing. In the end, I think it was the cards that kept me sane. Every couple of minutes, I had to look down at four hole cards and try to evaluate the hand. With every deal my universe would narrow to the cards and somehow I think that was what I kept doing, over and over all that night. In between hands I kept telling myself, "Don't do the meth. Don't do the meth. You're not going to die." Then I'd focus on the next hand to push the hallucinations aside. Bet, raise, check, fold; those weren't hallucinations. Hearts, diamonds, clubs, spades; these were real. For more than three hours it went on like that.

Later, I found out that the worst thing you can do when you are coming off speed is to dose yourself with caffeine and sugar. They just make coming off meth that much harder. Sugar and particularly caffeine increase your cravings and give you crazy mood swings. Caffeinated drinks will also dehydrate you, which is the last thing you want.

If you ask me about any other big tournament I've played, I can almost always give you a sense of how I played and who was at my table. I can recall hands, my cards, my chip stack, and sometimes even the blind levels. But if you ask me about Day One of the 2002 Omaha high-low tournament at the WSOP, I remember only misery and hallucinations.

One of the things that saved me was that, about six hours into the tournament, I was moved to a table that was literally full of fish. How this many bad players had entered a WSOP event and were seated at the same table that late in the day was amazing. There wasn't a real player at this table except, me—Matusow the meth head. I was able to play tight solid Omaha and increase my chip stack. Imagine, halfway through a World Series event, I got moved to a table that I could dominate even while I was withdrawing from meth. That was a gift from the poker gods.

I also remember that toward the end of the night, Daniel Negreanu was getting hit by the deck. In a way, that helped me as we played down from the final two tables. My mouth is one of the ways I stay in the game and being able to pick on Daniel from time to time helped me stay grounded. I don't remember much of what I said, but reporter Andy Glazer wrote that I wasn't making much sense. Apparently I was yelling stuff like, "The really cool thing is that Daniel has all these chips, and I guarantee you that he can't win this tournament if I do." Glazer also wrote that I was hyperventilating.

He didn't know the half of it.

Phil Ivey also made it to the last two tables. He was having a huge World Series. Ivey had already won three bracelets and had made a couple more final tables. A lot of spectators and players were hanging around that night to see if Ivey would win a record fourth bracelet in one year. Ivey couldn't hold on for the final table, but somehow I did. One minute I was wondering if the night was going to last forever and the next minute I was bagging my chips. That's how I remember it; the day just ended and I had survived.

Before that awful day, I had almost convinced myself that I couldn't play poker without speed. As much as I wanted to win that tournament, and as much as I'd already told everyone at Binion's within earshot that I was going to win it, I needed to do it without the meth. I was on a mission to prove to myself I could play without it and I had just played fourteen hours with the meth still in my pocket.

While we were bagging our chips, players came by and congratulated all of us for making the final table. I just kept saying: "You have no idea. You have no idea."

I didn't tell anyone the truth about my meth withdrawal. I didn't really know the whole truth myself.

When I woke up the next day, I was hurting, but not like I had been the night before. The panic and the hallucinations were gone. I started to think about the challenge in front of me: trying to take down the final table. I felt like I could focus on poker. That meant I had a real chance. Daniel Negreanu was going to start the day as chip leader and he had the rest of us outchipped by almost 2 to 1. But Daniel wasn't my only problem. It was going to be one tough final table. This was before Harrah's started giving out a gazillion WSOP bracelets every year, so it meant a lot more that the nine players coming into the final table had won ten bracelets between them.

Greg Mascio was starting the day second in chips behind Daniel. This was his second final table of the 2002 Series; he'd finished second in the $1500 Omaha high-low event earlier. I knew how bad I had wanted a bracelet after my second place finish in 1997, and I was guessing Mascio was feeling the same way.

"Miami" John Cernuto was no stranger to me or anyone else in the poker world. John had just won his third WSOP bracelet a couple of weeks earlier in the limit Omaha high event and he was coming into this event third in chips.

Dr. Max Stern, a great mixed game player, had already cashed in fifteen World Series tournaments. He was another player coming into this event with three WSOP bracelets, one of them in Omaha high-low. And while he was going to start today with only about eighteen big bets, he knew how to use them.

Everyone knows Marcel Luske now, but "The Flying Dutchman" hadn't really played in the U.S. before 2002. All I knew about him was that he had made another final table a few days earlier.

Hans Pfister, a European player with a great track record, was trying his hand at the World Series for the first time. Hans had finished fourth in an earlier Omaha high-low event, and had also placed tenth in a stud high-low tournament a week earlier, so he knew his way around split games.

Then there were the two short stacks. John McIntosh had won a bracelet just the week before. The other short stack was Mike Shi, with less than 8,000 chips. He had played really well at my table the night before, but had run into a series of second-best hands that crippled him. Mike had made a couple of final tables in limit hold'em events over the past few years. With blinds at 1,000/2,000, both McIntosh and Shi would be looking to double up or go home early.

I came to the final table fourth in chips. But I was going to win it. Or at least, that's what I had told everyone. By the time I drove downtown that afternoon to Binion's, went up the escalator, and entered Benny's Bullpen, the tournament room at the Horseshoe, I had myself believing it.

Could I actually win this bracelet? Could I keep the ice in my pocket? Could I do both of those things, or was this going to be another drug disaster?

As I walked into the tournament room, like I had done a hundred times before, I noticed for the first time that Binion's wasn't aging well. Of course, as psychotic as I had been the night before, I wouldn't have noticed if I'd been playing in a cave. The Horseshoe was never a palace; the ceilings were low and the makeshift bleachers around the final table wouldn't pass the safety inspection at a Little League field. Binion's had been the first casino to install carpeting back in the '50s, but I swear they hadn't changed it since. Once the casino passed to Benny's daughter Becky in 1998, she abused it like a meth freak. She ran it into the ground 24/7 without putting anything into it. It went through the repetitive motion of operating day after day, without thought—or maybe, without heart.

I know my own state of mind was probably affecting the way I looked at things, but Binion's was poker back then. I found myself wondering how long it could keep running on empty.

When I saw my opponents take their seats at the final table, Binion's stopped being the object of pity and instantly became the greatest poker room in the world. This was the World Series of Poker and I was playing at a final table. Daniel was seated immediately to my right, which was fine by me. He had been running over the table the night before and I was hoping he'd continue raising with any four cards. Luske was on my immediate left, with Mascio to his left.

I suppose I should have been careful about what I wished for because Negreanu started raising what seemed like every hand and his great run of cards continued. He doubled his chips within the first hour. His stack was so outrageous, I'm almost positive he stopped looking at his cards when he was going up against the short stacks.

I started "The Mouth" working on him. I figured that his good luck would have to end sometime, and if I was busting his chops, it might make him tilt faster when it did. I'm pretty sure I was singing something ridiculous, at the top of my lungs, about him being such a luck box. He was giving some noise back to me too. It wasn't going to be a quiet final table, not with Daniel and me sitting side by side.

Unfortunately for Mike Shi, his luck continued too. His bad luck that is. He pushed his short stack in with A-3-4-6, but no low cards came on the flop to help him. He busted out in ninth place after Pfister flopped three kings. Surprisingly, Mascio was the next to go. I think he was getting frustrated with Daniel raising and taking down pots every hand. I knew how he felt, as nothing much was coming my way. But in two quick hands that were bet all the way to the river, Mascio went out in eighth place. Most of his chips went to Daniel.

McIntosh's short stack also couldn't wait any longer. In the big blind, he had to call Daniel's raise. He ended up with four pairs, but Negreanu only needed one straight to beat him. We were down to six players with Daniel still running over the table. Then I started to catch some cards and took Max out in sixth place when I flopped a boat. One report said that this was when I started to heat up. The truth is, I had just started to feel steadier and definitely got my head in the game. I had gained some ground on Daniel, but he kept up the pressure by taking Pfister out in fifth. I found myself thinking about meth. It probably helped that the field narrowed pretty quickly, helping me focus and get better reads on the remaining players.

If you read any of the reports from this event, mostly what they talk about is how Danny and I were going at it. Both our mothers were there, but that didn't even begin to slow us down. My mouth was firing on all cylinders. I was telling Danny he was going to need all those chips when we got heads-up.

"We've played heads-up like twenty times and you almost won once," he said to me.

"You're a donkey who puts his money in the pot with the worst of it, then prays to catch card," I joked back.

I don't know if either of us was putting the other on tilt, but I know we had gotten under the skin of the foreign players. They don't allow trash talking at the European casinos and I could tell that Marcel thought we were completely out of line. Marcel has now become accustomed to us crazy Americans and he's always singing at the table. Hey, maybe I taught him that.

By the time we were down to four players, Daniel had a 4 to 1 chip lead on the three of us combined. But the 'three of us' were Miami John, Marcel and me, so there was still some poker to be played. As it turned out, we had been seated in seats 6, 7, 8 and 9. Of course, we had spread out a little but we were still all at one end of the table. With Daniel still winning—and of course, me still talking—Cernuto and Luske were in for an uphill and loud battle for the bracelet. Marcel may have been put off by all the trash talk Daniel and I were serving up, but for Miami John this was just another day at another final table. As it turned out, Cernuto's biggest problem was running his queen-high flush into Luske's ace-high flush. Miami John went out in fourth place.

Even after taking out Cernuto, Luske was still the short stack, and it got critically shorter when Negreanu scooped two big pots from him. Marcel was just starting to mount something of a comeback against Daniel when I stepped in and took a lot of his stack with a straight. If I remember right, it was a nasty suckout. Daniel finally sent Luske out in third place on an ugly hand. Short-stacked, Marcel was pretty much forced to play a weak Q-9-5-5. With the monster stack, Daniel called with J-9-4-3. Neither of these hands is what you'd really want to play, even short-handed. The flop came 3-3-4 giving Negreanu a full house and sending Marcel to the rail.

Once the tournament had started, I don't think there was a minute when Daniel didn't have a massive chip lead. He was still chip leader when we started heads-up, but I had gained a lot of ground. We both felt like we were going to win this thing. We both thought Omaha high-low was our best game and that few in the world could beat us. One of us was going to win our second WSOP bracelet that day and we both really wanted it. Neither one of us was willing to give up a potential edge by making a deal. And neither of us wanted to give up the trash talking. So it began. If you had asked anyone who would make for the loudest heads-up match, everyone would have said Danny and Mikey. We were ready to play for the bracelet. It wouldn't be pretty, it wouldn't be quiet, and it would take nearly four hours.

When Daniel ordered a Corona, I asked the crowd, "How can you beat a drunk? They don't know how to lay a hand down."

"Don't worry about it," Daniel said, "I can beat Mike with my eyes closed."

"See that gold bracelet? After I win this, I'm going to have it engraved: 'To Mike, from Daniel, with love.'"

In the first half hour, the lead changed hands as many times as we exchanged one-liners; neither one of us could gain traction. I finally won a monster pot with aces full. On the next hand, I check-raised Daniel on a flop of 7-7-2 and he laid it down. I didn't have anything, but I knew he didn't either. I finally had a decent lead on him and had him out-chipped by about 230,000 to 140,000. Daniel's run was ending, and I was turning up the heat.

"Later tonight, I'm going to go out celebrating my big win over Daniel Negreanu," I played to the crowd. "What are you going to be doing, son?" I turned to Negreanu and asked.

Two hands later, I check-raised him again.

"You can't change destiny. Don't you know that?" I said to get under his skin, but I believed it too. I felt the win coming.

"Take care of him tonight, because he's going to be very upset after he loses this chip lead," Daniel said to one of my friends in the audience after slowing me down a little bit by taking a big pot with two pair, holding K-J-5-4.

"You finally won a pot, and now you've found your voice?" I countered.

I took a pot by betting the flop and Daniel folded, showing one pair. "All I got to do is bet and take it. You're getting easy. At least try to put up a little fight, Danny."

Daniel might have taken that one to heart, because the next thing he did was take down a monster pot when he made a Broadway straight to my king-high straight. We were almost back to even. I'd been pushing him around pretty good with next to nothing, but I could tell that he was thinking he finally had a second chance to win this thing. I didn't want him to think that way for long. We had been at it, heads-up, for over three hours.

I looked down at a pair of aces with a couple of rags on the next hand. Two aces in Omaha aren't as strong as pocket aces in Texas hold'em, but heads-up they still work pretty well. I raised, hoping that Daniel would think I was steaming a little bit. It worked because he called me all the way to the river and couldn't beat my aces for high and didn't have a low. On the very next hand, I was dealt aces again. Again we went to the river and again Daniel couldn't beat the high pair, although he was close. He had a couple of kings. For the first time at the final table, Daniel was under $100,000. And it only got worse for him. On the next hand, I really hit big, scooping the pot with the nut low and trips for high. We were both quiet at this point, probably for the first time all day.

A few hands later I bluffed to take the pot and showed him that I had no pair and no draw. The expression on Daniel's face said that he wanted to be anywhere else but at that final table right then. On the next hand, I flopped a set and a nut low draw. Daniel had a few outs for a split pot, but no low came and my set held up.

And that was it. It was over. I had won!

There are two stories about how I came back to win the Omaha high-low bracelet that year. Daniel will swear to this day that I got unbelievably lucky and the deck ran over me. I will always say that I outplayed him. If there had been hole card cameras for that tournament, everyone would know how badly I had outplayed him.

Did I hit cards? Yes. Did I outplay him? I took him to school.

I was proud of this win. I came from behind to beat a tough opponent, but that's not why I was proud. I played the tournament without the speed. I know how that sounds. You win a World Series bracelet and the thing you're the most proud of is that you didn't do it on drugs. How sick is that? But that's where I was. I had been clean for over two months before the World Series and I went back to the drugs. I was totally fucked up and realized that if I didn't gut it out, I'd always feel like I needed to be on speed to play. If the meth had won this time, it would always win.

While they were taking my picture and conducting the interview, I felt like I was celebrating two come-from-behind victories, a public one and my private one. It was an exhilarating feeling, higher than any drug could take me. It was the biggest sense of personal accomplishment I had ever felt. I'd just taken down the biggest Omaha high-low tournament against some of the best Omaha players in the world. Only a few months earlier, I'd lost my girlfriend, my game, and most of my money using that horrendous drug. Even after I had kicked the physical addiction, it looked as though I might never beat the psychological dependence. But as I raised the stacks of money above my head at the final table, I felt like I had beaten all my demons.

You'd think Danny and I would have been sick of each other at that point, but we walked across Fremont Street and had dinner together at the Golden Nugget. From there, we went over to the Bellagio. It was almost like an insider tradition for a bracelet winner to strut his stuff through the Bellagio poker room. I felt great as the guys from the big game patted me on the back and congratulated me.

Just when I thought the night couldn't be more perfect, I ran into Teri and Roy. The look in her eyes said it all: She had backed the wrong horse. Here I was, her ex, celebrating a World Series of Poker victory. Now that was a sweet moment!

I played the main event, but didn't survive the first day. There has always been some controversy about me and that event and I want to set the record straight. During the television coverage of the final table, Phil Hellmuth said that if Robert Varkonyi went on to win the championship, Phil would shave his head. If you've seen that event on television, you know that Robert did go on to win it and Phil had his head shaved on camera. But some of you may have heard that I also said I'd shave my head, but that I slipped out a backdoor when the final table got to heads-up. Not true! I did say I would shave my head, although not on camera like Phil, but the spotlight got a little crowded. Phil really wanted the publicity for the stunt. This was one year before Chris Moneymaker accelerated the poker boom, and poker publicity was hard to come by. But Phil was a master at grabbing the headlines. I left Binion's and let Phil have the camera time. And I got to keep my hair.

When people ask me what the greatest poker accomplishment of my life was, they're always surprised when I tell them it was winning my 2002 WSOP Omaha high-low bracelet. I'm outgoing and confident at the poker table, sure, but I've never thought of myself as being a particularly brave person. I felt brave that week. Even now, there are times when I look back on that week to remind myself that I can, and should, be a stronger person.

I'm also an honest person. And I would like to tell you that this victory over meth was the first step to my getting clean. But it wasn't. It would be another year before I finally got the message and kicked illegal drugs once and for all.

Chapter Fifteen

Stuey's Ghost

For poker players, the day after the WSOP is like the day after Christmas for kids, or the last day of summer vacation. These days, a lot of players just jump online and play day after day and night after night, blocking out the fact that they have to wait another long year before the next Series. You do anything you can to throw yourself back into a routine that convinces you that there's life after the Series.

Before the 2002 World Series, my routine was cash games and drugs. And when it was over, I returned to my cycle of weekend Ecstasy parties and the four day poker week. I still had "Black Tuesdays" when I switched from partying to poker, but I still looked forward to a long party weekend.

I was the guy with the money. It wasn't like today with all the online poker millionaires. I had a lot of money and the party was always at Mikey's house. It had been two years since I discovered Ecstasy and the Vegas party circuit. I'd really just begun to get to know the whole club and party crowd when Teri and I had hooked up. I had been the party guy with the great girlfriend. Now I was the professional poker player with the big bankroll, great party house, and no girlfriend to hold me back.

The party scene in 2002 was a whole lot different than it had been just two years before. Earlier, we'd party at the clubs and then come home to crash and recover before we did it all again the next night. In 2002, the party would basically follow us home. When the club was too tame or was closing, I'd bring home the really tasty pieces. Sometimes the party started at one of the many strip clubs in Las Vegas. Those after-parties took on a very different tone. The ride home with a limo full of strippers was a party all by itself.

A few years later when the poker boom hit, a lot of charity poker parties were held at the Playboy Mansion in L.A. One young player told me, "It was unbelievable. All these girls were just walking around topless and even bottomless. It's like they just got naked at every party!"

I remember smiling and thinking that it was just like the parties at my house. It got to the point that the "right" girls and the "wrong" girls all knew my address. They all knew my schedule—four days of poker, then three days of partying. Week after week.

I began using meth to focus at the tables again, but it hadn't gotten out of hand. I didn't have any big losing streaks, but I was dipping into the bankroll to cover my expenses. My monthly nut had the added cost of the partying, and price of partying was higher now. But I was still doing well enough at the Bellagio to keep my bankroll from running down too far. I knew partying was a leak in my game, but it seemed like a controllable leak. I was having the time of my life. I was playing decent poker. I was getting laid a lot. I really enjoyed the party scene both in public and at my house.

The drugs were actually helping with some of my problems. I was basically self-medicating my bipolar disorder and ADHD. Unfortunately, the drugs were also doing a number on my long-term health. I know now that drugs probably caused my ADHD and made it worse the longer I used them. So while my street drug solution helped some problems, it caused problems that will be with me for the rest of my life. Of course, I didn't know any of that back then.

I look back at my party years and it doesn't even seem like that was me. I did all that shit—the drugs, the strippers, the partying—but eventually you grow up or grow out of all that. Or in my case, you recognize that you just can't keep living that way. We've all done some things in our lives that we're not that proud of, but on some level we still like to remember our wild days. If I had to pick

just one party story, it would definitely be the night of the Pimp &
Ho party.

That night also changed my life in a way that I never could have
predicted.

The annual Pimp & Ho Ball in Las Vegas happened in September
of 2002 at the Palms Casino and Hotel, a party as big and as over-the-
top as they come. Everyone got dressed up real sexy — guys in outrageous costumes and lots of ladies in nearly no costume at all. I had
a pre-party and after-party at my place. I rented a big limo to take
a bunch of people to the party and I also bought the number-one
party booth at the Palms for $5,000. While everyone really appreci-
ated all the parties I threw at my house, they thought all this was a
little extravagant, even for me. They decided they would all toss in
$250 apiece for the evening. I thought it was really cool of my friends
to pitch in and offer to cover some of the costs. So along with all the
food and drinks I got for the party, I also included a couple of hits of
Ecstasy for everyone.

This was my third time going to Pimp & Ho Ball and I was looking to make it a truly outrageous night. I decided I'd had enough
of the party scene and wanted to get back to my game, so I told all
my friends that this was going to be one final, big blowout. The pre-
party was my way of getting us going for one last great night. I invited everyone, even my personal physician, who also played poker
at the Bellagio a few days a week. I'd never really partied with him
before. Besides being my doctor, we were friends. He'd heard about
the big party and asked if he could come and bring a friend who was
in town from New York. "Of course. It's a fucking party!" I said. In
the end, I had no idea how many people I actually invited.

People started showing up at the house around nine or so; the
Pimp & Ho Ball didn't even open its doors until at least eleven. A
few strippers I knew came by to help get things warmed up. Even
though we all tried to pace ourselves for the marathon party ahead,
people were already rolling pretty hard by the time we headed over
to the Palms. Not everyone could fit in the limo. I remember that
my doctor and his friend Mike Vento decided to drive their own car.
They didn't think they would be staying as late as the rest of us. I
didn't get the impression they were very hardcore partiers to begin
with.

Our party booth was filled with naked women—some of them I actually knew.

I wandered out on the balcony and ran into Doc's friend, Mike Vento. He seemed like a nice guy and we shot the shit for awhile. He told me at least three times how much he appreciated that I had gotten him into the party. Mike said he was moving to Vegas from New York where he'd been running some underground strip clubs, and that he and some investors were planning to open a few clubs here. We talked a lot about poker, Vegas, and X. He told me the Ecstasy was really smooth and he asked if I could get more of it.

As nice as it was to talk with Mike, he was no competition for naked women. I headed back to the very friendly, and very naked, girls in the booth. It was still pretty early when I noticed that Mike and Doc had left. I still had a long night ahead of me—I was rolling at my last big party ever and I wanted to make the most of it. At some point a porn star and her husband joined us in our booth. When things started to break up at the Palms, we all headed back to my place. We packed the limo and a few more cars full of partiers, including our new friend the porn queen.

The after-party erupted as soon as people walked through my front door. There was a big off-white leather couch by the fireplace. I like that couch, I still have it today. I guess the actress liked it too, because she staked it out for the post-party action. It wasn't long before she and another girl started making out on it. Pretty soon they were both naked and the porn star was doing the other girl right there in the middle of the party. Over the next maybe three hours, the porn star did ten different girls. I'd say she did them back-to-back but it was more like front-to-front. You couldn't buy wilder entertainment. Well, in Vegas, you probably could, but it would cost you. It was ridiculously hot and the party just kind of flowed around it. People would stop to watch. Girls were negotiating their way into the lineup. Just like in baseball, there was an on-deck circle where the girls were warming up. It was as over-the-top as any of the parties at Mikey's place. I really like telling that story to people while they're sitting on that same leather couch.

The party kept on rolling all night and through most of the next day. That might not have been the biggest party that ever happened at my place, but it was the one I'll always remember, a truly fitting end to my party days.

After it was over, I backed off my party weekends. I stop doing X and spent more weekends at home watching football and a lot less time at the clubs. I became pretty good friends with the porn star and her husband and I partied with them and their friends from time to time. Interestingly, they were into a much calmer lifestyle than you might think, which was perfect for me. I wanted to focus more time and energy on the Bellagio poker room than the clubs.

Toward the beginning of 2003, I decided that I needed to get my tournament game back in shape for the World Series. I played the L.A. Poker Classic in February, cashing in one tournament and breaking about even in the side games. Then I went to Reno for a World Poker Tour event at the beginning of April. While I had cut out the Ecstasy completely, I was still using meth for poker. I remember that trip to Reno because I was running on empty and had a really bad reaction to the meth.

I'd been at the tables for over thirty hours when I started to lose it. I was forgetting when I was in a hand and slowing the game down. I was exhausted. Fortunately, someone had the sense to talk me into taking a break and catching some sleep. Unfortunately, that suggestion came a little too late because in the elevator up to my room, I nearly collapsed and started to hallucinate. I had no idea where I was, but it didn't look anything like a casino elevator.

I want to thank whoever got me to my room. I know you probably weren't the green gorilla I said you were; maybe you just had a beard.

Reno was the warning bell, the signal that I was about to hit bottom. But then again, I don't know too many people hooked on meth that heard the warnings until after the crash. I just kept hammering away. A couple of weeks later, just before the 2003 World Series of Poker, I made the final table of an Omaha high-low tournament at the Five Star Poker Classic at the Bellagio. I finished seventh at a table with Phil Ivey, Miami John Cernuto, Toto Leonidas, Howard Lederer, Greg Mascio and Minneapolis Jim Meehan.

I remember it well, not so much for that final table, but for what happened the next night.

I decided not to play the next Bellagio event. I took the day off and slept until the late afternoon. I remember sitting in my living room as it slowly got dark outside. I flipped on the TV and surfed around until I saw the opening credits for a show about Stu Ungar.

That caught my attention, so I sat there alone in the dark and watched Stuey's life play out. You didn't have to be a genius to see the parallels between his life and mine at that point. Stuey never came close to breaking his drug habit. Eventually, it took his life.

A lot of well known poker players were interviewed for the show and told great stories about Stuey. But they were all talking about someone who was dead, someone who'd lost his life to drugs. I began to think about the very real possibility that I'd be the next great dead player they'd be talking about. I didn't want to be poker's newest poster boy for drug addiction. But as I sat there, I realized that I had the potential to become the next Stu Ungar. At that exact moment, the 1997 championship final table flashed across the screen, the main event that Stuey had won out there on Fremont Street. And there I was, sitting in the front row watching Stuey's last victory.

I wish I could say that I quit drugs right then. I really wish I could say that, but I can't. I'd seen the light and I was very, very close to turning my life around. But you know how it is—people with serious problems have to hit rock bottom before they make the change.

I was still a couple of inches away.

Chapter Sixteen

Up for Another Series

For almost a year I'd tried to maintain my bankroll while paying the high costs of partying. But by the time the spring rolled around, I wasn't what I'd call financially healthy. It wasn't just the extra expenses of my out-of-control lifestyle, but the partying had also affected my win rate.

To help my bankroll situation, I got my friend John Brody to stake me for some of the events at the Series. John and I had talked about some kind of backing deal a few times, and he stepped up. I let him choose which events he wanted to back me in. As it turned out, John knows something about picking winners.

I knew that I was going to need meth for focus. I didn't have another "meth withdrawal" Series in me. When John agreed to stake me, he said that if he caught me using any drugs, he would never stake me again. So I had to be more careful with the meth than I'd ever been before. I couldn't let anyone know I was using, no one. I had tried and failed to control meth during past Series, but in '03, I had a strategy and I lined up a secret weapon. First, I was only going to do meth during the tournaments. I wouldn't do it between events and ecstasy was totally out.

I also had a "holistic" drug connection, a pharmacist who gave me amino acids to clean my system of the extra garbage in the street meth. I was trying to purify the meth inside my body, or at least counteract some of the side effects of street meth. My prescription medications today do the same thing, just in a more direct way. Amphetamines that are chemically processed in a laboratory are clean of all the crap that can cause tweaking, the compulsive, repetitive behavior and fidgeting that totally fucks up meth heads. I was taking 5HTP and some other supplements that definitely helped. With my new system of only taking small amounts for focus at the tables and using my "cleaning" supplements, I was actually doing what I hadn't been able to do before. And for a time, it really worked.

I played break-even poker in the cash games during the first two weeks of the World Series and hadn't really connected with any good runs in the tournaments I played. Then in the $2500 No-Limit Hold'em tournament, I made the final table along with T.J. Cloutier, David Singer, Steve Zolotow, Kenna James and Phi Nguyen. Tom Jacobs was also there playing his ninth WSOP final table; two weeks later he would make it to his tenth and win his first bracelet. The other players were Eric Holum and Jim Miller, both Vegas pros. Eric had won a bracelet in 1999, and Jim wound up playing a key role at the critical end of this event.

I was super locked in at this event, on meth, of course, but it was working perfectly. We ran through the first six players in short order. When it got down to three, there was me, Phi Nguyen and Jim Miller. Jim was short-stacked and I wanted him gone so that I could get Phi into a heads-up match. But Jim did an amazing job of surviving. He went all in time after time, and managed to pull out win after win. When we were at five players, he had moved all in with K-10 against someone's flopped set of jacks. Jim stood up to shake hands with all the other players and leave, but the board came runner-runner to give him the Broadway straight. He was super short-stacked for over an hour; we just couldn't shake him.

Then there was Phi Nguyen. Twice he had come over the top of me after I had reraised his initial raise. Both times I had A-Q suited and both times I laid it down. I decided to put him to the test the next time. I got pocket jacks and moved all in. He called with pocket queens. The Q-J-4 flop gave both of us big sets, but I was drawing dead to one jack. I busted out in third place. I wasn't unhappy with my play; I just got unlucky on that last hand. It really stung that I missed out on the $60,000 difference between second and third place. If we had just gotten Jim Miller one time, I would have had a heads-up situation and a shot at the win. But we didn't. Phi quickly ended the event and won the bracelet.

My second money finish came about two weeks later in the $3,000 Limit Hold'em event, the one where Tom Jacobs finally won his bracelet. When we were playing short-handed on two tables, Rob Hollink went out in fourteenth and Devilfish Ulliott was twelfth. I got snapped off in tenth, sending Phil Hellmuth, Bill Gazes, David Chiu, Jennifer Harman, Toto Leonidas, and Jim Meehan to the final table.

My third and final money finish in 2003 was in the last limit event, the $5,000 Limit Hold'em. I went out with two tables to go late on Day One, in fifteenth place. I was playing short for the last hour or so, just looking for a good place to double up, but it never came. I did nothing in the championship that year, going card dead right from the start. I was out on Day One.

I had three cashes for about $80,000, but my backer got about half of that after the make-up for all my tournament buy-ins. I was also a small loser in the cash games, so overall, the Series was a little bit of a downer. I had needed to get my bankroll back in shape and that just hadn't happened.

Even though I didn't cash in the championship tournament, that main event changed everything in the world of poker. The night before the final table began, a bunch of us went out to dinner and ended up talking about the players at the final table.

"Chris Moneymaker has a huge pile of chips going into tomorrow," somebody said. "He's looking good to go the distance."

"Great, another unknown idiot is going to win!" I said.

"If this guy wins, we're all going to become so rich, we won't know what to do with all the money," Erik Seidel told us. He was the first guy to really get it.

Erik, who has eight World Series of Poker gold bracelets, was one of the few players who understood that the poker boom needed a fuse to light the fire. Poker needed an unlikely hero, someone that every quarter-ante home game player could identify with. Chris Moneymaker was that guy. Not only was he an amateur, but he'd won his seat in an online satellite tournament. All of the stars had aligned for Chris to win and jumpstart the big poker boom. In that respect, I don't think that Chris got enough credit for his win and certainly didn't do enough with his celebrity.

I think about the line you often hear from golf pros, even today: "We all ought to give Arnold Palmer a cut every time we win."

Serious golfers know that without Arnie making golf popular to the general public it wouldn't be the billion dollar business it is today. Moneymaker was the right guy at the right time for poker. The poker boom is always explained the same way: first, the movie *Rounders*, then Moneymaker and then the Internet.

The World Series was over and life would go back to normal—which for me, really wouldn't be the case. Poker players' lives were anything but normal, and mine was much farther out on the edge. And I was ready to fall off.

In the first few days after the Series, I started sliding into another depression. But this time, I kept on slipping deeper and deeper into the dark. I just sat in my room shaking. Going downstairs, even for food, was a long trip. I had no clue what was wrong with me. It seems insane that someone who had gone through meth withdrawal a year earlier during a WSOP tournament wouldn't recognize the symptoms the second time around, but that's what was happening. That's a sick aspect of this drug: You know you can stop the pain by doing more meth, but you really don't understand that the reason you're suffering is because you're coming off it. Meth takes away the pain, but it's also the cause of the pain.

I got worse and worse to the point that I couldn't even go out and buy any meth. I couldn't leave the house. Hell, I couldn't even leave my room. Fortunately or unfortunately, a couple of my very close friends, Sam and Andrea, were coming to visit me for July 4th weekend. By the time they arrived, I was a complete basket case. I wasn't eating or sleeping, and I was suicidal. I didn't have a story this time. There had been no back-to-back drawouts against me like in 2000, no huge suckouts on the river, no Carlos super bluff that I just couldn't get over. There was no poker reason why I should be in such bad shape.

Sam and Andrea had to take a cab from the airport because I wasn't answering my phone. They showed up at my house to find me curled up in a ball in my room. For the first three days of their vacation they tried taking care of me, dealing with a suicidal idiot who made no sense about anything. They couldn't figure out what was wrong with me. They knew that I'd had depressions before but there had always been some reason why I felt that way. I couldn't tell them what was wrong, only that everything was wrong and I wanted to die. On the third day of their visit, Andrea told me I should do a line of coke and everything would be better.

"No," I told her. "I'm not doing any drugs. I've been doing them and I'm a total wreck."

"Mike, this is not about partying, this will make you feel better." Andrea said.

If I'd had any of my senses left, I might've remembered that long night three years ago when some other friends had told me that taking Ecstasy would make me happy. Or I might have remembered when Teri told me how meth would just wake me up and help me focus. But I was in too dark a place to remember that. I was too desperate. Finally, after almost a day of trying to get me to do some coke, Sam had had enough. He spread a line of coke on a mirror and looked at me.

"I don't give a fuck what happens," Sam said. "You do this line right now or I'm going to beat the crap out of you."

I had to stop feeling so bad. I snorted the coke.

Coke may not have been the correct medication, but in the short term, it did the trick. In less than a minute, all the depression was gone. Sam and Andrea were totally relieved. Now they could enjoy what was left of their Vegas vacation. And they could spend it with their buddy Mikey, who was now in a great mood. For the last three days of their trip, we had a great coked-up time. Remembering just how dark and depressed the last few weeks had been, I was afraid of going back there again. So I kept doing coke. And more coke. We did the coke they brought with them, the coke I went out and bought the next day, and some more coke we got at one of the clubs.

We were out in the world and going to clubs where everyone knew me. Sam and Andrea couldn't believe I was the same messed-up, suicidal guy they'd found curled up in his room just a few days before. Now I was the guy that walked past the line outside of every club and was greeted by the doorman like a long lost friend. Every club manager knew me and we got VIP treatment wherever we went.

But during those two or three days while I was having a great time and feeling really happy, I kept wondering in the back of my mind, "Why do I need these drugs to be normal? What is so wrong with me that I have to do drugs?"

I was close to asking the right questions, really close. But after my friends left, I didn't have time to think about it because I had to get my ass to France. During the Series, Erick Lindgren and I had decided that we were going to Paris in July to play the Grand Prix de Paris, the biggest event in Europe. Besides the poker, we also wanted to have a European adventure, do some sightseeing and have fun. Sam and Andrea left on a Sunday and I was supposed to board a plane with Erick the next day to Paris. I'd been partying on coke for three days, I'd barely slept, and I was in no shape to play poker. I was also afraid that the dark depression would come back.

As I was packing my bags, I went out and picked up a baggie of meth for the trip.

Chapter Seventeen

Last Tango in Paris

It's amazing how things can change in such a short time. Between 2000 through 2003, Erick Lindgren, Daniel Negreanu and I were really close friends and most of the time, one of us was broke. Well, broke probably isn't the right word: We were "struggling with our bankrolls." It was a time when we always had to be aware of which way the money was flowing—in or out. Even though we were watching our bankrolls, Erick and I just couldn't resist the World Poker Tour's Grand Prix de Paris tournament. There really hadn't been many opportunities for players to play in Europe before then, since the European Poker Tour didn't yet exist. So with my little bag of focus powder and my $60,000 bankroll in my pocket, I boarded the plane to Paris.

After checking into our Paris hotel, Erick and I spent the day shaking off our jet lag. My plan was to jump right into action at the Aviation Club. I had heard that the cash games around the Grand Prix could be really good, but you never truly know about them until you show up at the casino. Some tournaments have only one or two good games going, and you can be stranded on the wait list for six or seven hours. By that time, the really big fish might have busted out. As it turned out, almost from the moment I set foot in the Aviation Club's poker room, there was a big H.O.R.S.E. game going. With Phil

Ivey, Barry Greenstein, David Benyamine and me in the game, there was always a full table with lots of European players and "wannabes" eager to sit down with us. The stakes were €800/€1,600; at the time, a euro was about equal to a dollar. Those high stakes didn't stop the table from running around the clock.

I regularly dipped into my bag of meth, but I was doing my best to keep it under control. After what had happened to me after the World Series, I was afraid of slipping back into a depression. I tried not to overdo the meth, but I didn't want to go off it either, so I tried to maintain a low-level meth high. I was playing some ungodly long sessions, but so were most of the other professionals. I doubt that anyone suspected I was doing meth, if for no other reason than I was winning, and winning big.

After seven days, I was up about $180,000 in the cash games. These were some of the wildest games I've ever played. David, Barry and Phil were making totally sick prop bets on every hand and getting some of the other players in on the action. It was crazy. The pot would be €10,000 but they'd have three or four side bets for €10,000 each. No one was paying attention to the poker game. Well, no one but me. They were too busy paying off on the "all low" flop or the "all red" flop, totally out of control. Everyone was laughing and drinking and prop betting like absolute idiots. Jeff Lisandro and I just kept raking in the pots and staying out of the way of the prop bet craziness.

The table was playing so good that we were actually skipping the tournaments. Considering what our win rates were in the cash games, the payouts for a sixteen or eighteen hour tournament didn't make sense. A simple math calculation said to stay and play cash games, which were way more profitable than the tournaments. With the meth keeping me focused and awake, I played for a week straight, taking a break to sleep only twice.

I didn't get very deep in the main event, but Erick made the final table and cashed in fifth place for about $60,000 and David Benyamine went on to win it. When Erick made the final table, I suggested that he take a hit of my meth. I wanted him to do well and I knew that with that extra focus, he would play great. That was a fucked up offer to make, but I was just trying to help. Erick said he was focused enough and he was right. He played a great final table without my "help."

The Paris trip wasn't entirely about the poker, Erick and I were anxious to do something outside of the casino. Howard and Suzie Lederer and David Grey had plans to take a train to a Radiohead concert and asked us to come along. Suzie was so great; she arranged all the hotels, trains and tickets while all of us were playing poker. So she had the whole trip set up for us. A day or so after the tournament ended, we hopped on one of those great European trains and took about a four hour trip to Nimes.

I had been playing for seventy-two hours straight and had planned to crash on the train. But even though I'd stopped taking meth that last day, I just couldn't sleep. Besides, Erick thought we should spend some quality time in the bar car. That was the most fun I've ever had on alcohol. We were drunk the entire time. Once we were back in the compartment, I suspect our group wasn't too happy about all the noise Erick and I made. But we were just having a great time. We talked about everything except poker. Eventually we got off the train in Nimes, practically falling down drunk. Okay, not practically—I could barely stand up. We hit the hotel and I took about a two hour nap.

When I woke up, it felt like I'd slept for days. I have no idea why that combination of residual meth, food, alcohol, and hardly any sleep made me feel refreshed, but it did. I felt great and the concert was excellent. I remember having a kind of out of body experience, but I think that had more to do with the kick-ass joint some kids shared with me.

Then it was back on the train to Paris and to the airport for the flights back to Las Vegas. I totally crashed on the plane ride home and got in some solid sleep. But as soon as we touched down in Vegas, I wasn't tired at all. Maybe it had something to do with the hit of meth I did in the airport bathroom while we waited for our bags. Erick was heading home to sleep but I was supposed to meet someone at the Crazy Horse, so I headed over to the strip club for a quick drink to wind down before I crashed.

I had about two nights of sleep in seven days in Paris. I figured if I had a drink or two after the long flight home, I could probably hit the bed for twenty hours straight. Instead, I started talking with a stripper and she had a much better idea for me and my meth—we partied nearly non-stop for two more days. She was really hot and very into lots of meth and sex, so we had a blast. I got my third night of sleep in nine days when the stripper and I finally passed out sometime on day two of our meth orgy. After we woke up that second day and had a couple more rounds of sex and meth, she left to go back to work.

I thought she was crazy, ruining her life like that.

I was so wired I couldn't get the sleep I knew I needed. I remember lying there in bed and thinking about what my last two weeks had been like. I'd partied on cocaine with my friends because I'd been depressed after the Series, played poker in Paris for a week on meth, and followed it all up with two days of meth and sex with a stripper whose name I didn't even know.

I was totally out of control and I knew it.

This was no way to live my life. Something was seriously wrong with me. If I didn't know I had a problem before then, the previous two weeks provided too much evidence to ignore. I knew that I didn't want to do drugs anymore; I knew that ten straight days on speed was insane. I was slowly figuring out that the meth was probably doing me a lot of damage. I also knew that if I simply quit again on my own, things would probably get ugly. I could feel the depression just waiting to take me down again.

While I knew that being on meth kept the demons at bay, I still didn't get the real connection between withdrawal and my depression. I thought about all of that for a few hours before I passed out. When I finally woke up fifteen hours later, I felt the depression creeping back in and I knew the shakes weren't far behind. I wasn't going to let this happen again.

This time I was determined to get whatever help I needed.

Dosing myself with street drugs wasn't a cure. If there was something I could do, a professional would be the one to know what it was. Before the depression could get a firm grip on me, I looked in the yellow pages under psychologists. Confused by all the listings, I called my mom and told her I needed help, but just didn't know where to get it. She made a few calls and phoned me back with the name of a psychologist recommended by one of her friends.

Dr. Carlissimo agreed to see me immediately. I told him my situation as clearly as I could give it to him.

"I don't want to do drugs anymore. But when I don't do drugs, I get severely depressed."

I told him I couldn't deal with drugs or depression being my only two choices. We did word association and memory tests; he did a bunch of different things to evaluate my current mental condition. He also asked about what drugs I did and how much of them I'd taken in the last three years. We talked about why I used the drugs. I told him about how meth affected my poker game and how Ecstasy had changed my life. He told me that some of my brain functions were working at a first or second grade level. It was pretty clear to him that I was starting to suffer from the long-term effects of drug use and the immediate effects of drug withdrawal.

He explained that Ecstasy had damaged my brain. This is when I first heard about serotonin receptors and the potential damage to my short-term memory. He also told me that the depression I was going through was partially a side effect of meth withdrawal. He said that he couldn't make a complete and accurate assessment of all my problems, including how much damage I'd suffered from the drugs, until I was totally clean. But even then, he said, there were strong clues that I was fighting something more than drugs.

"Totally clean" meant that I had to be completely drug-free for thirty days. Once that was behind me, then he could get me the help I needed. He explained that I had been self-medicating myself for over three years. Once he had a better handle on my psychological problems, there were much better, and definitely cleaner, prescription medications we could try. But before all that could happen, I had to keep clean. He must have said "thirty days" a dozen times. Dr. Carlissimo was up front about what the next thirty days were going to be like. He said that during the first two weeks, I'd be severely depressed and probably suicidal. The shakes would come back and I'd need someone to drive me to his office to see him. He also told me that using medications to get me through my drying out period would only delay a correct diagnosis. He painted a dark and nasty picture of the next month.

Then he told me that I was probably bipolar. It was just his best guess at that point based on the tests and everything I'd told him about my life. If I was bipolar, there were medications that could help, but we'd cross that bridge after the next month was over.

"You have to trust me, Mike. This is the only way to get out from under all of your problems."

I must have thought about those words a thousand times over the next thirty days: "You have to trust me, Mike."

That's what I grabbed onto. I did trust him and I wanted to be off the drugs. It seemed like there was only one way to do that—I had to quit everything. Cold turkey. I know there are people that freak out when they hear the word bipolar, or when they're diagnosed with a mental illness. But to me, just knowing there might be a reason for the problems I had suffered for so many years was a relief.

"No drugs for thirty days? Why would I do that? How could I do that?" is what the old Mike may have thought. But now, finally, I was ready. I heard what Dr. Carlissimo said and knew he was right. It was time to begin. If I could just get through this, then I could say, "July 23, 2003 was the last day I did any illegal drugs."

But first I had to survive the next thirty days.

On the very first day I decided that the only way this was going to work was if I put my complete faith in everything the doctor said and told me to do. And it wasn't like he left me hanging out there on my own. He saw me at least once a week during the month to check on my progress. At one point he told me that even after I was clean, I would probably experience bouts of depression over the next eighteen months. That wasn't quite the news I needed to hear, but he assured me that we could probably control them with medication once we had a firm idea as to what was wrong with my brain.

Those thirty days were the toughest and the longest days in my life. I'll never forget them. Coming off drugs again put me in full suicide mode. I spent a lot of time just shaking in my room, thinking I was going to die. I counted off the days like a prisoner. I would wake up, go to the calendar and check off another day. It was brutal. I started reading online about meth withdrawal and saw that a lot of people went back on it because they just couldn't take it. The meth would ease their pain and that's all they could see. I had started to understand that the pain was the meth.

Most of my party friends forgot I existed once I decided to quit. I guess once I stopped footing the bill for the parties, I wasn't much use to them. But I had one friend who was there for me. That was Mike Vento, the guy I had met at the Pimp & Ho party in September. We had been friends on and off since then. But when everyone else kicked me to the curb while I was struggling to quit drugs, he stepped up to the plate to help me win that battle. He knew how hard I was trying to fix my life. He knew I wasn't partying and understood my goal. He stopped by to check on me regularly, and I think he even drove me to the doctor's office once.

The second two weeks were easier then the first, just like the doctor said they would be. I'm not saying they were easy, but I felt like I was in the home stretch. And when the thirty days were finally up, I felt much better. I was still shaky and depressed, but I was not suicidal anymore.

Dr. Carlissimo sent me to a psychiatrist. The psychiatrist agreed with his first instincts—that my history of deep depressions and occasional bursts of happiness were symptoms of bipolar disorder. He was confident that a lot of my drug use was mostly an attempt to self-medicate through the bipolar swings. I was also diagnosed with Attention Deficit Hyperactivity Disorder. He thought that I probably had a mild form of ADHD before I took drugs, and that my drug use had made it severe to the point where it had become an issue.

The psychiatrist immediately put me on Depakote for the bipolar disorder along with an antidepressant called Lexipro. It was amazing how quickly I felt stable. I had zero desire for X or meth. I felt comfortable. I was happy. There is no better way to describe what stabilized means other than just being happy. It was the first time in three years that I had been happy on a consistent basis. I guess if you've never been depressed for a long time, it might seem a little strange to describe my life as just being happy. People take happiness for granted. Not me. For me, happy was a luxury and it was a pretty damn good feeling.

I took street drugs for the first time on May 5, 2000 when I took Ecstasy. July 23, 2003 was the last day I did any illegal drugs.

I told Mike Vento how good I was doing and how happy I was. We worked out together a couple of times a week and went to the movies together. He seemed like a guy who just wanted to be my friend. I told him that I really didn't trust anyone and that I never knew when someone was trying to take advantage of me.

"Mike, you can trust me," he always said. "I'm just here because you are my friend."

Then one day, out of the blue, Mike asked me if I could get him drugs. I was shocked. Why would you ask a guy who had just come off drugs to get you some? Why would he ask me when I was seeing a psychiatrist because of my drug use? He knew I wasn't into selling drugs and that I'd never sold drugs. He told me that he had some friends coming into town and he didn't have any connections and he really needed me to do him this favor. I told him I was uncomfortable with his asking me to do this for him and thought that would be the end of it.

Then he asked me again a couple of days later. He said all he needed was a couple of ounces of coke. He just wanted to set his friends up while they were in town. I told him that I was really nervous about buying that much coke. I was never really that into coke and didn't want to get involved with it.

"I just can't do it," I said. "I'm totally uncomfortable making that kind of buy."

The next day, my personal physician called and asked me if I could help Mike out. Doc was the one who had introduced Mike to me back at the Pimp & Ho pre-party and now he was pressuring me to get Mike the two ounces of coke.

What the hell was going on?

They both had started to make me feel like I wasn't helping out a friend, the same friend who had been so good to me the past couple of months while I was in such bad shape. And that's why I finally decided to make some calls to see if I could find the coke for him. I was just sick about it. I had to make about fifty phone calls to find the right people with enough product to sell me two ounces of coke. I didn't feel right about it, but my friend needed a favor. Eventually, I found the right connection and made the deal. I felt totally over my head making a buy that big. I'd never bought more than an eight-ball of coke before, and it was always from a dealer that I knew from the clubs. But Mike had been almost the only person who had stood by me while I was getting off drugs. And that meant a lot.

Another friend called and said he had about a hundred Percocets he wanted to unload. I guess he had heard that I'd been calling around looking for stuff. He had a chronic back disease and got about a thousand pills at a time. He was short on his rent and thought maybe he could sell his extra pain pills for some quick cash. When Mike heard about that, he was all over it. Somehow the pills got added to the deal. In a sick way, it's funny that my friend with all the pain killers chose that one time to sell some.

I'll never forget picking up that coke. Even though I knew the guy casually, the quantity made me nervous to the point that I was shaking. "Why am I doing this?" I kept asking myself.

When I got there, I even told the guy, "A good friend of mine asked me to do him this favor. I'm not even making any money off this and I don't want to make any money. I don't even know why I'm here. But I appreciate you going out of your way for me."

I was babbling like a complete cokehead.

When I got back to the house, I called Mike. "I just wanted you to know that this is the worst thing I've done in my life" I said. "I've never been in this awkward a position. Come and get it the fuck out of my house. I'm never getting anything again for anybody. I'm not into this anymore. I don't want to be into this any more. I hope you appreciate me doing this for you, because I'm never doing this again."

Mike came right over to pick up the coke and the Percocets. He brought a new girlfriend I'd never met before. I thought it was kind of strange that he brought a date to pick up drugs, but whatever. When I gave him the package, he wanted to give me an extra two or three hundred bucks for doing the favor for him. At that point, I went a little ballistic:

"This is what it cost me from these guys. I don't want a fucking quarter from you. I play poker for $10,000 a hand every single day. Do you really think I need your $200?"

"But I want you to have something for doing this."

"I want nothing but your friendship. I don't want your money. If you want to take me out to dinner tomorrow, you can take me out to dinner. Here's what he charged me for it. Don't ask me to take any money from you. And don't ever ask me to do this again, because I've never felt as scared as I did when I picked up this stuff. I'm done. Never again!"

That's the drug deal that I did for Mike Vento. For the next month, we were friends again and the drugs were never mentioned. We continued to work out and go out once in awhile. He told me that he was proud of me for getting off drugs, but in the back of my mind, I always remembered how hard he had pressed me to get that coke for him. I kept wondering if he'd ever ask me again, but that never happened and we were back to being buddies. I told Mike everything, so he always knew how I was doing in the cash games. We talked about the tournaments coming up. He always told me how impressed he was that I had turned my life around.

But Mike also kept pushing me to go out to clubs. Once I was off drugs, I didn't want to hit the party scene any more.

"C'mon, I'll take you out for drinks."

"Whenever I drink it makes me want to do drugs and I don't want to do drugs, so I don't want to drink."

"I promise, I won't let you do drugs. Just c'mon out for drinks with me and my friend. We'll grab a booth and have a good time."

Finally, one night we went to Light, the nightclub at the Bellagio. While we were there, my friend Bill showed up. When I introduced him to Mike, I said, "He's the guy I used to get my fucking coke from back in the day." I didn't even think about it; I was drinking. "But he's a good guy and he's a good person to know. He knows everybody in town."

Mike and Bill seemed to hit it off right away. I actually started to wonder if that's why Mike wanted me to go to clubs with him, to hook him up with drug connections. Mike and Bill yakked it up all night. Later Bill said, "Your friend is really cool."

"Yeah, he's a real good guy," I said. "He's really helped me out ever since I stopped partying and doing drugs.

It looked as though Bill and Mike had become buddies.

In late September, I headed to Atlantic City for the World Poker Tour event at the Borgata. It was the first time I had left Vegas since I had gotten clean. About an hour before the tournament was ready to start, I checked my cell phone messages. There was one waiting for me:

"Mike, this is Bill. You gotta call me right away, it's an emergency. It's important."

"What the fuck? What could possibly be wrong?" I thought. Bill sounded really upset so I called him back.

"What's the matter, man?"

"Dude," he said, "you totally fucked me. You fucked me."

"What the hell are you talking about?"

"That guy Mike you introduced me to, he's DEA."

"What are you, crazy? He's not DEA," I said.

"Trust me," he said. "One of my neighbors is DEA and last night he was on a stakeout—and they were fucking staking out my ass."

Bill told me that while he was hanging out with Mike Vento, his neighbor had called him and asked what the fuck he was into. He told Bill that he was on a stakeout that Vento had set up and the last person he had expected to see was Bill. The neighbor told Bill to get the fuck out of there. While Bill was waiting to hear back from me, he had probably called everybody else he knew to put out the word about Vento, which meant that Mike's cover was blown.

When I hung up with Bill, I immediately called Doc, who had introduced me to Mike. When I was sick or needed tests or a prescription, I went to him. Here's a guy that I trusted with my health and with my life—not to mention the $35,000 I had loaned him. How could I have possibly imagined that Doc, who brought this guy into my house on the Pimp & Ho night, who insisted this guy come over, and insisted that I hook this guy up with coke, could have done this to me? No way!

"Doc, what did you do to me?" I almost cried over the phone. "Mike is a fucking undercover cop? And you're pushing me every single day, calling me to go out and hook him up with people and get drugs for him? I didn't want to get him that coke, but you kept insisting that I do it as a favor. This guy's DEA! Why would you do something like this to me?"

"Mike, he's not an undercover cop. You're crazy. Where did you get your information?"

"Dude, I can't tell you, but I know that Mike is an undercover cop. My life is ruined," I moaned. "What did you do to me?"

Doc kept denying everything. I started to wonder if maybe he had gotten busted for something and had set me up as his "get out of jail free" card. Or maybe Doc was telling the truth. Maybe Bill didn't know what he was talking about.

This hell broke out just as I was getting ready to play the main event at the Borgata. I busted out that day and flew home to Las Vegas on Sunday. On the flight home, I kept thinking about Vento. Maybe all the DEA agents knew I had been in Atlantic City for the tournament. Were they waiting for me to come home?

Was he really an undercover cop? I still wasn't completely convinced, although on one level, I'd always had a funny feeling about Vento. I had even told some people that I thought he might be a cop. Of course, that was at a time when I was totally paranoid about everything. One question kept rattling around in my head: Why would a cop continue to hang out with me after I had left the party scene and stopped doing drugs?

Vento knew I was clean. He knew that he had set up the only drug buys I had ever done. Worst case, I figured the cops might try to force me to turn in people that dealt drugs. I was a little worried, but not that much. I mean, they weren't going to barge in and arrest me—hell, I'd never been arrested in my life. Sure, I might have to come clean about some stuff. But I was past all that, and Vento knew it.

When I arrived home Sunday night, I threw myself into bed. Between playing the tournament and working all this Vento stuff over in my mind, I was beat. I slept through the next day. I woke up Tuesday morning to ridiculously loud knocking on the door.

"Bang! Bang! Bang! Bang! Bang!"

What the fuck?

Chapter Eighteen

Judas Revealed

"Who in the fuck is waking me up at this time in the fucking morning?"

I'd just come out of a post-tournament 24-plus hour sleep, and I was in a complete stupor. I stumbled downstairs to the front door. It was Tuesday September 23rd, 2003.

"Hello. Who is it?" I asked through the door.

"Hi. We just got into a car accident," a woman said, "Can we use your phone?"

"Hold on." I got the phone and opened the door. "Yeah, here you go. What's going on?"

"This is Metro police. You know why we're here, Mike."

I wasn't awake enough to be thinking. I had only gotten up so I could kill the asshole banging on my door. Still confused, I stood there in a daze with about a half dozen cops standing on my doorstep.

"We really are Metro, I'm sure you know why we're here and we want to come in to talk to you. We have a warrant to come in or you can let us in."

"You guys can come in. I'm not hiding anything."

"That's good, it'll go a lot better for you if you cooperate."

Then things started clicking pretty fast: I'd been set up by Mike Vento, my good friend, my buddy, and the cop who had arranged for this drug bust. They started asking me questions but I was barely listening: All I had running through my mind was how my friend had betrayed me.

"Where the fuck is Mike?" I wondered. Where was this guy who had pretended to be my friend all this time? What a fucking coward he was to send other cops to do his dirty work. You'd think he'd have enough fucking guts to show his fucking face while they're asking me questions about his lies. He had more answers than I did, but he was nowhere to be found that morning. I was still in my boxers so they let me grab some clothes. I quickly threw on a t-shirt and sweat pants.

When I got back downstairs, the first thing I asked was, "Look, I have an appointment to see my psychiatrist in about an hour and a half. Am I going to be able to make it?'

"You'll have plenty of time to make the appointment. All you have to do is answer some questions," they assured me.

"I'm willing to tell you anything you want to know," I said, "but I definitely need to keep that appointment."

I know it seems crazy that, with a bunch cops in my living room with guns and badges and shit, I was more concerned about my appointment than what could happen to me. But I was at a critical point in my treatment and that seemed more important than anything else. I had been clean and under the care of a psychiatrist for exactly two months when Metro knocked on my front door. I also saw the psychologist every week. That's why I hadn't left town except for the tournament in Atlantic City. I needed to stay close to home, because the medications for bipolar disorder are tricky to get right. Every patient is different and it's a balancing act for the first few months to get the meds working together. Also, a lot of the meds are toxic, particularly to the liver, so I needed regular blood tests to watch for any sign of trouble.

Once my bipolar problems were stabilized with medication, the doctor started to treat me for my Attention Deficit Hyperactivity Disorder. The ADHD was what made it hard for me to focus at the poker table, where I did my job and lived my life. But controlling my ADHD meant taking additional medication and those drugs had to be balanced with my bipolar meds. We were at the point where we were trying different medications and we still had to be sure my original prescriptions weren't killing me.

Two things were front and center in my mind: I was worried that I was going to miss an appointment to get my blood tested and my meds adjusted and I didn't want anything screwing up my relatively new drug-free life. The last thing I needed was to fall off the wagon after everything I'd been through. And I was pissed that my "friend" Mike Vento—whose real name, I would soon find out, was Sergeant Mike Gennaro of the Las Vegas Metropolitan Police Department—was not sitting there asking me the questions that a bunch of strangers were grilling me with.

"You know everything about me," I told the cops. "I play poker. You know all I do is play poker. I don't deal drugs. So, whatever you guys want to know, I have no problems telling you. I'm not hiding anything."

"That's good. How do you know Bill?"

I thought about the call that Bill had made to me in Atlantic City. I guess he was right after all: My friend the doctor was a lying prick and Mike had set me up. I told them that Bill was a good friend and that I'd picked up an eight ball of coke from him maybe two or three times in the last few years. We went out to the clubs once in awhile. Other than that, I didn't know that much about Bill. But yes, I had bought coke from him.

"Whose phone number is this right here?" they asked, showing me the number on a piece of paper.

I didn't recognize the number. "I have no idea." Over the next hour, they asked me about that number about twenty times.

"You're lying to us, Mike."

"I'm not lying to you. I don't know who that number belongs to."

Then they started yelling at me. "You've called this number a hundred times! You called it this time and this time and this time."

They had copies of my phone bills and they showed me the number. If I'd been thinking more clearly, I should've said, "Let's call the number right now and see who it is."

But I don't think they cared about the number. Wouldn't they have already checked it out themselves? The question about the number was just to see if I was really going to cooperate. I couldn't, because I didn't know whose number it was. A few weeks later, it finally hit me. That phone number belonged to my roommate's boyfriend; she probably called him every single day. I didn't recognize it because I never called it. I'd had a roommate for a few years, but

I almost never saw her. She worked a day job like a normal person and our schedules didn't overlap much. I had friends who had been at my house dozens of times and never even knew I had a roommate. I'm not even sure if Mike knew I had one and he'd been at my house at least thirty times.

She had a phone extension in her room and I always used my cell phone. When the phone bill came, I paid it without looking at the numbers on it. I don't know what the cops thought, but they were completely focused on that damn phone number. It became pretty obvious they were after something totally unrelated to phone numbers or drugs or anything else I could imagine.

They started getting angry with me because they assumed I was lying to them. They explained that if I played ball with them and answered their questions, I'd make my appointment on time and they wouldn't have to arrest me.

Arrest?

As soon as I heard that word, I got totally nervous. If they had other questions, they didn't ask them. If I wasn't telling them who that number belonged to, then I must not be cooperating and I was going to jail.

They were also doing the good cop/bad cop routine. The lady cop was the good cop and a big, fat nasty asshole played the bad cop. In real life he might not have been all that bad a guy, but for the interrogation he had the bad cop act down. He did all the crap you see on television cop shows. He'd walk behind me, out of my view while the other cops questioned me. Then when I couldn't answer a question, he'd leap in and yell at me, telling me I was a lying bastard and that I was going to jail. I knew it was all some stupid cop game to try and trick criminals into telling them what they wanted to know. I really wanted to cooperate, but they just had that one question that I didn't have an answer for. They'd ask me some shit that I could tell them, but then they'd always come back to the phone number. Did they think I was going to suddenly regain my memory and tell them, "Oh yeah, that's Pablo Escobar, the Columbian drug lord. I forgot. We go way back."

Finally, the fat prick cop yelled in my face, "You know what? You don't want to play straight with us. You don't want to answer this. Book his ass and take him to jail."

I started crying. I was in total hysterics. I didn't expect to be going to jail. I didn't do anything. In my mind, I'd never done anything. Yeah, technically I picked up coke for this guy, but he begged me to help him and he was a cop. On top of that I was pressured into it by my doctor, who was probably in on it the whole time. So I was pretty fucking scared. I never thought in a million years that I'd be going to jail.

The cops pulled their car into my garage, so that none of my neighbors saw me being led out in handcuffs. I guess that was just more of the good cop/bad cop thing, but after an hour of getting yelled and screamed at in my own house, I was at least grateful for that.

Sitting in the back seat of the police cruiser, I assumed we were going to the Clark County jail. Wrong. We pulled up to a building underneath the freeway by the airport, they rolled up a warehouse-type gate, and in we went. Apparently this was where all of the undercover work was based. They took me into a small office. I was expecting Mike Vento/Gennaro to be there. I thought at least he would have the guts to show up here, right? I mean, why would all these other cops go through all this shit and ask me a ton of questions when he had seen everything? Why not just bring Mike in so that we could lay it all out and be done with it?

Apparently, that wasn't going to happen.

The same cop from my house started asking me a lot of the same questions. Then he said, "We have your co-conspirator in the next room."

I thought that he must mean Bill, the guy I had introduced Mike to, the same guy who called me in Atlantic City and told me I had set him up with a DEA agent. Even though he wasn't the guy I had made the big "set up" coke buy from, they had to know that he was a low-level dealer. Other than a few guys around the clubs that I bought X from, Bill was the only guy I knew that sold drugs. Who else could my "co-conspirator" be?

"Who is Jerry Wayne?" the cop asked me out of nowhere.

"Jerry Wayne?" I asked in amazement. "Don't worry about Jerry Wayne. Jerry's a family man. He sits at home and we bet sports together. He's not into anything. If that's who you have next door, just let him go. You've got it all wrong."

"We don't believe you."

So they had tagged Jerry as my co-conspirator, not Bill the coke dealer. They might as well have said my co-conspirator was Mother Teresa. Jerry could barely walk; he had to take pain pills just to survive. But when he had brought me 200 pain pills to give to Vento, they started to build a case against him. I felt really bad that Jerry was getting dragged into all of this.

Then I remembered that after he dropped off the Percocets at my house, Jerry had been pulled over by the cops. It seemed like a routine traffic stop and all they did was ask for his ID. Clearly they had been watching the house and setting up all of this. But Jerry and I didn't piece it together until later.

I wanted to know where Mike was, but they never mentioned him and I never asked. Was it some kind of secret that he had set me up? Did they think I hadn't figured out this great conspiracy they had cooked up? I couldn't figure out what they wanted from me. They never asked about any specifics of any drug deal. They never mentioned the coke or the Percocets. They only asked questions about people I didn't know and phone numbers I didn't recognize. I just figured it was all part of some game, but it made no sense to me. They wouldn't ask me about the stuff I could tell them about, just the shit I had no clue about. We spent about an hour or so with more questions, which involved a lot of yelling, fist banging, and their best impersonation of the cop intimidation act. They kept saying that if I didn't tell them what they wanted to know, I was going downtown.

Finally, I just said, "Look, just take me downtown because I don't have the answers to any of the questions you're asking."

Although I don't think they believed me, they finally figured out that I either wasn't going to talk or maybe they'd just gotten the wrong guy. Either way, they weren't getting what they wanted for their undercover operation. They loaded me back into the cruiser, and this time we headed for the Clark County jail.

On the ride there I became really hysterical. I was crying and the cop kept yelling at me saying things like, "You need to shut up. You have no idea what you're in for. This shit ain't gonna play where you're going."

I knew I had to man up and pull myself together. I didn't have any experience with this side of life, with jail and cops and criminals. But this is where I was and I had to find a way to deal with it.

As soon as they got me downtown to the Clark County Detention Center, they stuck me in a cell by myself. I should've dressed in warmer clothes. The temperature was around fifty degrees. I thought I was going to die, it was so fucking cold. I thought it was strange that they didn't just toss me into the holding tank with the general population, they put me in a segregated room instead. Then I realized why the cops had kept me in isolation and not in the holding tank with other detainees: They thought they still could use me undercover. They didn't want me with the general population, talking and running my mouth. In their minds they had somebody that was afraid of jail and might be willing to do anything to stay out.

I actually overheard one of them say, "We don't want him in population. We don't want anybody to know his story or that he was in jail or arrested or anything. We've got to keep this real quiet."

They had mentioned something earlier in the interrogation room about me wearing a wire on some guys. I had no idea what they were going to do with me.

Finally, in the early evening, I was allowed to make a call.

"Mom, I'm in jail," I told her. "I've been arrested for selling drugs, which I didn't do. Doc begged me to hook this guy up with something so I went out of my way to do it. I don't know what's going on. Mom, please get me a lawyer. I need to get the fuck out of here. I'm scared to death!"

She paid a lot of money for a lawyer to come down to the jail that night.

"This is what they've got you on, Mike, but everything is going to be all right," he said. "We're working on getting bail for you right now, but we probably won't be able to get you out until about five a.m. since you didn't enter the system till early afternoon."

It wasn't the best of news, spending the night in jail, but at least I'd be getting out the next morning. I spent the next ten or more hours alone. Apparently their plan was to use me to get other people by working undercover for them. The cops eventually came by and told me that I could save myself by wearing a wire for them. But when they told me the names of the guys they wanted me to set up, I told them I would never, ever do it. They didn't want me to set up people I knew or low-level drug dealers. They wanted me to get into some heavy shit, shit I knew nothing about—shit that had nothing to do with drugs.

When I told them I wouldn't do it, they moved me to the general holding cell. Maybe they were just trying to scare me, figuring I'd crack when I was surrounded by the finest criminals Clark County had to offer.

Finally, at about 5:30 in the morning, I got out of there. I had been in jail for about fourteen hours.

I went home and slept for another sixteen hours. When I got up, I went to see the lawyer my mom had hired and gave him $10,000 as a retainer to represent me. He said he couldn't believe all the things they claimed they had on me. They had me down for four different cases of drug trafficking. When I had the Pimp & Ho pre-party, they said I charged everybody $250 for drugs. Sure, everybody got pills, but the $250 each was to cover the $5,000 booth and limo driver.

According to the cops, that actually amounted to two cases of trafficking, one for buying the drugs and another for distributing them at the party. They also had me down for getting pills for Vento and for the two ounces of coke.

As I walked in my front door coming back from the lawyer's office, the phone was ringing.

"What's going on?" Jerry's wife asked. "The cops have arrested Jerry!"

"They arrested Jerry? For what?"

I knew he'd been taken in for questioning, but I figured it was just a ploy to get at me. Jerry was just a poor bastard selling a few of his meds at cost to make rent. Not only did they arrest him, but he was still in jail waiting to post bail. I felt worse about Jerry being behind bars than I did about myself. We figured the cops had seen him bring a bag to my house, and had identified him leaving my house, so they figured they had some shit on him. But for all they could prove, there was a six pack of diet Pepsi in that bag. Jerry and I were being made out to be big drug dealers, while neither one of us made a dime getting the drugs that Sergeant Gennaro had set me up to buy.

Jerry and his wife were pretty scared, especially when I told them that I had been arrested for drug trafficking.

The cops were nothing but legal criminals, in my opinion. They set up me up knowing that I didn't deal drugs and was completely drug free at the time. They even had one of their gang help me get through the ordeal of kicking drugs, only to turn around and try to put me back into the drug world.

They weren't just trying to ruin my life with a drug set up, there was more to their plan. At one point Vento had asked me to help him with all of the cash he had from his supposed strip clubs. He said he was loaded down with twenty dollar bills and wanted to change them for bigger bills. Since he thought I probably had a stack of hundreds for tournament buy-ins, he wanted me to help him out. Actually I hardly ever carried that kind of cash. In Vegas, Bellagio chips were pretty much the only form of currency poker players used. He was trying to set me up in a money laundering scheme, pretending to wash his illegal cash to hide it from the government. In hindsight, I don't really understand how his cop cash was ever going to actually be illegal. But the money laundering thing never went down. I think, in this case, being naïve actually helped me for once. It sounded strange to me that he couldn't just take his cash to the bank and change it himself, so I never changed any money for him.

Later I found out that the money laundering charge, even though it was entrapment, would have landed me in federal prison for ten years. It just pisses me off that these legal criminals set up people for no reason, getting them involved in something they would never do on their own.

I got a great education from the Metropolitan Police Department of Las Vegas. They set me up as a drug dealer, they tried to set me up as a money launderer, and then they tried to get me to wear a wire. The really sick thing is they never really wanted to bust me for drugs. When it all came down, they used the charges against me so that I'd wear a wire on a couple of other guys they wanted. They were willing to drop the charges against me if I'd set up a few guys, otherwise they were threatening me with ten years mandatory for drug trafficking. While ten years in prison scared the shit out of me, it was a walk in the park compared to what could have happened to me if I had agreed to wear a wire.

The club dealers and small-time guys I knew weren't the ones they wanted me to set up. They wanted hardcore Mafia shit—organized crime, weapons dealing, money laundering. I had heard of most of these guys they wanted, but it wasn't like I knew them. How they expected me to get them to even talk to me was beyond stupid.

When the police offered to drop my drug charges to set these guys up, I told them I'd never do it.

"You can send me to jail for as long as you want," I said when the police offered to drop the drug charges in exchange for wearing a wire. "Doing jail is a lot better than being dead."

Once I was released from jail, I actually tracked down some of the guys they wanted me to wear a wire on. I told them everything the cops had said. If they were willing to set me up, they were willing to set anybody up. I wanted them to know they were being watched. But mostly, I wanted them to know that I wasn't the one watching them.

My first court appearance, a preliminary hearing, was two months later on Tuesday November 25th at the Clark County Courthouse. The prelim is where the judge decides whether there is enough evidence to hold you over for trail. If I didn't show up, the judge would issue a bench warrant and throw my ass in jail for a long time. Missing the hearing would almost be like pleading guilty.

So what's the problem? Just be there, right?

It would have been a no-brainer, except that I was in Atlantic City for the Showdown at the Sands tournament the weekend before my hearing. The main event started on Saturday, Day Two was played on Sunday, and the final table was Monday September 24th. You just gotta know that I played well and made the final table on Monday. While I was pumped to make it that far, I was starting to sweat about the timing. The finals were starting late in the afternoon and the heads-up could easily go past midnight, which was long after the last scheduled flight to Las Vegas. If I won or played later than midnight, I figured that I could charter a private jet for $25,000 to take me home right after the tournament ended.

On top of my other time pressures, the tournament was being taped for television and the crew frequently took long breaks to re-set the lights and cameras. I was a basket case. Every break or delay made me antsy and I nervously watched the clock. The winner got $1 million and second place was around $400,000, so I could easily afford the private jet if I needed it, but still I was afraid to miss that flight. Unfortunately, or maybe fortunately, I busted in eighth place and had just enough time to make the last flight to Vegas for my court date the next morning.

My lawyer had told me that the preliminary hearing was our first chance to get the charges dropped or reduced—but he hadn't prepared me for all the other shit that went down that day. Before the hearing actually started, he talked with the judge, the district attorney and the undercover police to see what he could work out. The judge needed to decide whether I was a dangerous drug dealer. Knowing he was looking at those exaggerated charges, I started to get pretty upset. There I was, alone in the hallway, crying to myself and wondering if my life was about to be ruined forever. I started thinking about all the clues I had ignored. Why had Vento been so nice to me? Why did he ask all those questions that first night at the Pimp & Ho Party? I never did see him or Doc take any X that night; in fact, I never saw him ever take any drugs. How could I have been so stupid?

Just then someone sat down beside me and tapped me on the leg. It was the long lost Mike Vento AKA Sgt. Mike Gennaro.

"Mike, are you okay?" he asked. "How are you doing, buddy?"

"How am I doing? How the fuck can you ask me that? You know I don't deal drugs. You know I've been drug-free for months."

"I know, I know."

"You begged me to find someone to get you that coke. You begged me. I told you no over and over, I wasn't into that anymore. I did it as a favor, a favor for a friend, my only friend, and you had been there for me."

"I know, Mike, I know," he said, "but I had to do my job. Now I'm going to talk to the prosecutor to do what I can to get this dropped. I'm sorry."

He gave me a hug and said everything was going to be okay. He went inside to talk to the district attorney and my lawyer.

When my lawyer came out about fifteen minutes later, I was feeling a lot better because of Mike's visit. I really believed that I had been arrested because the cops wanted something else. I started to feel like it would all be over soon. Maybe they just wanted the names of a few people that sold drugs. Hell, I would have given them some names; I was out of the drug scene.

But in the end, they weren't interested in the truth about me. The cops and prosecutor had their own plans.

"Mike, it's going to be tougher than I thought. They want to prosecute you." I was caught completely off guard when my lawyer said those words to me. "Your friend, the undercover cop, insists that he's seen you selling drugs more than once, and he wants you prosecuted to the fullest extent the law allows."

"Are you fucking kidding me?" I asked, astonished. "The guy hugged me and told me he knew I wasn't into anything and that he was going to fix everything."

But he didn't. Instead he stood in front of the judge and the prosecutor and claimed that he'd seen me selling drugs, that I sold drugs for a living. The preliminary hearing was going to go on as planned, and the cop and the district attorney weren't going to settle anything. On one level I could understand why Sgt. Mike Gennaro would lie to get a conviction. But why take the time to stop by and lie to me first?

By the time the preliminary hearing started, I was shaking. The district attorney started it all off by saying that they believed I had financed my poker playing through drug deals. They had me selling drugs at places I've never heard of. I guess they never thought to check my wins in tournaments or my tax returns. They made me out to be some big criminal. I felt like I was stuck in the Twilight Zone.

I totally broke down in the courtroom. My attorney tried to calm me down, telling me that prelims were always part fiction and part posturing. But when Sergeant Mike Gennaro took the stand, the lies got wilder. He wasn't even a convincing liar. He couldn't remember any dates, probably because most of them never happened. At one point he had me playing the World Series of Poker in Los Angeles. I guess someone should tell Harrah's it's been moved. The cops didn't have the tapes, or even transcripts of the tapes, they claimed to have. Then it came out that my doctor was an FBI informant. There was a lot of discussion about whether everything that had happened to me started with a violation of doctor/client privilege. After all, I had confided everything about my battle with illegal drugs to my personal physician.

At some point, my lawyer got Gennaro to admit that I had told him before the drug buy that I had never done that kind of thing before. He sort of admitted that I said I didn't want any money for it, although he was going to have to review the tapes that Metro no longer had in their possession. But it didn't seem to matter how lame his testimony was—he was a cop and I was a drug dealer. The preliminary hearing finally ended and the bastards got their trial. Gennaro walked out of the courtroom behind us, and I totally lost it.

"You dirty lying cocksucker!" I yelled. "You evil prick. I'm gonna beat this!" I went absolutely berserk right there in the hallway outside the courtroom. And so did he.

"You're going to jail, you cocksucker!" he screamed back at me. "I'm gonna do everything I can to fuck you over."

My attorney had to hold me back. I've never been in a rage like that in my life, I wanted to kill him. It was an unbelievable scene. I'm not sure why they didn't arrest me, except that they might have had to arrest Gennaro too.

Of all the things that have happened to me, all the hurtful things people have said or done, this was the worst. Not just that he lied on the stand; I've come to realize that's what cops do. No, what I couldn't believe is how or why he came up to me in the hall before the hearing and told me that he was going to help me. I mean, if you are going to lie and fuck me, then that's what you do. But why tell me something completely different in the hall outside the courtroom? Apparently it wasn't enough to fuck me; he had to fuck with me. What kind of man does that?

Over the next month, I just couldn't get Mike Vento/Gennaro out of my mind. How could a guy pretend to be my best friend, even help me get clean, and then set me up?

"Stop calling this guy your friend. He was never your friend," my lawyer told me time and time again. "The guy was there to destroy you at all times. And he's still doing it today."

I paid the attorney about $15,000 for the work he did for me at the preliminary hearing. But he told me that, considering all the "evidence" and the prosecuting attorney's case, it was going to be a long, hard fight. I needed to find someone that could go the distance in a big case. It was then that Chip Reese stepped in and hooked me up with David Chesnoff. Poker players could always count on Chip when they needed a loan or a tournament buy-in to get by. But I don't think too many people know just how often and how far Chip reached out to help people in any way he could. He was an exceptional person and I still can't believe he's gone.

David Chesnoff was the best lawyer in town. I was now playing for high stakes and I wanted the best defense possible. Chesnoff couldn't believe what the cops said they had against me. I was surprised, too, when I finally read all the records after the whole thing was over. I heard them lie in front of the judge, but I just couldn't believe they had the balls to actually put it in writing.

I was broke and lawyers aren't cheap. I borrowed $50,000 from my parents for my legal fees and a couple of poker players stepped up and lent me another $50,000.

During the six months after my arrest on September, 2003, I went from being a stable guy who was off drugs and on good prescription meds to someone who could barely cope with waking up each morning. The case hung over my head every single day. Did I think I was ever going to jail for it? No. But they were after me and I saw that the truth didn't matter to them. If they lied at the preliminary hearing, they'd continue to lie.

With David representing me, they again made the offer to drop the charges if I would wear a wire and introduce them to the list of guys they wanted. I told David I wouldn't wear a wire for those people if they fucking put a gun to my head and pulled the trigger. Let them put me in jail. I was just some guy they thought they could scare into working for them. They were worse than the criminals they were after and I wasn't going to help them. To my surprise, David agreed with me completely. He said I shouldn't give them anything. He agreed that they had entrapped me, that they did this sort of crap all the time. He wanted to go after them and see how much he could get thrown out. They were narcs and didn't give a shit about me. They had thought that I would fold under pressure.

"These are serious, serious charges they have against you," David said. "These guys will do whatever it takes to get what they want. It's my job to convince them that they don't want to screw with you."

For the next six months, I played poker full time, traveled the world, and tried my hardest to win. I was scared and stressed out, but through it all I found a way to survive and break even at the tables. I had all of this hanging over my head but I didn't really tell anybody about it.

This was something I wanted to keep quiet, and believe me when I say it's really hard for me to keep anything quiet.

Chapter Nineteen

A Phone Call in the Alps

The day after my preliminary hearing I was back at the table, playing a tournament at the Bellagio, and I made the final table. It's not like the arrest and all the legal discussions weren't on my mind, they were, but poker was my job and I went to work when I was scheduled to work. Poker was also my safe haven, where I went to escape my problems. When I was younger, I used poker to escape my isolation and shyness. Later, I used it to fight through my depression. Poker was something I could wake up to rather than thoughts of the arrest, a trial and jail. I always balanced the negatives in my life with poker; it was always the plus. I could always escape from the bad things in my life by going to the poker table.

I was still seeing my psychiatrist. When you're on the kind of meds I was taking, you gotta have them monitored all the time. After my arrest, it was pretty embarrassing to have to walk into the shrink's office and say, "Sorry I missed my last appointment, I was in jail." I'd only been seeing him for a few months and he had to be thinking "What did I get myself into with this one?" However, with all of the crap—the entrapment, the arrest, and all the legal negotiations between the district attorneys office and my lawyer—I never considered heading to a club to pick up a little somethin' for the weekend. I was so happy to have found a balance, I never thought about using illegal drugs for one minute. Never.

In November the shrink started me on Ritalin, the ADHD medication they prescribe a lot for kids. There were some concerns about my taking Ritalin because it is a methamphetamine-based medication. Since I was just coming off a speed problem, maybe Ritalin wasn't the best medicine for me. But street meth had given me the focus to kill in the cash games, and Ritalin was able to do much of the same, but without the creepy "tweaked" high.

During the first months of taking Ritalin, I had only one serious side effect: depression. I was already taking an anti-depressant, so the Ritalin was actually counteracting it and bringing me down. My doctor increased my anti-depressant dosage to overcome the depression. I eventually suffered stronger and harsher side effects from Ritalin, but during that first year, I was able to control the depression side effect I had. In late 2003 and early 2004, I controlled my ADHD with Ritalin so that I could focus at the tables and play decent poker.

In March of 2004, a bunch of us decided to take a vacation. It was going to be a nice getaway before the high season in Vegas poker. The Bellagio Five Star tournament started in early April with the 2004 World Series kicking off immediately after Bellagio. After all the fun we'd had in Paris the year before, Italy seemed like the next great place to visit, so we rented a villa near the Italian Alps. Howard and Suzie Lederer, David Grey and his wife, John Juanda and a couple of other non-poker friends all went in on it. We spent about $24,000 to rent the Italian villa, but it was worth it; the place was spectacular.

We basically went there to relax. We saw some of the countryside, drank Italian wine, played Chinese poker and took it easy before the next couple of big months in poker. I just wanted a chance to put all my legal problems on the back burner for awhile.

Right before I left for Italy, I talked with David Chesnoff and he said that another negotiation had been set up with the district attorney's office. David was still hopeful he could get me out of this mess, but said it would take time. I really didn't want to think about the case. We'd been getting extension after extension for all kinds of procedural reasons, so I wasn't expecting anything to happen while I was in Italy. David told me that if we had to go to trial, we would, but if he could pull off a last minute deal, he'd rather do that. He really didn't want to rely on twelve random jurors to believe what I said over the testimony of the well-rehearsed police. Knowing he was taking care of things for me, I was able to kick back and relax for the first time in months.

Then one morning, I checked my phone for messages: "Mike, this is David Chesnoff. It's very important that you call me right away. I need to talk to you about the case."

"Mike, I want you to sit down and listen to me," were David's first words when I returned his call. "I had a long talk with your guy Gennaro and then with the district attorney's staff. There's no way to get around this, Mike. You're going to have to do six months in jail."

"I'm not doing six months in jail. I didn't do anything." I completely broke down.

"You did do something." David was calm and clear. "You bought this guy coke."

"But my doctor and Mike coerced me into doing it. They know I'm not into selling drugs. Why should I do six months in jail for doing a favor for a guy who begged me to do it?"

"Well, you didn't have to do it. If someone asked you to kill somebody, would you kill somebody?"

"Well, that's different."

"It's not different," David said. "You broke the law, Mike, and you're going to have to do six months in jail. There's no way around it."

Clearly, I was in no shape to hear the details of the negotiations or review my options. With all of the charges they had manufactured, I was looking at ten years in prison if I went to trial and lost. From what I could understand, the deal involved dropping all the charges except the one they were pretty sure they could make stick. But I could barely follow what Chesnoff was telling me.

By the time we hung up, I was crying. I told everyone that I just wouldn't go back to the States. Howard, Susie and David didn't know what to do with me. I was so hysterical I could barely breathe.

All I could do was gasp, "Six months in jail!"

Finally, I caught my breath and told Howard, "Look, you gotta call David. You gotta tell him that I can't go to jail. I won't survive in jail."

Howard called Chesnoff and they must have been on the phone for an hour. Howard, who is always logical and calm, was the perfect guy for the job. He was able to listen to all the details of the negotiations and ask David the right questions. Apparently, I had two options. I could take the deal and spend six months in jail and never worry about it for the rest of my life. Or I could go to trial—which involved taking the risk of getting a fucked up jury that would believe the cops over a guy who plays poker all day and has a history of drug use—get convicted, and spend ten years in prison.

Howard was clearly convinced that there was only one option. He laid it all out for me in terms that any poker player could understand.

"You can't take that kind of chance," he calmly explained. "Even if David is 75 percent sure that he can get you off, it's not worth a 25 percent risk of spending ten years in jail. In other words, you could fold and give up a small pot, or you could put all your chips and ten years of your life in the middle. If you go all in, the most you can win is six months. If you lose, you're out of the game."

I was gambling with ten years of my life. My opponent not only was drawing to a lot of outs, he was the dealer. Everybody was 100 percent convinced that I needed to fold and take the deal.

Thinking about doing jail time didn't make me any less nervous about the deal, but I finally began to understand the reality of my options. I can't say I was rational enough to understand everything my friends told me, but as the day wore on, it sank in. Sometimes, even when you think you're right or have the advantage early in a hand, the odds don't justify the risk. I knew I needed to fold. Actually I wasn't even laying down that strong a hand. And to make matters worse, the other side was free-rolling—they had nothing to lose. I was the only one at risk.

I was finally able to relax enough for us to go out to dinner and everyone did their best not to talk about the case. I'll never forget what Howard, David, and Suzie did for me that week. It really helped having people around me that supported me, understood me, and wanted me to have the best outcome.

"Mike, this is all going to be over before you know it," they assured me. "We're all going to visit you."

Still, I seriously considered staying in Italy and never returning to the United States. I had some money and there was online poker. But everyone else was convinced I shouldn't go that route. Chesnoff didn't need an immediate answer; the deal was on the table, but I had plenty of time to consider it. The legal system moves at a snail's pace.

Papers had to go back and forth and then the court calendar had to be considered. It was early April and with the World Series coming up, I wanted to either get it done before the tournament started or wait until it was over. But eventually the decision was clear enough. I told Chesnoff that I would take the six months and he assured me that was by far the only sane course of action. The paperwork could wait until after the Series, but the decision had been made.

I was going to jail.

Chapter Twenty

Playing on the Precipice

For the next couple of months, I focused on playing my best poker, knowing I was going to jail. I was going to be playing in the two most important tournaments of the year, Bellagio's Five Star Poker Classic, which ended with the World Poker Tour championship event, and the 2004 World Series of Poker.

At the time, the World Poker Tour championship was the world's most expensive event. It cost $25,000 to enter and in 2004 it drew 343 starting players. I played well and was either in the lead or second in chips with about eighteen players left. But I ran into three tough hands that ended my run in fifteenth place for an $83,000 payday. With only two tables left, I went all in with pocket jacks against pocket fives. A 5 fell on the flop, giving my opponent a set and a good chunk of my stack. One round later, the exact same thing happened. I got pocket jacks and my opponent with pocket fives hit a set again. Miraculously, I still had over a million and a half in chips when I got pocket jacks for the third time. This time all the money went in on the flop of 10-10-3. I was clearly ahead when the other player flipped over A-K. Of course an ace came on the turn, and to add insult to injury, a king fell on the river. I lost with pocket jacks three times in a row, and each time I had the advantage when all the chips went in.

I could have gotten really depressed about that, but when you get hit back-to-back-to-back, you have to look at it as just a huge run of bad luck. You can play really well and still run into a cooler or two or three. I wasn't depressed at all. For one thing, I realized that even with jail hanging over my head, I could still play my "A" game. Although I was stressed out about all my legal shit, I felt pretty confident going into the World Series, which would start at Binion's Horseshoe just two days later.

Playing the World Series, however, ended up being very tough for me. I was a basket case. It was a struggle just to drive to Binion's every day. I kept thinking about having to spend six months in jail. It had already been eight months since I'd been arrested. I was also worried that I could still get screwed. While we had the offer of six months in jail with all but one of the charges dropped, they hadn't sent the paperwork yet. What would prevent the same guys that had messed with me before from pulling the offer and trying to make me go undercover for them one more time? I was still haunted by their initial threats of spending ten years in prison. Chesnoff told me not to worry, a deal is a deal. Still I felt that I couldn't trust the bastards until it was signed, sealed and delivered.

Another thing that was driving me crazy was that I couldn't talk about what was going on. My attorney had warned me not to say anything to anyone about jail or the negotiated deal. "The Mouth" had to be quiet about the one thing that was on his mind every second of every day! Other than the gang from Italy, maybe only five other people knew, including my parents. The more I tried to keep everything bottled up, the more the pressure built up inside. I tried to channel my anger and frustration into motivation. I would tell myself the same thing over and over, with every hand and every card: "I'm going to win to fuck those cops who fucked me." I wanted to prove to them that I was the great poker player I knew I was, not the drug dealer they had made me out to be. Those bastards had lied about me and I was going to show them who the real Mike Matusow was. For five weeks, that's all I thought about.

For most of my life, everything revolved around poker. If I had to prove something, I tried to prove it at the poker table. My game defined me not just as a player, but as a person. So, with jail hanging over my head, poker was my only outlet.

A year later, Daniel Negreanu would tell me that he sensed that I wasn't focused solely on poker anymore, that there was something else going on. He couldn't have been more right.

During the first week of the Series, I made the final table of a $1,000 No-limit Hold'em event with rebuys. It was a pretty solid final table with Lee Markholt, Ram Vaswani, John Juanda and Daniel Negreanu. We were down to five players when I limped into a hand with K-10. No one had limped into a pot all day; it was all raising or folding. But I decided to change things up, so I limped and Paul Phillips, in the big blind, checked his option. The flop was K-7-7 and Paul led out. I was certain that he didn't have a 7, so I moved in on him and he called me with a flush draw. He hit his flush and knocked me out of the tournament. I played the hand poorly; it was just a brain freeze not putting him on the flush draw. I finished in fifth place for $75,000, but I had clearly played myself out of a higher finish.

In the second week of the Series, I just missed the final table, finishing eleventh in a $2,000 Limit Hold'em event. Daniel went on to win that tournament for his third bracelet. What I remember most about it was a hand that came up about eight hours into Day One. "Syracuse Chris" Tsiprailidis had pocket queens, Cecilia Reyes Mortensen was dealt pocket kings, and I looked down at two aces. Not surprisingly, the betting got capped preflop. I really didn't know what Chris had, but I figured Cecilia for kings.

When Q-4-4 flopped, Chris bet out with his full house, queens full of fours, and both Cecilia and I just called. I suspected Chris for the boat at this point, but the size of the pot was sitting on the borderline of being worth a call to try to spike an ace. When the turn came with a king, Chris bet out again and Cecilia flat-called. The pot was huge by then, but I was sure Cecilia had kings and was laying a trap for us both with her kings full. In a cash game, you still might make a call, but saving a bet in a limit tournament is a lot more important. Although I was almost sure I was beaten, I went in the tank for awhile with my aces, wondering if I could be wrong. If there were two boats against me, they would clearly pay me off if I hit an ace on the river. This one pot would ensure that the winner would go deep in the tournament. I eventually called, hoping for a miracle ace on the river.

Miracles do happen! When that big fat perfect ace hit on the river, Syracuse Chris led out again and Cecilia raised. I reraised. Chris immediately showed his pocket queens to the spectators sitting behind him and folded. Cecilia went into the tank for about three minutes.

"I can't believe I only called on the turn. I know you have aces. How could I play this so badly?" she moaned.

These were not deep stack tournaments in 2004; saving one bet at this point in a tournament could make a huge difference. I knew she was thinking about all that, but she finally made the call. I showed my aces full, Cecilia showed her kings full, and Chris flipped over his folded queens full. Everyone at the table went wild when they saw our cards, and tournament players from the other tables came over to ask about the hand.

That win kept me in great shape for a long time, but later that night I went totally card dead. With two tables left I was at the table with Daniel. He was on another of those big card rushes, just like the 2002 WSOP Omaha High-low event where he ended up playing his hands in the dark. Daniel was building a huge stack with monster hands and I couldn't even steal a blind to save my tournament life. When I busted out in eleventh place, I was disappointed. I had a lot of chips early, but couldn't maintain enough of a stack to stagger to the final table. Granted, I won a lot of those chips on that monster two-outer, but it's always a letdown to get so close and not make it.

Two weeks into the Series, I had two money finishes, one final table and one almost-final table.

The 2004 World Series was the first year after Chris Moneymaker's championship run. Everyone figured the championship tournament would be big, but nobody knew just how big. In '03, the main event had drawn a record 839 entrants, which was up from 631 players in '02. We were all making bets on how many people would play the event in '04. I figured there might be as many as 1,200 players. I lost all bets, of course, when 2,576 players put up the $10,000 entry fee. No one had predicted it would be that ridiculously high.

The day before the main event started, the staff at Binion's was just starting to whisper about "maybe 2,000 players," and even then no one believed them. I mean, nobody saw that monster field coming, nobody. A lot of the pros were wondering just how big a donkfest it was going to be with all those amateurs and Internet guys in it. But Allen Cunningham had the right attitude. With that much money just sitting there in the prize pool, he said that we should just get in there and take it. Sure seemed like a good plan to me.

On Day One of the main event I was just fighting to stay alive, but on Day Two I went on a monster rush to win more than 100,000 in chips. The rush didn't last and before too long, I was staring at a much smaller stack. Then I received one of the few gifts I've ever been given in a big event. A player raised preflop and I reraised him with pocket aces. The flop came 10-7-5 and he shipped it all in. I called. Overjoyed, I watched him turn over A-J. With his generous donation, my stack was back up to 100,000.

Another hand came up late on Day Two that I'll always remember. I started with pocket sixes, raised, and got reraised by another player. We both checked the K-K-4 flop. When a 6 hit the turn, giving me a full house, he bet and I called. When the river came with a blank, he checked to me again. I had a pretty strong read on him, so I checked my full house, sixes full of kings, because I was almost certain he had kings full. When I turned over my full house, he turned up quad kings! He couldn't believe that I hadn't bet on the river. If I'd done that, he would've check-raised me trying to get one more bet out of me. He was pissed.

"How can you check down a full house?" he said, going ballistic.

"The next time you flop quads, bet them yourself," I answered. "Don't try to trap me, buddy, 'cause that's not gonna happen!"

Everything about that main event in 2004 was a struggle. I had to mix it up and play a lot of hands, which is not really my game. Every chip had to be earned the hard way, so I got into fighting mode and slugged it out. Even though I was reading my opponents really well, I still got snapped off a few times. Luckily, I was able to avoid getting busted. Days Two and Three were roller coasters.

On Day Four, Greg Raymer and I ended up at the same table. If you watched the Series on ESPN, this is the table where several "incidents" took place. They didn't show everything that went down that day, and I want to explain three hands in particular from my point of view.

In the first hand, Raymer and I got into a big confrontation. It's what people remember as the "Cojones Hand." You can still find it on YouTube. But what ESPN didn't show was everything that led up to that moment.

I didn't know who Greg Raymer was. Of course, two days later, he would win the championship event, but the only thing I knew about Raymer on Day Four was that he and I had big stacks at an incredibly soft table. With about 200 players left from the starting field of over 2,500, we found ourselves at a table with seven conservative and tight, even bad, players. What two professional players will do at a point like this is carve up the table and stay the hell out of each other's way. It's not collusion; it's just the strategy with the lowest risk and the highest return.

But Raymer kept coming after me. Instead of picking up the chips when I folded and letting me pick up chips when he folded, he decided to take on the only guy at the table who could bust him. And on top of that, he knew I was a pro. You have to learn to take what the table gives you. Tournament poker is tough enough. When you're given an easy path, you gotta take it. Both of us could have easily fattened our stacks by dividing up that table. But no, he had to keep coming after me.

So, when the Cojones Hand happened, I wanted to send a message: "Stay the hell away from me! Play like a professional and quit putting your tournament life on the line against the only other good player at the table."

In the hand, I had something like 5-high. We both checked the 9-6-2 flop. Another 9 hit on the turn, I bet out with nothing, and Greg raised. I reraised him right back with no pair and no draw—I had nothing. He folded and I flipped my cards face up.

"Stop fucking with me," I said. "I've got big cojones. You've got little cojones. And I'll bust your ass."

I was trying to make a point. Raymer needed to stop fucking with me and start taking advantage of our amazingly soft table. The other players were the path of least resistance. With only about twenty tables left in the main event of the World Series, why continue to take on the only guy who could hurt you? That is what I was trying to get Greg to see.

I rarely play it up for the cameras; usually what you see on TV is just me being me. But I did play to the cameras on that hand. I wanted my message to be that obvious. Even though I didn't know much about Greg at the time, I knew he was a good player. But playing your cards and playing your opponents isn't enough. You've got to play the tournament. There was no reason why both of us shouldn't have come away from that table with much bigger stacks, without ever putting our tournament at risk. Strong players know how to work the table.

They'll only go after another strong player if they sense he is taking unfair advantage of the situation by not sharing the wealth.

Greg just didn't get it. Even after I tried to make my point—loud and clear—he didn't change gears. When I realized my message wasn't getting through, I tried to apologize. Greg refused to shake my hand. I'm not sure I would have accepted an apology at that point either if I'd been in his shoes.

Don't get me wrong, I think Greg is a great guy and a solid player. In the year that he was reigning champ, he was one of the better representatives poker has ever had, and he was very good about sticking up for players' rights. But I still think he's too aggressive at points in a tournament when he could go on cruise control and pick up chips in nearly risk-free situations. Those situations don't come up often enough, so when you see them, you have to use them to your advantage.

I regret that incident with Greg, I really do. I shouldn't have played to the cameras like I did. Maybe if I hadn't been so in-your-face about it, Greg might have gotten what I was trying to say. But you can't take an opponent aside on the break and tell him how to play; that would be collusion. You have to show them at the table, which is what I was trying to do by playing and saying what I did. But Greg wasn't buying it.

Six hours later, we played our second big hand together. With only 100 players left in the tournament, Greg and I had been moved to the feature table since we both had chip counts that put us in the top five of the leader board. At this point, we still had no reason to confront each other, unless it was a situation like pocket kings up against pocket aces.

I raised with the 9-7 of spades from late position and Greg reraised me from the small blind. He made his raise very fast, and he was looking directly at me. I knew what that look meant, and I immediately put him on either A-Q or A-J. I was certain he didn't have A-K or better. So I made the call for another 125,000. I figured if no ace, queen or jack hit the flop, the pot was mine to take.

The flop came 10-9-3. Raymer pushed all his chips to the middle.

"What the fuck?" I wondered. "Does he want me to fold?"

I was 100 percent sure that my two nines were good. And I wasn't going to make the mistake I had made in 2001 against Carlos when I laid down to his big bluff. If my read was right, I could win this hand

and take a 2 to 1 chip lead on the field in the main event. I was looking at an opportunity to get my chips in with a 4 to 1 advantage. I sat there for five minutes considering my read and weighing all the possibilities.

"I know I'm right, I know I have this read correct," I said to myself. "Don't let me be wrong!"

I called.

I'd been watching Greg for ten hours and I could tell by the way he reraised me and the way he moved his chips that he had a decent hand. I was sure it was an ace with a face kicker. When he turned over the A-J of diamonds, I was happy—right up to the second that I saw his flush draw.

It never even crossed my mind that there were two diamonds on the flop and that he might have the A-Q or A-J of diamonds. Even though he didn't have a pair, his flush draw and two overs made my middle pair an underdog with two more cards to come. Immediately, another diamond hit the board—Greg had made his flush on the turn.

I had worked my way up to third in chips before that hand, so I wasn't busted. But if I'd won that hand, I'd have made it to the final table at the very least, which is exactly what happened to Greg.

When the turn card was a diamond, I jumped up and shouted, "No! No! No!" But I didn't regret making that call. I would have regretted not making it, just like I'd done against Carlos three years earlier. I had a perfect read and I made one of the best calls of my life. Would he have shipped it with A-J offsuit? Maybe. Greg was after me and he wanted to take me down.

After that hand I kept repeating to myself, "I play to win. I play to win."

It was going to be a little harder now, but I was still focused and ready to play. I didn't tilt because I knew I had made the right play. I had the read and I followed through.

"I am the master of the short stack," I told the table. "I've probably got a better chance winning this tournament with a short stack than I do with a big stack. I ain't givin' up!"

And I didn't.

It was another two hours before Greg and I would be involved in our third, and final, memorable hand of the 2004 main event, the hand that set up the #1 rated Matusow Meltdown of all time. Before the flop,

Greg raised to 14,000 with pocket eights. Ed Foster looked at A-Q and raised it to 45,000. Everyone else folded around to me, and I pushed all-in for 110,000 with A-K. Greg looked as though he wanted to call, but instead folded his eights.

Ed asked for a chip count and went into the tank. He finally said, "Well, I think you have me beat. I hope I'm at least in a coin flip." He called the extra 65,000. When the hands were turned up, I was ecstatic. With an A-K against Ed's A-Q, I was a 75 percent favorite to win pre-flop. The flop came 8-7-5.

"Come on," I mentally begged. "One time. Let me get lucky. Let the best hand hold up!"

The turn was a 7 and all I had to do was dodge a queen on the river to double up and get back in the tournament. But no! A queen hit on the river and Ed raked all my chips into his stack. I was devastated. The ESPN camera followed me away from the table and caught me sitting in the corner with my head in my hands.

"I played the best damn poker of my life," I was sobbing. "I thought this was my year. Why do I deserve this?"

That's what I said, but I was really thinking, "I wanted this so bad for what those motherfuckers did to me!"

Later, I gave the interview to ESPN, the one that everyone talks about, where I was crying and apologizing for all the really bad decisions I'd made in my life. Did anyone really think I was apologizing for moving all in with A-K, or for making the big call against Raymer with middle pair?

I was crying and upset because I was going to jail. I had pissed away three years of my life and countless millions of dollars in a meth fog. I had made all kinds of bad decisions, including who to trust as my friends. Winning the Series wasn't going to change all that. But for everything I had lost, had given up, or was about to have taken from me, I wanted to prove I still had the most important thing in my life—I had my game.

I never knew that a display of honest emotion on television could be so misunderstood. It changed how some people looked at me or thought about me. I had been so focused on the main event, and then with one card it was over for me. That was what hit me so hard during the interview. I was emotionally distressed—but not about a hand or two of poker. I was upset because a half a year in jail was staring me in the face.

Chapter Twenty-One

Island Payday

The morning after I busted out of the World Series, I wasn't thinking about my crushing loss in the championship event. I was thinking about my legal battle, which was about to come to an end. My parents and I scheduled a final meeting with David Chesnoff to officially sign the deal he had made on my behalf with the district attorney for six months of jail time. I didn't really want to sign it, but I did. Until the day I die, I'll say I'm not guilty. I'll admit to being stupid. I know I picked up drugs for an undercover cop, which is technically a crime, and I know I shouldn't have done that. But there's no way I would have done any of it without being pressured by my doctor and entrapped by an undercover agent.

"You did it," David said, "so stop saying you're not guilty." David never minces words.

The lesson I learned the hard way is that even when you have the letter of the law on your side, it doesn't buy you much. Sure there are laws against entrapment, but who can go up against the testimony of a narc and risk ten years of his life on a coin flip with a jury? It's not like I'm the only one in the world who's had to face that decision. That shit plays out every day of the year for some poor bastard. I'm guessing that most of them get an even sharper end of the legal stick—after all, not everybody gets to have David Chesnoff on their side.

All I can say is that I made the correct laydown. I folded and signed the deal. Just like the hand when I held middle pair against Raymer, I thought I had a solid read. I'm accountable for my decisions.

The frenzy of the 2004 World Series had been a good distraction for me, although it wasn't much of a boost for my bankroll. The final table appearance in the $1,000 rebuy event was worth $75,000 and the other two cashes put me just over $100,000 in gross wins. After subtracting all my buy-ins and the cut for my backer, the Series was only a small plus in my bankroll column. And now that it was over, the reality of six months in jail started to sink in. I had a tough time keeping my mind on poker and my game really started to suffer.

I started playing most of my poker online, not doing well. I also got knocked around pretty good in the live cash games. Knowing it was just a matter of time before I had to go to jail, I wasn't able to focus. The actual date of my jail time was up in the air. I still had to appear before a judge to get the deal formally approved and the sentence confirmed. For a couple of months, I just waited; no one knew how long it would take. It was an unsettling time, with my poker game continuing to suffer right along with my bankroll.

While I was waiting for the final word, I flew to Paris for the big tournament at the Aviation Club, where Erick Lindgren and I had gone the year before. I played about even in the side games, but the big story out of Paris that year had nothing to do with the tournament or the cash games. That was the year the Aviation Club got robbed. Even before it happened, Jeff Lisandro told us that, with all the big money in town for the tournament, he was concerned about a robbery going down. Somebody had pulled a knife on him outside the club just a week earlier, and he warned all of us to be careful when we returned to our hotels. Jeff was sure the club was being watched, maybe by more than one group of robbers.

Sure enough, the day before the final table, two guys wearing ski masks and black helmets barged in with shotguns and robbed the cage. The club had publicized that the tournament would have the biggest prize pool in European poker history, over €2 million. Apparently, the robbers thought all that money would just be sitting in the cage waiting for them. Tournament poker pros knew that the money pictured on TV at a final table was just fake bundles of cash for show. Most of the prize pool actually gets paid out in casino chips or checks. Obviously, the robbers weren't poker players.

So there we were, hiding under a poker table: Phil Ivey, David Grey, Jeff and me. I remember looking up and seeing one of the robbers holding his gun, thinking how fucking crazy it was for all of us to be in Paris, huddled under a poker table for cover. The robbers got away with about €75,000 and were never caught, despite the fact that they lost the keys to their motorcycle and had to steal a truck to make their getaway.

That was the biggest tournament the Aviation Club would ever have. A year later in 2005, the World Series changed its schedule, ending only days before the start of the Paris WPT event. Fewer people felt like going to Paris after playing six weeks nonstop at the Series. And I'm sure the 2004 robbery made a few people think twice about going back the next year. Then the French government screwed around with gambling laws, making it almost impossible to have tournaments there. It's too bad because the Aviation Club treated us really well.

When I got back from Paris, I began to make financial plans for the six months I'd be away. My legal bills had risen to over $150,000 and I'd borrowed about $100,000 to cover them. Paying my bills month to month was one thing, but putting aside six months of my mortgage and other bills in advance was eye opening. That made me realize how much six months of my lifestyle really cost me. I could see that I was in for a very close call with my finances.

Finally, word came from the court that my official sentencing date would be sometime in late September or early October. I was able to choose from a few dates, so I figured I might as well have some fun and play one more tournament before my ass got locked up. I found the perfect event: the Ultimate Bet Aruba Poker Classic September 28th to October 1st. So we locked in on October 6th for my court date and I started planning for a trip to Aruba, a last chance to party in the Caribbean before I went to jail.

Once the court date was set and the warm tropical week was booked, I began to focus on the tournament. I didn't want to go to jail dead broke and this was going to be my last chance to win some money. For some reason, I always did better in a tournament when I had something to prove, so I started convincing myself that I needed to take down the Aruba Classic.

I didn't want to go into jail depressed and broke and come out six months later the same way. If I could go in with a win, it would change everything. Winning the tournament in Aruba wasn't just a financial mission, it was an emotional mission. I knew that walking into jail would be the lowest point in my life. Walking in broke would make it even worse; I would feel like the bastards had won.

If I could find a way to win this tournament, with its $1 million payday, it would prove that the bastards couldn't control everything. They could take six months of my life, but they couldn't take my game. After backing Scotty Nguyen in 1998, I needed to prove I was a world-class player, not just a guy who backed a champion. When I won my first bracelet the very next year. In 2002, I needed to prove that meth didn't own me, that I was stronger than the drug that was ruining my life. My second bracelet was proof that I could stand on my own and play my game.

My determination to win in Aruba was stronger than it had ever been going into a poker tournament. I wanted to prove that I had control, not those bastards back in Vegas who'd screwed me right into the Clark County Jail. If I did the full six months, I would be released right before the WPT championship at the Bellagio and I would need a bankroll for my inevitable comeback. There was no way Mike Matusow was getting out of jail and missing the very next big tournament.

I took my cousin Greg with me to Aruba. We planned to visit some friends of his in Miami after the tournament. I had only recently told Greg about me going to jail. The list of people who knew about my troubles was still pretty short: my lawyer, my parents, my good friend Michael Craig, Chip Reese, and a couple of people I played poker with, like Howard Lederer and David Grey. I explained to Greg that while we were definitely going to have some fun in Aruba, I had a lot of work to do there and that once the tournament started, I was going to be in the zone. Not much money was left in the bankroll, and my cash game losses over the past four months had made a bad situation worse. I probably shouldn't even have tried to play poker; I was way too emotionally fucked up. But everything would be cool once I won the tournament.

The Aruba Classic was huge that year, nearly 650 players made it to the island for the $6,000 buy-in tournament. In 2003 it had only attracted 436 players, and the year before that, only 100 players had made the trip. But after Chris Moneymaker's win at the 2003 World Series, more and more players were competing for tournament seats on the Internet. Online poker sites kept offering more and more qualifying tournaments into the big events. So, they were almost guaranteed that at least one player at the televised final table would be wearing their logo and would talk about how little they had invested to win a chance at a million bucks. You couldn't buy better advertising than that. The more players who won seats online, the bigger the prize pools got.

The field for the Aruba Classic in 2004 was pretty huge. Why wouldn't it be? You could play for $5, $10, or $50 online and if you got lucky, you not only won a seat in a World Poker Tour event, your plane ticket and hotel were also paid. It wasn't just recreational players coming in for the event. The pros loved this tournament too. It's hard to convince your girlfriend or family to travel with you to Tunica, Mississippi or Elizabeth, Indiana. But not too many people turned their noses up at a week in the Caribbean. It was one of the few places where the pros could kick back and relax with their families and still get in a little work.

The field for my Day One turned out to be a pretty tough crowd. I looked around the room expecting to see a lot of unknown Internet players and instead I saw Scotty Nguyen, Freddy Deeb, Josh Arieh, Carlos Mortensen, Barry Greenstein, David Benyamine, Allen Cunningham, Russ Hamilton, Marcel Luske, Blair Rodman, and my buddy Erick Lindgren, the defending Aruba Classic champion. Erick had won this event in 2003, just a few months after his final table in Paris and our Radiohead concert trip.

I was totally focused the minute I sat down and chipped up pretty steadily throughout the day. In the last half hour of the night, I got all my chips in against Debbie Burkhead. I remember that hand like it happened yesterday—strange how some hands just stick with you forever. I was holding the K-6 of hearts and two hearts hit the flop. I pushed all-in with the flush draw and Debbie made the call holding pocket queens. It was a good read by Debbie, who put me on nothing better than the draw, but my flush got there on the river. That pot was good enough to move me to the top 25 percent of the combined field going into Day Two.

Day Two was a perfect day for me. The combined field was much softer than my pro-heavy first day. I was on cruise control; my reads were incredible and the amateur players seemed reluctant to play against me. I began to dominate the tournament. Over half the field qualified online. A lot of the online players were new to the game and hadn't developed their chops yet. Since they were freerolling in an island paradise, with bikini-clad women, great bars, and beautiful beaches, they weren't completely focused on the tournament. One kid told me that his trip to Aruba was the first time he'd ever been on a plane and the first time he'd left his home state of New York. Half the field was playing like they were on vacation, which to some extent they were. It set up some pretty juicy situations for a determined pro. I had soft tables all day long and finished the day as the chip leader with thirty-three players left.

I wasn't the only pro left in the field. Chris Ferguson, Bill Gazes, John Juanda, Eric Brenes, Layne Flack, Chris Moneymaker, Johan Storakers, Mark Kroon, and Shawn Rice all made it through Day Two as well.

On Day Three, we had to play from thirty-three players down to the final table. The Aruba Classic was a World Poker Tour event, which meant the televised final table would start with six players, not nine as in other tournaments. With twenty players left, I narrowly escaped getting myself into some trouble. I had the A♦ K♦ on a flop of A♣ 7♦ 6♥. Tom Kopit checked the flop and I checked behind him with top pair and top kicker, a trap play. I wanted him to catch something on the turn so that I could get more chips out of the hand. When the 2♠ hit on the turn, Kopit pushed all in. I had him covered and I called.

Thankfully, he didn't have me beat, but he did have about fifteen outs with the 9-8 of spades. Writer John Vorhaus described the action that followed: "The river was a brick and Matusow's hand held up, giving 'The Mouth' a chance to thank—rather exuberantly—a God who would not, in Mike's confident estimation, allow him to lose the hand."

I wasn't so confident when I saw his fifteen outs, but you can bet your ass I was confident after the hand.

I pretty much went on a tear after that. I took out Johan Storakers in fifteenth place when my pocket aces held up against his K-9. Right after that, I flat-called with pocket kings, a short stack pushed all in, and a third player called as a bonus. I lost the third guy when I moved in over the top and faced off against the short-stack's A-J. He caught a jack on the flop, but that's all he got, and I took him out in fourteenth place.

I had a pretty outrageous chip lead at that point. Layne Flack was the only other player to have over 1 million chips and I had a sizeable lead on Layne. Then, with about ten players left, I ran into two monster bad beats. On the first hand, a medium stack went all in and was drawing to just two outs; he got there on the river. Five or six hands later, the same exact thing happened. I put another medium stack all in with only two outs that could save him, and again his miracle card hit on the river. If I hadn't had a monster stack before those two hands, my tournament would have been over.

I was down, but not quite out. I pulled a quick double up with a weak ace against John Juanda's K-9 and survived to make the final table. But I was going to have to start Day Four as the underdog. There were about 7.8 million chips in play and I only had 713,000 of them; everyone else had over 1 million.

Even though most of the starting players had qualified online, the final table was pro-heavy. Layne Flack, John Juanda and Eric Brenes joined me in the final six. Even with my short stack, I still believed I was going to win the tournament.

The two bad beats from the night before hadn't fazed me at all. The only other time I was so convinced I was going to win a tournament was when I won the 2002 WSOP Omaha high-low event against Daniel Negreanu. But this was like the next surest thing in my life, even stronger than my Scotty Nguyen dream. I don't know how to explain these feelings I get. It's more than just confidence or a game day psych-up. I just knew that if I played strong, the million dollars would be mine.

I wanted to keep the whole jail thing out of the media, so when I did the interview before the final table, I told the television crew I would talk about the tournament, but nothing else. They acted like they didn't know what I was talking about, so I figured they hadn't heard any of the rumors that had started to pop up in Aruba. My arrest never came up in the interview. Nothing was mentioned on the telecast either, even though I was already in jail when they edited it. By the time the show actually aired, I was already out of jail. Today, they would probably have sent a camera crew to the court to try and catch me being led away.

The Aruba final table is always filmed outside on a balcony of a nearby restaurant. Although the setting makes for a beautiful television shot, the weather can really mess with the television equipment and the players. Everyone was pretty loose during the TV set-up time and Layne Flack and I were joking around. But when we got ready to play, most of the players got pretty tight and quiet. One of the write-ups on the tournament described it this way: "Five of the six players barely spoke at all. They let their chips do the talking. But Mike Matusow on the other hand...."

Well, of course I was talking; I was going to use every tool I had to win this tournament.

Layne and I tangled a couple of times during the first hour. He won a decent pot from me with A-9 when I had A-8 and our kickers played. Then we got into it when I moved in with A-K. He called with A-Q and lost to my higher kicker. Finally, the two of us stopped clashing and we began to dominate the table. I really thought that Layne played great poker and I played second-best, and both of us completely outplayed the rest of the table. Layne had started the day as the chip leader with over 1.5 million and I brought up the rear with my short stack. But within the first couple of hours, we both had added chips while everyone else lost theirs. One way Layne added to his stack was by taking out Vic Fey in sixth place and John Juanda in fifth.

At one point, I made a huge mistake against Layne when he opened for 150,000 and I called with K-J. When the flop came K-3-2, Layne bet 300,000 and I moved all in with top pair. Layne snap-called with pocket aces. I was in deep trouble! But I rivered another king for a huge suck out and doubled up. On that hand, I finally got back the chip lead that I'd lost the night before.

That's when I went crazy with my famous "Vindication, baby!" rant. I let it all out. It probably wasn't the best idea to be jumping around like a madman. Outside on the deck it felt like 120 degrees and it was humid as hell. Everyone was so hot, we all had towels wrapped around our heads. The television crew was having problems getting the shots they wanted because all of us were hiding under towels and our clothes were soaked with sweat. I was taking Ritalin to help my focus, but one of its side effects is that it can mess with your body's ability to control temperature. So, I was dying from the heat, my emotions were over the top, and there I was jumping around.

I'd been losing a legal battle for a year and a half and I was about to pay for it with six months of my life. But against Layne, even going in with the worst of it, I got to win one. With only three players left between me and a million bucks, I took a monster chip lead. On a scale of one to ten, my emotions were easily an eleven. I had to slow down. I knew I could make a mistake if I continued to let my emotions rule my actions. Our next break when we could all duck inside to cool off wasn't anytime soon. I needed to try to calm down and keep playing till then.

I knocked out the guy who finished in fourth place when he pushed all in with a weak ace and I woke up with pocket jacks. That guy still owes me $24,000, by the way. Why does no one ever pay me back?

Anyway, we were down to a three-horse race between me, Layne and Eric Brenes. Layne and I were nearly even in chips with about 3 million in our stacks, and Eric was under 2 million. Brenes really seemed to be struggling most of the day, maybe it was the heat. He'd stayed alive the night before by getting it all in with A-J against two fours. The other guy flopped a 4, but a straight came on the board so Eric got his money back on a split pot. He survived that hand and stayed alive to make it to the final. Looking back on it, once we were three-handed, I should have moved in on the button more often. The blinds were so high and the steals were really worth a lot. I think that's a mistake that both Layne and I made: We let Eric see too many cheap flops. With a chip lead and ridiculously high blinds, I really shouldn't have been gambling on all those flops. I should have pressed every hand. Layne started to creep up on me, and after winning a couple of medium size pots, he regained the chip lead.

Suddenly, everything changed when Eric pulled off what I thought was a really bad play.

Layne raised before the flop, and I flat-called with K-J. Brenes pushed all-in. If Layne had folded, I definitely would have called. I knew that Eric's brother Alex had told him to come over the top a lot, and there was no way I would have let Eric steal that pot. But Layne didn't fold—he called. And once he had made the call, there was no way I could also call. I folded.

I really thought Eric picked the worst possible time to take his brother's advice. He moved in on both of us when we were both already in the pot with a raise and a call. There's no way that one of us wasn't going to play that hand against him. As it turned out, Eric moved in with pocket deuces. If you're going to put it all in with two deuces against two players and both of them play, you're about 20 percent to win the hand. If only one of them calls, the best you can hope for is about 50-50. Pushing with deuces can only succeed if you're sure that both players will fold. At that point of the tournament, and especially after Layne's raise and my flat call, there was zero chance that we would both fold, absolutely zero. Eric should have known that, but clearly he didn't. Or maybe he was willing to push, thinking his deuces would hold up.

Layne showed A-3. Eric's deuces held up against Layne's weak ace, but the flop delivered two kings. All I could think of is that if I had called, I would have busted Eric. Then I would be heads-up against Layne with close to a 2 to 1 chip lead. But instead, Eric had made an incredibly bad play and because Layne's table position was superior to mine, he had gotten to make the call instead of me. After that hand, our chip stacks were within three or four big bets of each other and the blinds were astronomical.

Then Eric and I played a big hand. Layne folded on the button, I limped in the small blind with Q-9 offsuit, and Eric just checked behind me. The flop came Q-8-5. I led right out with a pot-sized bet of 120,000. Eric shoved all his chips in, over 2 million. I called him with top pair, and he showed 8-6 offsuit for middle pair. He caught a 6 on the river to win the pot and double through me. I sent my last 100,000 to the middle on the very next hand with pocket sixes. Eric made the big-stack call with K-7, hit a 7 on the board, and sent me out the door.

That Q-9 cost me three quarters of a million dollars. If Eric hadn't hit that 6 on the river, I would have been up against Layne with a 2 to 1 chip lead and I would have liked my chances. Instead, I finished third. I don't know how I didn't win it. At one point when we were three-handed, I had better than a 4 to 1 lead. In any normal tournament structure, I would've won with that kind of lead. But back then, the WPT was using a totally bullshit television structure. With blinds going up like fucking rockets, the final table became a crap shoot. The only move you could make was all in. Eventually the WPT fixed their structure for the better, but in 2004 we had no room to play. A single suck-out could mean three-quarters of a million dollars, the difference between first place and third.

Not winning the tournament sucked. I felt pretty dejected and probably was suffering from a mild heat stoke. I also knew I was going to jail in four days. I kept thinking that if I had won it, it would have been God's way of saying, "They ain't gonna take you down, Mikey." But I got over the bust out pretty quickly—scoring a quarter of a million dollars really eased my pain. That was a lot of money in 2004. Hell, it's a lot of money today. Of course, now I play online where people play for those stakes all the time. I see guys tossing around six figures every week like it was nothing. Regardless, a quarter of a million dollars made a huge difference in my life.

Greg and I flew to Miami; he had some very cool friends there and we were going to party with them for a couple of days before I had to head home for my court appearance. We stayed at a great hotel in Miami; I mean, why not? I had just scored $250,000. I also have to confess that having sex was definitely on my agenda. After all, I was going to be doing without for a long time. So I wasn't disappointed when we headed out to one of Miami's classier strip clubs.

We were throwing a lot of cash around at the club. And this great, and I do mean great-looking, twenty-one-year-old stripper sat down on my lap and asked me what I did for a living. I told her I was a professional poker player.

"Do you win?" she asked.

"He just won a quarter of a million dollars yesterday!" my cousin answered, laughing his ass off.

"I'm gonna tell the boss I need tonight and tomorrow off. I'll be right back." She smiled this unbelievable smile, and hopped off my lap.

"So you must live in Las Vegas, right?" she asked when she came back.

"Yeah, I do, but the day after tomorrow I'm going to jail for six months. I got set up by a narc."

Her reaction was unbelievably perfect. She leaned in really close and whispered, "Well, it sounds to me like we need to get this celebration going. Where's your hotel?"

I guess the best thing I could have hoped for before going to jail was winning the Aruba tournament and taking a million dollars back to Las Vegas with me. But I gotta tell you that right there in second place was stopping over in Miami and finding that absolutely hot twenty-one year old. She knew exactly what I really needed before I went away for six months. It was only about twenty-four hours in a hotel room, but I remembered that day for way more than the six months.

When I got back home to Vegas, I had about two hours to make some money moves. I'd been thinking about what to do with the $250,000 I won in Aruba. I ended up making one good decision and one decision that I'll always regret. I put $50,000 into my bank account, so that all my living expenses would be totally covered for the next six months. My monthly nut then was right around $8,000, and I had already arranged for those bills to be paid on time. Before I went to Aruba, I didn't have enough money in my account to cover the whole six months. Now I did.

Howard Lederer had contacted me right after the Aruba win and insisted that I take the rest of my Aruba money and invest in Full Tilt Poker. The site was in the middle of fund raising and I would have become an owner, which would be worth untold millions today. What I did instead was place the rest of the Aruba money, almost $200,000, with a buddy of mine in Vegas so that he could place sports bets for me while I was in jail. I knew that Howard was offering me a great opportunity, but I just wasn't ready to commit all my money before I went to jail. I knew I was going to be craving some action in jail and, without poker, having money riding on football every Sunday was about as much as I could hope for. My six months would be over just before the 2005 World Series began, and I needed to know that I'd come out of jail with a bankroll.

Finally, it was time to do the time. My dad and lawyer took me to the court house; my mom was too upset that morning to come. Although I already knew what my sentence was going to be, this was actually the official sentencing hearing. Once you accept a plea bargain, you go before the judge and plead guilty. So that's what I did. Then the judge asked me if I had anything to say. Okay, so this was just one more time when being "The Mouth" wasn't a good idea.

"I don't believe I'm guilty," I answered. "I don't believe I intentionally did this on my own."

"Oh, don't tell me that. You're a druggie and you deserve this. Six months flat."

The judge banged his gavel and it was over.

Chesnoff had been hoping to get me just "six months," which meant I could get time off for good behavior. But no, I had to say something that pissed off the judge. He gave me "six months flat," meaning I had to serve the full six months with no time off. Later I heard that the judge was a real hard ass anyway, so maybe it wouldn't have mattered if I'd just kept quiet, or even lied and said I was sorry. But I said what I said. The judge said what he said. And it was done.

They handcuffed me and took me away.

Chapter Twenty-Two

Six Months Flat

I guess I thought jail worked something like a hotel—the court made your reservation and the jail prepared your room as soon as you were sentenced. But as it turns out, jail doesn't know you're coming until the side door of the courtroom swings open. Then you get dumped into booking. I wasn't too worried or scared as I walked down the long, dark hallway to the booking area in the basement of the courthouse and jail complex. I was still pretty happy from the Aruba score and the great stopover in Miami, and my psychiatrist had made sure that my meds were working well before I started my sentence.

After sitting in booking for two hours, they finally called my name. Why, I don't know, because I had another two-hour wait before getting booked. And then they didn't even have a bed for me. So, I got tossed into a holding cell with around thirty of "my closest friends." It was another one of those cold, fucking 50-degree rooms.

For the next thirty hours, no one told me anything. I'd been dropped off the face of the earth—no one knew where I was and no one really gave a shit. My thirty roommates were all like me, waiting for a bed, or waiting for the paperwork that would send them home, to court, or to jail. The only place to sleep was on the cold cement floor. I kept thinking that I might never do my six months; I might just freeze to death in the damned holding cell.

My memory of the next six months is a bit sketchy. Although it seemed like it would never end while I was in there, I tried to just forget everything when I got out. It seems like one isolated blur in my life. I don't remember all the details, but the parts I do remember, I'll probably never forget.

When I finally got assigned a bed, I remember thinking, "One down, another 179 days to go." The Clark County Detention Center had an overcrowding problem, so they set up a bunch of cots for the medium security inmates in what used to be the commons area of the North Tower. North Tower is the maximum-security section where hardened and violent criminals are housed. Let me tell you, it was full of mean, nasty assholes. The two populations weren't supposed to mix, but there just weren't enough beds, rooms or cells when I got there, so about forty of us were "temporarily housed" on cots in North Tower. The real inmates of North Tower were kept in their cells. We basically hung out and watched TV on the floor of the common areas. Even though it wasn't a regular cellblock, the guards made it clear that they weren't going to tolerate any bullshit as long as we stayed there. They didn't really need to tell us that; we could see how they kept the hardened criminals in line in the cells around us. We were all new prisoners, and a few words of encouragement or intimidation went a long way with us. During my first few days, a guard asked me what I was in for.

I had told him about a sentence and a half of my story when he said, "So, you were selling drugs to kids." Clearly, my tale of entrapment wasn't going to win me any points with the guards, so I tucked that story away for the rest of my stay.

After three days or so, I was transferred to South Tower, the medium security facility where less dangerous inmates were housed. I was put into "population," which meant I was living with forty other guys. One of the first things the other inmates asked me was, "Where do you want to work?" Apparently, where you worked and where you lived were related.

"Work? I don't wanna work," I told them.

I mean, I thought I would just sit there for six months, play some cards and a little basketball and do my time. I hadn't worked in fifteen years. I'm not sure I would have taken the plea deal if I'd known I had to work. But I found out that when you are in jail, you've gotta work.

However, just like getting into jail took some time and then getting a bed took more time, apparently it was going to take even more time to find me a job. Nothing happens fast in jail.

About two weeks after I was transferred to South Tower, I was assigned to the commissary work gang, one of the easiest jobs in jail. I bagged up candy, cookies or soup for the inmates to buy. Inmates bought a lot of commissary stuff because the regular meals they gave us were so fucking bad. Working actually didn't totally suck because you got so bored doing nothing all day, you actually looked forward to doing something with your time.

But I still had a few problems to sort out in my new prison life.

First, there were rules. When I got the commissary job assignment, I was moved into a module where all the commissary workers stayed. The first rule was that you had to make your bed each morning. Now I never, I mean, never, had made a bed in my entire life. And nobody told me I was supposed to do it, so the very first day in the module, I got written up for not making my bed. I also didn't know anything about what it meant to be "written up." I found out that if you got five write-ups, you went into a 24-hour lock down. If you got too many write-ups, you could lose privileges or even your job. If you lost your job, you could end up losing one of the better places to live.

I didn't understand any of this shit. I didn't realize how good it was living in the commissary module. I basically shared it with about eight other guys and we each had our own room. I just assumed that was how all of South Tower was set up: Once you had a job, you lived in a module with your own room.

I was wrong.

The other problem was that even though commissary was only a four-hour-a-day job, you had to stand up the entire time. I have severely flat feet and I can't stand for long periods. So within an hour of my first day on the job, it felt like someone was jabbing ice picks into my feet. As soon as I'd sit down, I'd get yelled at. The corrections officer (CO) knew that I was some guy from TV and that gave him a reason to dislike me right away. So, I got yelled at a lot. And I got written up a lot. I'm not sure exactly how many times I got written up for not making my bed, for sitting down on the job, or for talking too loud.

I figured that things weren't exactly working out between me and that CO. But what were they going to do, put me in jail?

I really had three problems. I didn't know the rules. I couldn't stand up to do the commissary work. And one of the COs didn't like me, which meant he was going to be on my ass all the time. He also was going to try to get rid of me by writing me up for anything and everything he could dream up.

The other CO on our module told me that I should just stay out of the way of the other guy. So, I started trying to be more careful. The other inmates clued me in that the commissary was the five-star job of the entire jail. They told me that the last thing I wanted was to get moved to one of the really hard jobs in the kitchen or laundry. So I tried to toe the line. I tried to be quiet and I definitely tried to stay out of the CO's way.

While I wasn't exactly a model inmate, I thought I was getting by. But what did I know? There was also a woman who ran the commissary work line who was getting really pissed that I sat down so often. She told my bad CO that I wasn't doing the work, which really wasn't true. Between the two of them I lost the job. I guess the CO thought that would mean I would get kicked off his module, but that didn't happen. I know he wanted me out, and I'm not really sure why he didn't get what he wanted. It was probably just screwed up paperwork. So while I did lose my job at the commissary, I didn't get booted out of my room in the module. I ended up with a new job at lawn service.

There just aren't a lot of jobs where you get to leave the jail. Lawn service inmates got to go outside to cut lawns on county property, like at the courthouse. The CO running the service was one of the good guys, not some prick who just had it in for the prisoners. He liked me and we didn't have any problems at all. It was a really sweet job; we were outside and there were no hassles. Since it was November by then, the grass wasn't really growing much, so we were only working a couple of days a week.

The downside was that I spent even more time on the module because I didn't have work detail every day. Naturally, that just got under the module CO's skin even more. One day, the sink in my room had a horrible odor coming out of it. I told the CO and he sent me to the closet where all the mops and brooms and cleaning stuff were kept. I got a bottle of drain cleaner and poured it down the drain. When he saw that I had used the whole bottle, he went totally off on me, and wrote me up for "wasting county property."

I'm not kidding.

This was a big infraction, so big that it cost me my job with lawn service. And worse, I got kicked out of the commissary module for having too many write-ups, which is really what the fuckhead CO had been after all along. I was off the module and out of his sight.

They moved me into a big dorm-style module with fifty other guys. I didn't have my own cell and I definitely didn't have any privacy. For the first time, I actually became pretty scared. Instead of having my own room in an eight-person module, I lived completely out in the open. I mean, this was the kind of place you imagined that bad jail shit happened, where bad prison movie scenes took place. The other inmates in the commissary module knew they had it good and they didn't want to end up here. But what the fuck did I know? I hadn't been to jail before. I didn't know that your sentence doesn't have anything to with where you end up or what job you get. Your job has everything to do with whether you do easy time or hard time.

I'd been warned about kitchen and laundry and how tough they were. They were right about kitchen. My new job assignment was a fucking nightmare. Kitchen duty was a real job, nothing like commissary or lawn service. I had to get up at six in the morning, and work until two in the afternoon—eight hours straight without being allowed to sit down. After a few days, I was in horrible shape. Tears were pouring from my eyes because the pain in my feet was so bad. The work itself was pretty nasty. I swear they must have searched high and low for the COs with the worst fucking attitudes to run kitchen duty. They basically got off busting your ass and treating you like a fucking slave. Kitchen was the bottom of the job pile and that's where I found myself.

Luckily for me, some of the inmates who worked the kitchen were cool. They saw that my feet really did hurt me a lot. One guy came up with the idea for me to wear really big boots, like size 13, over my shoes. That totally helped, and for the first time, I could actually get through a day of work on my feet. Unfortunately it wasn't long before some asshole CO noticed the boots.

"Them boots are only for washing dishes!" he yelled. "Take them off right now."

"I can't work without them!" I yelled back at him.

He didn't give a shit, of course. It's just amazing what incredible assholes some of those COs were. Or maybe it was more amazing that there were some smart, kind and compassionate COs that actually survived in that job. But the bottom line that day was that I lost the boots, and my foot pain got worse.

Then I got caught stealing food. Really. Part of your job in kitchen was getting the meals ready for the inmates and the employees. Needless to say the officers and other employees got much better food. I think you'd probably get arrested for animal cruelty if you actually fed your pet what the inmates ate. So inmates snatched food all the time from the employees' menu. Some guys stole it for themselves, but others had a little racket going by selling stolen food on the module. I had a buddy who was really good at stealing food, so he and I would steal stuff together just to share with our buddies.

Anyway, I got caught stealing chicken. I had been entrapped into buying drugs, but sure as shit, I was guilty of stealing chicken.

I spent the next two weeks in the hole.

The hole was supposed to be solitary confinement, but most of the time you had a roommate and there were other cells close by. You stayed locked up in your cell for twenty-three hours a day. One hour a day, you could clean your room, shower, make phone calls, read a newspaper, watch TV, or whatever. Otherwise you were locked down. I got an amazing education in the hole. I realized that with enough time on their hands, guys can create anything.

The inmates made these long strings out of unraveled blankets. Using a pen as a weight, they'd toss the string between cells, exchanging notes, magazines and even food. They could sail those things down stairs and around corners. Of course, if they got caught doing it, it was another week in the hole. But they were geniuses with a string. I think that with the right training, these guys could have gotten shit to the moon. It was amazing! I used to laugh so hard, I almost forgot where I was. I got to know my roommate and a couple of the guys close to our cell pretty well. I have to say that those guys really watched my back, and once we were out of the hole, they stayed on my side.

When you get out of the hole, you have to appear before the Classification Officer to find out where you're going next. Since you had been sent to the hole, they thought that maybe it wasn't the best idea to send you back to the same place where you had gotten your butt in trouble. I told the Classification Officer about my feet and how I wasn't able to do kitchen work because of the long hours standing up. I also explained how I had found a solution by wearing boots, but that they weren't allowed. I begged him for any job that I didn't have to do standing on my feet. He was another one of the good guys, and he sent me to the laundry.

Oh shit, I had been warned about laundry duty. But he explained that, on the day shift, I could sit down to do my work.

I'd been told that kitchen and laundry were the two worst jobs you could have. They were right about the kitchen, but I think they were lying about the laundry. Maybe they wanted to keep it a secret. For me, the laundry was the best job in the whole place. Why? Because all you did was fold clothes. The night shift guys had to wash them and dry them. But on the day shift, we had benches and we just sat there and folded and talked. You could talk all you wanted and as loud as you wanted. Of course, that was a big plus for me.

We also had the coolest COs. The main CO on laundry was a close friend of the CO I'd had on lawn service and they operated the same way. Their attitude was to "be fair, be firm and be consistent."

The laundry CO also spelled out the rules up front. Since I always seemed to be in the slow group about the whole rule thing, this really helped me out. He let you know that he operated on the three-step rule. First, he would ask you to do something. Then he would tell you to do it. On the third time, he would make you do it. It was real simple and unless you were just looking for trouble and willing to lose the easiest job in the jail, you just did what you were asked and everything worked out fine.

The module for the laundry crew was small and there were very few hassles of any kind. I was about halfway through serving my six months when I landed in laundry, and that move was going to make my last three months much easier.

That is, until some weird shit started happening to me. I'd been in laundry for about a month, when out of the blue they rousted me out of bed at five in the morning.

"Hey Matusow, get up. You're being transferred."

"What do you mean, I'm being transferred?"

"Get up! You're being transferred to the kitchen."

"The guys in the kitchen already know I've got flat feet and can't work there!"

"It don't say nothing about that here. You gotta go."

"You either stay in this cell, or go the hole," the guard said.

I chose the hole.

The first time I was sent to the hole, I deserved it. I got caught stealing food. The second time, I chose the hole over going back to the kitchen. This time I chose going to the hole in North Tower to avoid getting my ass kicked by a hardcore fucking lunatic. To this day, I have no idea how I ended up in North Tower, but at the time, I was convinced that Sergeant Mike Gennaro and his buddies had something to do with it.

I did over a week in the hole, but it wasn't too bad. My roommate was a pretty decent guy. His story wasn't too different from a lot of the guys I talked to in jail. They didn't have many chances or choices outside in the real world. After they got out of jail, they had even fewer choices. They weren't dumb guys and they wanted a better life. But once they were out, they couldn't find their way from the life they had known to something different.

It's not like there are a lot of people out there helping them find their way either. It's fucked up that we spend so much money to put guys in jail and keep them there, but we don't spend anything to help them from ending up back in jail. Sure, there are a few organizations that do help, like Chicago's Safer Foundation. Four out of five ex-inmates they find jobs for stay out of jail for at least three years. Illinois reduced its number of parolee arrests by more than 20 percent and saved over $60 million in prison costs with programs like that. But most states don't have much of anything to offer former inmates. Maybe the people that are trying to help aren't getting enough support from people like us. Inmates usually cycle back to jail, costing the state money, and living pretty shitty lives. I actually tried a couple of times to help my North Tower hole roommate when he was released from jail, but I'm not sure it really helped him in the end.

Someone finally figured out I was in the North Tower hole. I got called back in front of the same Classification Officer.

"What are you doing back here? Didn't I just get rid of you ten days ago?"

"Yes, sir, but I got another early morning transfer," and I told him the story of my time in a North Tower cell.

"This can't be right," he said. "There's no way someone like you would ever end up in North Tower."

He looked through all the paperwork. Then he got on the phone and started screaming at people. "What's this kid doing in North

Tower? No way this kid goes to North Tower. I want to know right now who's doing this!"

He was pissed. For one thing, he was the guy in charge of where we were all supposed to be. He wasn't just mad on my behalf; somebody was fucking with his turf. This CO one of the nicest, calmest guys I ran across in jail, but he'd gone totally ballistic—he was going to get somebody's head for this.

"He goes back to laundry and he goes nowhere else! Am I clear?" he shouted into the phone.

Whatever else was going on, this guy stuck up for me. I think he had figured out that someone out there was pulling some strings to fuck with me.

"Mike, I don't plan to ever see you again," he apologized one last time.

Ending up in North Tower was one of the scariest things that ever happened to me. Getting slammed up against the wall was the closest I had come to fighting in jail. If you get in a fight and neither one of you ends up dead, both inmates are sent to the hole. But you also wind up with a much bigger problem: A big bad hardened criminal is out to get you. That makes the hole look like a suite at the Wynn. Actually, the North Tower hole wasn't that bad. I think I read more books there than I had read in my entire life. I was pretty sure someone had sent me to North Tower to intimidate and fuck with me, but I couldn't figure out why. What would the cops gain by harassing me? They knew I wasn't going to change my mind and slap a wire on my chest for them just to get my sentence reduced by a couple of months. I guess some people don't need a reason to fuck with you, they just do it.

One of the more reasonable COs that I talked with told me that the growth in Vegas had caused the overcrowding and other poor conditions. The Department of Corrections had to hire a lot of guards that didn't have the proper background and training. Most of the older correctional officers were former military, so they had good, solid backgrounds with a lot of experience. But with so much demand for workers in Vegas, they weren't getting the same caliber of guys they needed in corrections. Some of the young COs would do shit to inmates out of spite, vengeance or just plain ignorance. The CO also said that the fact that I was a young professional poker player who had been on television might've been a source of jealousy for the younger COs. He knew a lot more about how the prison system worked than

I did, so maybe there hadn't been a big conspiracy to fuck with me. Maybe the system itself was just fucked.

After my third visit to the hole, I returned to laundry where I spent the next five very uneventful weeks folding laundry and playing casino.

Then it was over. I was out.

Jeff Shulman and his wife picked me up at the jail. I asked Jeff to pick me up because I felt safe with him. A lot of my party friends had blown me off when I gave up drugs. Then there were the people that blew me off after the bust. Of course, one of my "best friends" had been the bastard that set me up. I knew I could count on Jeff to keep my release low key. I didn't want an over-the-top celebration. I just wanted it to feel comfortable.

The other thing I wanted was food. I'd been eating crappy jail food for so long, I'd forgotten what real food tasted like. On the way home, we stopped for pizza and chicken wings—a total disaster. All that rich, spicy food felt great going down, but when it hit my stomach, which was used to bland, tasteless stuff, I got major-league sick. I don't know what's worse: the fact that they get away with feeding inmates such total crap, or the fact that your body actually gets used to it.

I was thankful for all the players that came to visit me while I was in jail. Well, actually they came to talk to me through a video monitor on a strict thirty-minute timer. I found out afterwards that it was a big hassle to get through the visitor screening process, but these guys had done it. John Juanda and Erik Seidel came by to see me a couple of times and so did Daniel Negreanu. Michael Craig visited me five or six times, whenever he was in Las Vegas. Ted Forrest came by once and he totally angled the system. Apparently, they only allowed two people in at a time, but Ted showed up with Michael Craig on a day when Erik Seidel had also come to see me. Plus Ted didn't have any ID, so they told him that only Michael and Erik could come back to see me. Then they opened the doors and Ted just walked in with everyone else and I got a three-visitor day. I didn't expect any of them and that gave me a big boost when I was having a really bad couple of weeks. My friend Matt came whenever he was in town; Howard and Suzie Lederer did too. David Grey was another visitor. My memory is not the best, but I also remember seeing David Williams and Antonio Esfandiari.

When people visited, it meant a lot to me but at the same time, it was almost the only time I thought about the outside world. When

I was inside, the outside didn't exist. As soon as I got out, it was as though the inside wasn't real anymore. I can remember getting back from the laundry and playing casino for hours and hours, and I always won. But for the life of me, I can't even remember how to play casino now. It's one of those odd things you can't explain.

It's a totally different world in jail. Everybody talked about getting high and getting out. Some of them found God inside and talked about how they were a changed person. But the second they got out of jail, God took a backseat to getting high and the life they had come from. "Why would you want to get high instead of getting your life together?" I asked them. But no one was listening, like they didn't know what I was talking about. Being a career criminal was just what they did. For some of them, stealing cars was a rush. They'd heist a Toyota, use the money for drugs, get high, and then keep repeating the process until they got caught. They knew they would get caught and end up back in jail, but that was their life.

I tried to help some of the guys who had been so good to me on the inside. When they got out, I gave them some money to help get something going. It's sad to say, but they all were back in jail in less than a year. Most of the guys inside were repeat offenders. Although everyone one of them would tell you, "I'm never coming back here," most of them did. A good lawyer could have gotten most of them off for the shit they were eventually busted for. But once you have a rap as a repeat offender, the cops just bust your ass for any old thing. Most of the guys who did time lived in an outside world that was way different from the one I knew. Seeing the outside world through the eyes of the guys I did time with was probably the biggest revelation I had in my six months of jail.

I can't say I'm completely sorry I got to see it up close because it really opened my eyes. But I'll never go near anything again that would remotely put me in jeopardy of going back to jail. When I said, "I'm never coming back here," I meant it.

I came across some corrections officers who were real assholes while I was in jail. The shit they pulled on me isn't half as bad as the crap they pulled on other inmates. But there were also a lot of really good COs. These guys had common sense and compassion. They treated inmates firmly, but they treated them like people, with respect. And they were the COs that had the least amount of discipline problems. They gave respect. They got respect. It all worked. Sometimes they'd even bend the rules. The sick thing is that they could probably lose the jobs for showing that kindness, while the pricks who fucked with you had job security. Human decency, if it meant bending the rules, wasn't just frowned on, it was a firing offense. So if any of those "good guys" read this book—thanks for sticking your neck out. You know who you are.

There are two more things that happened while I was in jail that I need to mention. First, I learned something about my medications. The nurse came around every day at 7:00 a.m. and 10:00 p.m. So, I took my meds at the same time every day. That along with "lights out" meant that I was on a regular schedule of medications and sleep for six months. While I was on that schedule, my meds worked much better. But poker players don't live that kind of life. In a poker tournament, working a 14-hour day isn't unusual. If you're playing a hot cash game, a 20-hour session isn't out of the question. My hours are strange and my sleep schedule is sometimes out of whack. I never really thought about how my crazy schedule affected my meds until I saw how much a normal schedule helped while I was in jail.

I also did something really stupid while I was in jail. Really, really stupid, because it screwed me up royally when I got out of jail. Remember that $200,000 I gave to my buddy to bet on sports for me? You know, the money I won in Aruba, the money I didn't invest in Full Tilt Poker? Well, I used my phone privileges in jail to bet on sports every week. By the time my jail time was only half gone, I'd blown my entire bankroll. I lost all of it betting on NFL football from fucking jail.

Yep, after all that talk about needing to win in Aruba so that I could have a bankroll for the 2005 World Series when I got out, I blew all of it betting from jail.

Every last dollar.

Chapter Twenty-Three

Last Dance at the Horseshoe

I got out of jail just ten days before the WPT Championship at the Bellagio. It was my coming out party, or maybe my coming back party. Everyone in the poker world knew that I'd been in jail, so my appearance at the Bellagio was going to mean a lot to me. I wanted to announce I was back and ready to play some poker. At the same time, I was nervous about playing the tournament. Some players had avoided me since the first rumors of my arrest came out in 2003, and I didn't know how they would react. When I walked into the Bellagio tournament area, at least a dozen players came over to shake my hand and welcome me back. After six months in Clark County jail, I couldn't wait to play.

But from the moment the cards were in the air, I was totally lost. It was like I'd forgotten no-limit hold'em completely. I was trying to outplay everybody on every hand, completely forgetting that poker is about patience. I never even considered folding a hand. Even with 50,000 starting chips and a great blind structure, I was out of the action in four or five hours. I can't remember ever playing worse. When I got knocked out, I didn't even care. I was smiling, just so happy to be out in the world again playing poker at the Bellagio.

The 2005 World Series started in early June, the latest it had ever begun. But the late start was good for me, because it gave me about six weeks to raise a bankroll. I was pretty much broke after blowing almost two hundred grand gambling on sports while I was in jail. John Juanda and Erik Seidel agreed to back me in some of the events, but I needed some cash. After tapping some other sources, all of which turned me down, I went to Phil Hellmuth and borrowed a $5,000 stake on Ultimate Bet.

I was a Team Full Tilt member and spent a lot of my time playing on that site, but in 2005 Full Tilt wasn't running the great high-stakes games they do today. So Full Tilt understood that a lot of their pros spent some of their time playing the big games on other sites. In fact, just at the time I was getting my stake from Phil, Ultimate Bet opened its first $50/$100 no-limit hold'em tables. Until then, $25/$50 no-limit was the biggest game online.

With the $5,000 stake from Phil, I turned on my computer and brought up a no-limit hold'em cash table. Over the next two weeks I went on a monster rush. I needed a bankroll and I was determined to prove I could still play poker at an extremely high level. Everything seemed to come together and I crushed the online cash games for over $700,000 in about two weeks. It was a fucking amazing run. Sometime during the second week, I took a couple of hours off and bought myself a brand new BMW convertible. I paid cash.

My UB bankroll hit its peak in early May of 2005. Unfortunately for me, that was about the time that the player accounts involved in the Ultimate Bet cheating scandal started showing up in the high-stakes games. It would be years before anyone figured out what was going on. But it was hardly a coincidence that my bankroll started to drop just when those crooks started stealing ridiculous amounts of money in the Ultimate Bet high-limit games. By the time the World Series of Poker rolled around, my bankroll had backed off from its high point. But I was still going into the Series with a good cushion.

I was on a mission and I was really pumped for the '05 WSOP. But I made one huge error that nearly ruined it all for me. When I was in jail, the jail's medical staff controlled my medications. I took the minimum dosages and didn't take any Ritalin. The nightly casino game for high-stakes soup vouchers wasn't exactly that tough to beat.

Once I was out of jail, I felt good and happy, and began to think that maybe I didn't need all that medication. It had been over a year since I had started on prescription drugs and I resented having to constantly live my life on meds. Sometime around the middle of May, about two weeks before the World Series started, I took myself off all my prescription medication. I used to be a person that never wanted to do any kind of drugs and I guess I thought that I could go back to being that kind of person. It wasn't that I didn't like the way the drugs made me feel, although I know that's why some people go off them. That really wasn't my issue. I just thought that it would be good for me in the long run if I could get off prescription drugs. My psychiatrist was totally against it and warned me that after a couple of weeks the stabilizing effects of my various meds would wear off. He told me that I could be headed for a major depression. Still, I thought that I needed to give it a try.

About two weeks after I stopped my meds, the Series began at the Rio Hotel and Casino. Harrah's had bought the WSOP brand after the 2004 Series and moved it to the Rio in 2005. The first event was a $1,500 No-limit Hold'em tournament. On the first day, I played as well as I could possibly play. I was second in chips starting Day Two with about 50 players left in the tournament. That morning I was feeling great. Then in the middle of the day, I suffered a breakdown. I flat out lost it. Right in the middle of the tournament sitting at a poker table at the Rio, I just broke down. I started shaking and crying. I lost a pot and left the table to go hide in the back room. John Juanda found me.

"What's wrong, man?" he asked.

"I can't do this. I feel like I'm dying."

I knew that John and the players at my table were thinking it was just another Matusow Meltdown, but I had no control over what I was feeling. My psychiatrist had told me what was going to happen, but I had no idea it would come on so fast or that it would so completely overwhelm me. I realized I had to get back on my meds as soon as possible. But I still had a tournament to finish and I had tons of chips. I returned to the table and gave them all away over the next two or three hours, busting out without winning another hand. I barely knew what I was doing. I just sat there going through the motions of playing poker, wanting to kill myself.

"I told you that you couldn't go off the Depakote," my doctor said the next day when I saw him. "I told you what would happen."

The good news is that I started taking my prescriptions again. The bad news is that it would take at least three weeks before my meds built up in my system enough to stabilize me again. Over the next few weeks of the World Series, I was completely depressed and played horrible poker. On top of that, I continued to lose all kinds of money at home playing online at Ultimate Bet. Even in my condition, I just couldn't believe how bad I was running.

Coming into the championship tournament, my forty-fourth place finish in the first event was my only cash in the '05 Series. I'd made a final table at the Series every year since 1999, but it looked as though my streak was coming to an end. On the morning of the main event, I was still pretty depressed. The last thing I felt like doing was driving to the Rio to play poker. A couple of friends came over and literally pulled my ass out of bed, threw me in the shower, and drove me to the tournament.

"You're gonna win it!" they kept telling me.

They had no clue how hard it is to win the Series, even when a player is on top of his game. In the shape I was in, I had no chance.

I can't say that I started out on the right foot. I got back-to-back-to-back-to-back penalties for using the "F-bomb" during the first level of play. The "F-bomb" rule was totally ridiculous; you had to spend ten minutes away from the table for just saying the word "fuck." I swear, there were guys from New Jersey who were afraid to open their mouths during a tournament. You could say any other piece of filth under the sun, just not fuck. They've changed the rule since then so that you only get a penalty if you direct it at a player or dealer.

Today, "You're a fucking idiot!" would get a penalty, but just a random, "Oh, fuck!" wouldn't—which makes a lot more fucking sense.

In my case, I was talking to the guy sitting next to me and used the word in the conversation. I don't blame the dealer for calling the floor person: The WSOP rule had turned them all into language cops that year. But I did go kinda nuts and threw out a few more F-bombs at the floor person until I had racked up forty minutes in penalties. Looking back, it was probably the best thing that could have happened to me. I felt a lot better when I got back to the table. For the first time in weeks, I had my balance back. Maybe I needed the jolt of adrenaline from the F-bomb blowup, or maybe the meds were finally working, I'm not sure, but I immediately started playing better poker.

By the dinner break, I was playing the kind of poker it takes to win. My reads were good and I was able to make moves I hadn't even thought about for the last three weeks. It was the first time since my breakdown at the beginning of the Series that I didn't feel depressed. I even started talking at the table. More importantly, I actually started letting myself think about making a deep run in the biggest poker tournament in the world. During the late afternoon, they announced that the WSOP had a record starting field of 5,619 players. The total prize pool of over $52 million would go to the top 560 finishers. The winner would be taking home $7.5 million of it, the biggest single prize in the history of poker.

I not only survived Day One, I thought I played really well. I was still feeling good when I got home that night and I felt even better the next morning. I was convinced the meds were finally firing on all cylinders and that gave me even more confidence. I figured that if I could play as well as I did on Day One when my meds were just starting to work, I could probably kick some ass on Day Two. I would start the second day with about 26,000 in chips and the blinds were going to pick up at 300/600. We had started the main event with 10,000 chips each, so I was sitting in good position with an average stack.

I'd been taking all my meds except Ritalin. Until I had enough Depakote in my system, Ritalin acted as a monster depressant, and I had learned that taking Ritalin for more than a few days in a row was a problem for me. I would gain focus, but sometimes the side effects really whacked me out. I figured that if I made it through the first two days of the main event, I'd start taking it on Day Three and see how it worked out from there.

Making it past Day Two was harder than I had expected. About halfway through the day I raised with A-J. The guy next to me pushed all in, but I had a feeling he was coming over the top with air, raising me with nothing. I put him on maybe an ace-rag, so I called 13,000 more. I was pretty happy when he turned over the 8-7 offsuit. I wasn't so happy when he had made a 10-high straight on the turn. That hand knocked me down to 8,000 in chips, and within an hour my stack sank to 3,000.

That totally sucked. I'd spent six months in jail thinking about this World Series. My friends had me halfway believing I could make a run. Instead, I was short-stacked and nearly out of the tournament.

But I didn't give up. Barely looking at my cards, I moved all in on three or four hands in a row, picking up 1,500 in blinds and antes each time. I had built my stack up to 9,200 when I limped into a pot with pocket threes. A guy over-raised the pot, making it 2,100 to go, but I didn't think his cards were that strong. I was pretty sure I could bet him off the pot, so I moved all in. I was wrong on both counts. He insta-called me with pocket queens. Luckily, I hit a 3 for the set and doubled up to about 19,000.

With that hand, the yellow light turned green and I hit the gas. From then on, I shredded the table. I attacked every weak spot and no one saw a flop without a raise. I didn't let anybody breathe. At the end of Day Two, I had 120,000 in chips, which put me in the top 20 percent of the field.

Some people call Day Three at the World Series "money day" because that's the day the field gets reduced enough so that every-one left standing is in the money. In 2005, 569 players remained in the field for the start of Day Three, and only nine more players had to bust out before we cashed. But I call the third day "moving day," because that's when you really have to build your stack if you want to advance deep into the tournament.

I was a little worried about taking my Ritalin because I hadn't taken it for a while. Even when I had taken it, it had screwed with me about 30 percent of the time. But when I felt it hit on Day Three, I knew I was in for a good Ritalin day.

I was right: I moved up from 120,000 to 454,000 chips. As good as that sounds, it actually meant that I slipped a little further down the leader board. I remember one guy at my table who was really out to fuck with me that day. He actually started in on me while we were unbagging our chips before play even began. He came right out with a lot of nasty shit and was being a real dick. Some of the other play-ers actually told him to get off my back. Maybe he was one of those guys who hated me because of the drug charges or maybe he was just playing a poker mind game. But he was an amateur compared to me, particularly in the "mouth" category.

I decided to ride him back a little bit. I told him that if he kept talking shit to me, I was going to win all his chips. I predicted he'd come after me with a crap hand and I'd take him down, that he wouldn't even last an hour playing against me. The ESPN crew filmed his bust-out hand. I raised big with A-K suited and he called with J-7. He got all his chips in on a flush draw on the flop and lost. We'd been playing for about thirty minutes and he'd already given me all his chips, just like I told him he would. On TV, you can see me needling him and calling him an idiot. What you don't get to see is all his trash talking that led up to his bustout.

I think my final line was, "I told you what you were going to do; come after me with nothing and give me all your chips, you fool."

On Days Four and Five, I played a lot with Joe Hachem, the Australian who would go on to win the event and the $7,500,000. On Day Four, we got a really soft table. Unlike the year before with Greg Raymer, Joe knew that we were going to divide up the chips. We were playing the same game. Joe started the day with just over 200,000 and finished with more than 800,000; I started with 450,000 and had a huge day to finish with 2.5 million.

Joe and I spent Day Four chopping away. We didn't have to risk our chips on coin flips or play very many hands to the river. We were taking all the weak chips and staying away from big confrontations with anyone who could hurt us. A lot of people don't understand that when you play no-limit hold'em, especially in the World Series of Poker, you don't ever want to play a race. You don't want to get in a situation where you essentially have a 50-50 bet—what we call a coin flip—for all your chips.

Of course, once I got close to 2 million, no one wanted to risk their tournament life against me, which meant I could pick up even more chips.

The field had made it into the money the day before, so players who busted early on Day Four won about $40,000. But if you made it to the end of this day, you were guaranteed over $145,000. Those sorts of numbers tighten up a lot of players and create even more weak spots to attack. Day Four was probably the best I'd ever played the "chop strategy." I had control of the table and avoided Joe, the one strong player at the table.

However, I did play my first coin flip of the tournament, although I did it on what I thought was a perfect read. I raised under the gun with two jacks and a player sitting behind me flat-called. The small blind thought about it, and moved all in; I put him on a big ace, probably an A-K. The real question was: Did the guy who had flat-called my raise also have a big ace? I looked at him and decided he also had to have an ace.

With that extra ace accounted for, I was a 60-40 favorite. It was a big pot of over a million chips, so I made the call after the small blind went all in.

When the other guy folded, I asked him, "Did you have an ace?"

"Yeah. I threw away A-Q," he answered.

The small blind had A-K, just like I thought. He didn't catch an ace or a king and I won the race. That hand pushed me near the top of the leader board and I really started believing everything my friends had told me. Maybe I really was going to win this tournament.

Day Five was the final day of play in the Amazon Room at the Rio. Part of the deal when Harrah's bought the World Series of Poker the previous year was that the final two days of the main event would be played at Binion's Horseshoe one last time. On Day Five we started at the Rio with fifty-eight players and would play down to twenty-seven. The next day we would move downtown to Binion's. There were a lot of big stacks in that room and it was going to take a long time to lose more than half of the remaining players.

I went into our final day at the Rio in second place with 2,561,000 in front of me. I had another great day and doubled my stack to over 5 million. A big chunk of that came on one pivotal hand. Freddy Bonyadi started the day third in chips with over 2.4 million and he sat at my table. As the day played on, I was up around 200,000 more than my starting stack while Freddy had taken a couple of small hits. But we were both still sitting on big, big stacks compared to the rest of the field.

Freddy raised on the button, I came over the top of him with a 6-2 offsuit, and he called. The flop was came 5-5-J with two spades. I made a big bet and he called. The turn card was a deuce and I made another huge bet. Again he called.

The river card was the 10♠, putting three spades on the board. I moved all in with my pair of deuces. Obviously, I wasn't betting my cards, I was betting the situation. I would have less than a million in chips left after the hand if he called. Freddy stood up, as I was sweating my fucking balls off. I really had no idea what he had.

"I guess this is the tournament if I call," he said.

I played this hand because I was sure he wouldn't play a big pot with me, not with his big chip position. He knew that I wasn't coming after a guy who could hurt me unless I had a big hand. At least that's how it played out in my mind. The only time I go after a big chip stack is when I know it's somebody who thinks exactly like that.

Freddy went into the tank for nearly five minutes. He stood there playing with his chips. Finally, he mucked his cards.

"Just show one time," he said as he folded.

"I don't really want to," I answered honestly.

"Just show me," he insisted. "I know you have it."

So I flipped up the 6-2.

Everybody went nuts. Freddy left the table. I later heard that he was in the bathroom puking, at least that was the rumor. He said I had him beat, but I think he might have made a small flush on the end. That hand was big for me. It not only built my stack, but it got Freddy off the table for a while. When he returned, Freddy was still on tilt and gave up all his chips to Tex Barch in a horribly misplayed hand. Then I was moved to the TV table where I played extremely controlled poker.

I played small ball for the rest of the day, never having more than 10 percent of my stack at risk in a hand. I never played a coin flip and never called down a losing hand on the river. I seemed to know where I was at all times.

I ended Day Five as chip leader of the main event with 5,140,000.

Driving downtown on Day Six, I was thinking "Wow, we're going into Binion's Horseshoe for the last time?" I knew the World Series had to move because it had outgrown the Horseshoe, but it was still sad. I wish they could bring back the Hall of Fame tournament or hold the Tournament of Champions there. Before the poker boom, playing at Binion's was like a family getting together. You bumped into every player you knew and you could just feel the World Series in the air.

With twenty-seven players left in the main event, I was the chip leader. Phil Ivey was second with 4,635,000. Steve Dannenmann was in third place with just over 4 million in chips. Tex Barch was in fourth with 3.9 million. Amazingly, Greg Raymer, the 2004 WSOP champion, was in fifth place with 3.8 million. With such gigantic starting fields, making back-to-back runs like that in the main event was simply incredible. I kept thinking that if Greg and I went to the final table together, ESPN would cream in its pants. Their execs were still focused on the blowups Greg and I had had the year before. They thought it was good TV drama. They couldn't care less that, by the time the '05 Series rolled around, Greg and I had talked it all through and considered each other friends.

I was also dead certain that Ivey and I would make the final table. We had the two biggest stacks and I didn't think that either of us was going to make any costly mistakes. There was no need to. We had huge stacks, a great blind structure, and a lot of opponents who were willing to risk their chips on the wrong hands. I was just going to chop, chop, chop all day long. If the other players were smart, they'd figure out that I was deathly afraid to play a big pot. They could come over the top of me every single time and I'd fold. But none of them knew that. I knew they didn't have a read on my game.

I took a small dose of Ritalin and it kicked in just as the player introductions were winding down. As focused as I was on the tournament, somewhere in the back of my mind I was thinking about vindication. On some level, I was still playing to show down those bastards who had put me in jail.

I didn't go into Day Six thinking about winning the tournament. You can't play long days thinking like that; it drains you too much. You have to play one day at a time, one hand at a time. That's how I made it through every single day of the main event. At night, I might think about what my friends kept telling me, but not at the table. The only day I could start thinking about winning the tournament was when we went to the final table. Until then, it was one day at a time, one hand at a time.

Right out of the gate on Day Six, the shit with Shawn Sheikhan started. He hadn't played a lot of no-limit tournament poker back then, so his strategy basically boiled down to needling me. Nothing bothered me more than people who talked more than I did. If you wanted to get to me, all you had to do was keep talking at my table. At a WPT tournament once, a drunk was making me crazy and I had to put on my headset to block him out. If you talked non-stop, you could drive me nuts. Don't bother trying that now, it doesn't bother me anymore. I've plugged that leak in my game.

Shawn was berating me every single hand. I actually asked him to stop. "Please, Shawn, shut up. Please, Shawn, shut up. Please, Shawn, leave me alone."

But Shawn was in front of the TV cameras for the first time and craved the attention. And of course, the video crew was right there looking for a story. What better story than someone who was actually outtalking "The Mouth."

Then came the hand where he slammed his fist, basically telling everyone what he had. I was playing heads-up against another player and Shawn had already folded to the guy's raise and my call. The flop was something like A-9-K or A-9-8 and Shawn slammed his hand on the table. At this point, everyone knew that Shawn had folded an ace. This was totally unfair information for anyone to have and completely wrong for Shawn to do. I bet out, the guy raised me, and I moved in on him with only a queen-high. He folded.

I actually think Shawn's move made me more money. If he hadn't slammed his hand down, I don't think the other guy would have tried to make the play and reraise me. I think he would have just folded to my bet. I went berserk, mostly because I was tired of Sheiky being on my case every damn hand. The floor gave him a penalty when I pointed out what he had done, but I got a penalty too because I made my point with an F-bomb. I know it plays on TV as being funny, but it wasn't at the time. It was an ugly scene.

Just after midnight, I busted Shawn in eleventh place. Some people said I was after him, but I'd actually been avoiding him because of all the trash talk. In his bust-out hand, Shawn made a short-stack move with an A-7 against my A-Q suited. I won't say it wasn't a good feeling to bust him. I was just happy to get rid of his constant jabber.

With Shawn gone, we were down to ten players. The last two tables were combined into one. The hold'em final tables at the Series are always nine-handed, so we had to play until we lost one more player. This is where I made my only really big mistake. I wasn't aware that we were playing for a $1 million guarantee for everybody who made the final nine. The prize pool was set up that way so that Harrah's could say, "Everyone at the final table is a millionaire!" But it also meant there was a $400,000 difference between tenth and ninth place, a fact I wasn't aware of until the very end.

We played ten-handed for nearly three hours without losing a player. I was wondering why everyone was afraid to play a pot. Then I figured it out: They all wanted that guaranteed million dollars. If I had realized that people were playing tight because of the big jump in the payout, I would have raised every pot. I couldn't give a shit about the prize money; I just wanted to get chips so I could win the whole thing. I should have understood the payouts better at the start, but once I did figure it out, I started raising almost every single hand.

I picked up about 2.5 million in chips in the final twenty minutes. But I could've raised every pot for more than two hours, and probably could have gone to the final table with 20 million chips! I still kick myself over that.

Here was the final table and chip counts:

1. Aaron Kanter: 10.7 million
2. Tex Barch: 9.33 million
3. Andrew Black: 8.14 million
4. Mike Matusow: 7.41 million
5. Steve Dannenmann: 5.46 million
6. Joseph Hachem: 5.42 million
7. Daniel Bergsdorf: 5.27 million
8. Scott Lazar: 3.37 million
9. Brad Kondracki: 1.18 million

I made it to the 2005 main event final table with 7,410,000 chips, solidly in fourth place. Aaron Kanter was the chip leader with over 10 million and Brad Kondracki, the short stack, had just over one million. Phil Ivey and Greg Raymer didn't make it, which made me happy and sad at the same time. I really didn't want to play against them, but it would have been great television.

On the morning of the final table, I told everyone that as long as I didn't pick up kings against aces, I was going to win it. On the second hand of the day, Scott Lazar reraised Steven Dannenmann, and I pushed all in with pocket kings. Steven folded and Scott called. When he turned over his two aces, it didn't faze me. I would still have 3.1 million chips left if I lost the hand. I was still going to win this tournament. And I was still mentally composed. All I thought about was how much money I owed to the pot, and getting on to the next hand.

Then the worst thing in the world happened—I flopped a king.

I had been so calm and then bam! I hit a set of kings. Suddenly, I thought my friends were right: I was going to win the World Series. I couldn't believe I had hit a card like that. I was about to win 25 percent of the chips in play and we would be eight-handed. There's no way they were going to beat me. I figured worst case I'd get second place and $4 million. Either way I'd be set for life.

When the 2♥ came on the turn, I cried, "No! No! No!" That put three hearts on the board. Scott had the A♥. I ran over to my friend Matt in the corner and buried my head in his shoulder.

On the river, I thought he said, "You got it" and I jumped up and down in the corner. But what he said was, "He got it." And then I saw the fourth heart.

I was destroyed. I couldn't imagine one card being that cruel. I was so together when I turned over the kings against the aces. I really was. But losing to the four flush nearly killed me. I tried to collect myself, but it was hard not to think about it. I started playing a lot of hands. I stole some blinds and antes and built my stack back up to 5.1 million. I was back in good shape. But I couldn't forget about the hand. I wouldn't have been thinking about it at all if I just hadn't hit that king.

People still ask me about the hand I played against Andy Black. There's an unwritten rule in poker that only a few pros know. When the floor announces that you're taking a break after the next hand, you raise. You raise in the dark because nobody wants to play the hand, they want a break. So I auto-raise from any position when a break is announced. And that's why I raised with a lousy 9-5. Everybody folded to Andy. He called. I didn't want to play with Andy. But I figured he was probably sick of me running over the table. I figured he'd check-call me on the flop and lead the turn. I just knew that would be his play. Andy checked the J-6-5 flop, I bet out 350,000 and he called. The turn card was a 10. He led out 1 million and I made it 2 million. Then Andy pushed all in, and I had to fold. I was down to 2.7 million in chips after the hand.

Of course I should've just rolled it off and let the hand go without making another bet. That way, I would've had 4.4 million and could go right back to work. That was the big mistake I made at the final table.

When I played my final hand against Steve Dannenmann, I had about 2.4 million chips left in my stack. He raised up front and I wasn't sure whether he had a big hand or not. I thought he had A-Q, but I also thought he could have two queens. I had pocket tens in the small blind and debated about what I should do. Looking out of the corner of my eye, it appeared that he didn't want me to call. So, I called 750,000 with my tens.

I led out 250,000 on the flop of 2-3-5 and he pushed. The second he went all-in, I knew he didn't have shit. I slowly examined him up and down and around. I had 1.1 million left. Could I really go out in ninth here? Could I really fold this hand here? He was shaking. He was dying for me to fold the hand.

"Steve, I know you've got nothing, buddy," I looked him dead in the eye and said. "I'm positive you don't have anything. I call."

He turned over A-J. At first I thought he needed an ace or a jack, and figured I was a 4.5 to 1 favorite to win some big chips on the hand.

"Dannenmann needs an ace, jack, or a 4," I heard the floor announce.

When he said that, I realized Steve also had a straight draw, reducing me to only 60-40 to win the hand. The 4 spit out of the deck on the turn. I couldn't believe it! The only thing that could save me was an ace or a 6 on the river to put the straight on the board. No such luck. I just couldn't believe that I had played so well and gotten so unlucky.

It was over and it was over fast. I finished in ninth place.

Getting to the final table of the main event is like hitting the lottery. After 2001, I never thought I'd ever make it back. It had taken Phil Hellmuth twelve years to make it a second time. I knew that winning was going to be an unbelievable long shot, but I had started to listen to my friends and believed I could win it. Although the money helped, I was pretty devastated. Technically, I had won $1 million. But after I paid off my backers and other money I owed along the way, I ended up with a little less than $250,000 in my pocket.

In the end, I was proud of myself and proud of the way I had played. But the bottom line was that I was playing to win. Instead, I finished in ninth place, which was the same as eighth or fourth or second to me. I'm always after the win.

Chapter Twenty-Four

A Champion's Vindication

After the 2005 World Series final table, Harrah's told the final-table players that we were all getting seats in a Tournament of Champions (TOC) freeroll at Caesars Palace. The plan was to invite the final table players from the main event along with all of the "high finishers" from WSOP Circuit events that had been held around the country that year. Harrah's was putting up a $2 million prize pool, which would go to the top nine places. The winner would take home a million bucks.

Since this was a new event for Harrah's, there were some glitches in the qualifying process. One of the biggest problems came from their sponsor, Pepsi, which wanted Phil Hellmuth, Doyle Brunson and Johnny Chan added to the tournament lineup, even though they hadn't qualified under the TOC guidelines. At the time, "The Big Three" had all won ten WSOP bracelets and it was going to be a deal breaker if they weren't included. That started a shit storm in the poker community, but in the end, Doyle, Phil and Johnny ended up playing, and they played well.

In the months between the World Series final table and the TOC, I continued to play a lot of online poker and my losing streak continued. I lost most of my final table payday. I was starting to think online poker was rigged because my bad beats seemed endless.

The TOC finally rolled around in November and featured 114 top players. Even though the field was stacked with talent, it was a pretty small field for a $1 million first prize.

My luck started right out of the gate when I drew what had to be the only soft table in the room. I pretty much controlled it from the first hand. When that table broke, I looked around the room. There wasn't one easy table left. Every table was loaded.

I also definitely caught some cards on Day One. On one hand, I moved all in after a flop with a Q-7 when I sensed a weak player was trying to steal from me. He called 22,000 more with a suited A-8. It turns out he called with bottom pair. I don't know how he made that horrible call, but he got punished when I caught a runner-runner straight and sent him to the rail. Right after that, Kenna James and I tangled on a hand where Kenna had K-J and I had K-9. We got it all in on the flop of J-9-9, leaving Kenna drawing to just two outs. They didn't come and he was gone. At some point, Allen Kessler picked up about 10,000 chips from me when his aces beat my jacks. But late in the day, Allen put his chips in with A-Q and I called with the A-10 of spades. Allen picked up a queen on the flop, but I found two spades and rivered the nut flush to take him out in forty-seventh place.

After busting Allen, I was near the top of the leader board and pretty much stayed there for the rest of the night. In one of the last hands of the day, I took out Dennis Perry in thirtieth place. The plan had been to play down to twenty-seven players on Day One, but since it was past 1:00 a.m. they called it a day. Phil Hellmuth had been dominating all day and it was pretty clear when we were bagging our chips that he was going to be the chip leader. After the counts were made, Phil was in first place, but not by much. He had 110,900 chips and I was right behind him with 107,600. Hoyt Corkins was a distant third with 65,700 chips.

On Day Two, they decided to do something that had never been done in a major tournament before. They used what is now called the "Sommerfeld Redraw Method," named after tournament director Jimmy Sommerfeld. The top three chip leaders were put at three different tables. Then they took the players with the next three highest chip counts and divided them up the same way. They went right down the list like that until everyone had been assigned a table. I believe that all tournaments should be done this way. It sucks when all the big stacks end up at the same table. In the end, they almost get punished for their previous day of hard work. It sucks even more when you're a short stack and end up at a table with all short stacks. There's no way you can tap into the bigger stacks in the tournament when they're all at other tables.

When it gets down to just a few tables, I believe players should be reseated by chip count, especially when they redraw overnight. It can't be that hard to write a computer program that assigns players so the chip counts are more or less even at the tables. It gives everybody the same chance to win and doesn't bunch up the big or the small stacks.

Phil Hellmuth started Day Two with the chip lead and that's exactly where he ended the day. I don't think Phil lost the lead the entire day. He was playing really well and no one was able to get him off his game. When we got down to eighteen players, Phil and I ended up at the same table. I tried to get something going with him, but he wasn't into talking.

Mark "Big Daddy" Hanna was also at our table. Mark likes to sing at the table and of course, so do I. So we did a few duets to entertain the crowd. We still couldn't get a reaction from Phil though. I raised a hand preflop and when no one wanted to play, I announced that I was going to raise the next hand too. I said if they weren't going to play, I was going to rob them blind. As promised, I raised the next hand and they all folded. After the hand, I showed them my pocket aces, but even that didn't get a reaction from Phil. He was in the zone and it was going to be tough to break his concentration.

During the day I was never lower than fourth or fifth place. By the end of the day, I was in the same position I had started. Phil was in first, and I was right back in second place. You hardly ever see the leaders on Day One still leading at the end of Day Two, but that's how it was. Johnny Chan made it to thirteenth place and Doyle busted out on the bubble in tenth place. I think the Pepsi folks were pretty happy with the performance of their three horses. At this point, the rest of us were happy too. We had made it to the final table of the TOC.

It was a pretty spectacular final table lineup:

Phil Hellmuth: 281,500
Mike Matusow: 179,000
Brandon Adams: 135,500

217

Tony Bloom: 130,000
Steve Dannenmann: 122,000
Keith Sexton: 95,500
Hoyt Corkins: 95,000
Grant Lang: 61,500
David Levi: 41,000

Since only nine places were being paid, we were playing for the whole $2,000,000 prize pool, which broke down like this:

1. $1,000,000
2. $325,000
3. $250,000
4. $150,000
5. $100,000
6. $75,000
7. $50,000
8. $25,000
9. $25,000

After the Tournament of Champions, WSOP Media Director Nolan Dalla said, "It was, quite simply, one of the greatest final tables of all time. It had everything; drama, tragedy, humor, passion, laughter, tears, a fight, a downfall, a comeback, and an ending no one could possibly have predicted."

The Tournament of Champions was the best final table I have ever played. I don't believe any of us had ever played at a better final table. There were plenty of bad beats, but there were no bad plays. And there were no easy hands during the entire fourteen hours of play. I thought my patience was absolutely phenomenal. I don't think I ever slipped. I was taking Ritalin and it was working well. As the day wore on, I felt like my meds were giving me something of an edge.

The TOC was going to be a really big television event. We were told in advance that the show would air on Christmas Eve the following month, so everybody joined into the spirit of the holiday. Phil showed up in his new designer sunglasses. I knew Phil couldn't resist showing them off, so I wore my own "designer" glasses with a holographic middle finger on them. Part of my game plan was to needle him. We were playing at the same television final table, so it was almost required for the entertainment value alone. But more importantly, I had to get him off his game. He'd been playing incredible poker and had been the chip leader for two days. I wondered if even my most annoying behavior could rattle Phil's cage.

In keeping with the holiday spirit, Steve Dannenmann gave out presents. During the WSOP main event table, Steve had one of those world globe card protectors. I had teased him a lot about it back then. So he gave me one just like it for the TOC final table. Steve also had a nicely wrapped present for Phil. We told Phil it was from both Steve and me. The crowd got Phil to open it and even Phil cracked a smile when he saw the stuffed donkey doll. This happened between the first couple of hands, which was great for me. Talking and joking for the cameras played right into my game plan. A quiet, focused table would play into the comfort zone of most of the other players. I wanted it to stay loud and distracting for as long as possible.

We had just begun the second round at the table when Hoyt Corkins went all in against Brandon Adams. Hoyt had pocket queens, but Brandon was sitting on pocket aces. Hoyt was headed for a fast ninth place exit when a queen hit the turn. After that hand, Hoyt was right up there, leaving Brandon with the short stack. If Hoyt had busted on that hand, the amazing final six hours of the TOC would have been completely different. A few hands later, Brandon pushed in with Q-J and I called with pocket eights. Although Brandon is considered a pro now, he was basically an amateur at that time and the crowd was really in his corner. He was from New Orleans and his family had just lost their home in Hurricane Katrina. Brandon had pledged ten percent of his TOC winnings to the Hurricane Katrina Relief Fund.

But the fund had to settle for ten percent of ninth place money when Brandon was forced to make a move with a less-than-premium hand and my pocket eights held up.

Keith Sexton and Hoyt Corkins got into another pair-versus-pair contest. Hoyt had queens again and Keith was behind with a pair of tens. They got it all in on the 9-4-2 flop and it looked like Keith would be gone until his miracle 10 hit the turn. The crowd went nuts. They were still whooping and hollering when a bigger miracle queen came on the river to eliminate Keith Sexton in eighth place. Hoyt shook his head in amazement as he pulled in over 300,000 chips. He took the chip lead on that suck and resuck hand, knocking Phil out of the lead for the first time since Day One. I was hoping this very minor setback might let me get under Phil's skin a little bit.

I told Hoyt that he should really consider attending a Phil Hellmuth Fantasy Camp, but I still got nothing from Phil.

In the first hour of play, we had seen three big hands come down and had lost two players. The crowd was wired. This was already a great final table and we were just getting started. I can't describe just how wound up the fans were. I've never seen anything like it. I've never played to a more knowledgeable, more enthusiastic audience. I'm not sure whether the other players enjoyed playing in that atmosphere, but I thought it was great for poker. I was lovin' it!

David Levi eventually had to make his move. He started the day as the short stack, and had been on the sideline for nearly two hours. He committed all his chips on the very first hand he played. Unfortunately, the first playable hand he got was A-Q at the same time I woke up with pocket aces. David got a queen on the flop but didn't get any help after that. He went out in seventh place. I edged into second place behind Hoyt on the hand. We were just short of two hours into the day. We had lost three players and I had eliminated two of them. It was also the first time in the tournament that I had pulled ahead of Phil.

"When I go home at night, I think to myself, 'God, I wish I was Phil Hellmuth,'" I said to needle him.

After about an hour more of tight play, Grant Lang made a big bluff move into Tony Bloom. As the current short stack, Grant had been playing really conservatively. He just happened to pick the wrong time to bluff. Tony was sitting on pocket aces and snapped off Grant like a dry twig. We were at about the three-hour mark when Grant went out in sixth. Hoyt had a big chip lead at this point and Tony had moved into second. I was third and Phil had slipped down to fourth. Steve Dannenmann was the new short stack.

I did my best to stay out of the way in the next few hands. Steve made a short-stack move with the A-4 of hearts and Tony's A-K dominated him. But three hearts hit the board and Steve doubled up with the flush. Tony became the short stack and pushed in on a flop against Hoyt. Hoyt caught a pair against Tony's gutshot straight draw. A straight saved Tony on the river. The crowd always backs the underdog and they were getting what they wanted. Apparently, the media was a little disappointed because Phil and I hadn't really gone at it yet. It certainly wasn't because of a lack of effort on my part.

For some reason, Phil was uncharacteristically messing with his chips all day, stacking and restacking them, not keeping them in any order that could be easily counted. I got on his case about it four or five times. I knew that if I really needed a chip count I could just ask for one, but it was more fun to ride him about it. At some point though, Dannenmann got really pissed off about it. I didn't think Steve could ever get angry about anything, he's such a totally mellow guy. He asked Phil to stack his chips so that they could be counted. Phil refused and things got really nasty.

"I don't understand why you can't stack your chips like everyone else," Steve said. "You're disrespecting the game."

Phil said nothing. Neither did the floor. The tournament staff could have stepped in, but I think they were bending over backwards not to interfere with what might be considered "good" television. Or maybe they just thought it would blow over. But Steve was clearly annoyed, and he wasn't going to let it go.

"I'm here playing as an amateur, and I know I'm up against professionals," he told Phil. "You above everyone else should know the rules. You sell all those books and products. But you aren't a professional—you're a punk!"

Wow! Mild-mannered Steve Dannenmann had just called Phil Hellmuth a punk on national television. I can't remember if I was laughing my ass off or too shocked to speak. Wait, I've never been too shocked to speak. I must have been laughing. The whole place was in an uproar. Now the floor had to do something; it had gotten out of hand. But what did they really expect? Most people thought that Phil and I would be squaring off, but it was the good-natured Dannenmann calling Hellmuth a punk. The floor finally decided that this was a good time to take an unscheduled TV time out. They sent us on break to cool off.

When we got back, Steve was still really steaming and I tried to take advantage of that. I moved all in on him with A-K. Wouldn't you know it, Steve woke up with pocket jacks and we were in a race. No aces, kings or jacks hit the flop, but there were two hearts and I had the ace of hearts. At that moment, I remembered the World Series final table when Steve busted me after hitting runner-runner hearts for the flush. Here we were four months later and I had a chance to return the favor. When the third heart fell on the turn, I "knew" another heart was coming. An ace or a king would have given me the hand too, but I knew it was going to a heart. I was about to get payback for the Series.

I called it out: "Heart! Heart!"

Bingo, a heart fell on the river—I was alive! The crowd went crazy and Steve was crushed. If he had won that hand, who knows how far the Dannenmann-Hellmuth feud would have gone? One round later, Steve moved in with A-10 on a flop of Q-J-3. I made the call holding a queen. Nothing came to save Steve. He was eliminated. Grant Laing had been eliminated right before that, so we were down to four players.

During his ESPN interview, Steve was still steaming at Phil. "We don't need players like that in the sport," he said, adding, "Mike Matusow is the best player I've ever played with."

I was happy to have Steve's chips, but I also wished he was still at the table. I hadn't been able to rile Phil, but somebody had to. I really think Steve was starting to get to him. Not long afterwards, Tony Bloom made his move with K-8 and Phil called him with A-Q. They both flopped a pair but Phil's queens were bigger than Tony's eights. And just like that, we were down to three.

Strangely, it was the same three players who had led the event after Day One: Phil, me and Hoyt.

When we started three-handed, I truly believed I was going to win it. It turned into a brutal battle with the lead changing many times. But even when I was low on chips, I still felt like I was going win. I never thought it would be easy, but I had no idea just how hard it would be. I have never been more challenged at a poker table. Afterwards, we all admitted that the competition probably pushed each of us to the highest level we had ever played. Even the short-stack moves were made at the right time for the right price. I have never been associated with better poker than that, and I can't imagine I ever will be again.

About 15 hands into three-way play, Phil and I got into a pot where the board ran out Q-10-9-K-J. With the king-high straight on the board, I bet 25,000 on the river and Phil raised to 100,000. I had tried to trap Phil earlier in the hand with my Q-J. I'd hit top pair on the flop and made a straight on the turn. I'd bet both times and Phil had made both calls. I just couldn't put him on the ace for a higher straight. I finally decided he was trying to steal the pot. I called, but he wasn't bluffing. I have no idea why he called both my bets holding just A-6, but he did. With that hand, I put Phil back into the chip lead.

A couple of hands later, we broke for dinner. My friends at dinner were busting on Phil. They were saying stuff like, "Hellmuth has no chance. He's afraid to play a hand against you, Mikey. He's a legend in his own mind."

Although I'd been saying shit like that all day, that was all table talk. I explained to my friends that I was just trying to rattle Phil. The truth was that Phil had been playing so well that if I didn't find a way to get him off his game, I wasn't going to be able to beat him. Phil played phenomenal poker every minute of those three days. If he continued to keep that focus, all the pocket aces in the world wouldn't beat him. I was playing great poker also, but I wasn't sure that was going to be enough.

"Did you lose your voice box?" I asked Phil when we returned to the table after dinner. I had to keep trying.

About half an hour later, Phil spoke his first words to me. He raised 40,000 on the button and I moved in for 285,000.

"Is this where you have your Matusow Meltdown?" Phil looked at me and asked.

I just smiled back at him. But when he folded, I showed my 8-3! He had folded A-8.

Phil went nuts. Once he finally settled down, Hoyt told us that he had folded another 8-3. That just set Phil off even more. I knew that Phil wasn't ready to race for all his chips just yet. I knew he'd back off. But what made the hand a real winner for me was showing him a monster bluff and getting him to steam.

At this point, I picked up a tell on Hoyt. He did the same thing every time he had a big hand. I was so sure of it that I began playing as though Phil and I were already heads-up. If Hoyt came into a pot showing his tell, I just got out of the way. Any time he played a hand without the tell, I played him as being weak. If Phil was also in the hand, I played it like Hoyt wasn't even there. Tells work great when you first pick up on them. But too many amateur players think that tells are permanent. Not true. Professionals might show a tell for only a day, or they might lose it when we go on dinner break. Professionals are just too good to keep a tell for years or even for a whole tournament. In other words, Hoyt doesn't have that tell anymore—so don't waste your breath asking me about it.

Hoyt, Phil and I ended up playing for almost four hours and I talked the whole time. I got on Phil's case for even being there in the first place, calling it his "free ride to the freeroll." I teased Hoyt about a few of the lucky hands he'd gotten.

At one point I said to Hoyt, "You should have been broke three times, and Phil shouldn't even have been here!"

"You know, I finished second in this event last year. There's only one way to improve," Phil said. Finally, Phil was talking back.

"If you keep getting free invites to tournaments, it's easy to finish second," I shot back.

If you've seen short-handed play at a final table, you know it can get pretty boring at times. But that wasn't the case at the Tournament of Champions. Hand after hand we were battling and pushing chips around the table. The lead kept changing. I got short-stacked twice in those four hours, and one time I was down below 90,000. With 1,140,000 chips in play, that was a painfully short stack. Someone should write a book about this tournament, there were so many incredible hands. I know I can't do it justice, but a couple of the hands stood out.

One hand I loved came down between Phil and Hoyt. Phil limped from the small blind, Hoyt raised from the big blind, and Phil called. They both checked the flop and the turn. Phil checked the river before Hoyt bet out 60,000 with the board reading 9-9-8-7-8. Phil just sat there and stared. Any big pair would beat him, any 9, any 8 and any ace because Phil only had king-high. Then he actually made the call—and Hoyt lost when he tabled his queen-high. What an amazing read! Phil took down a 200,000 pot with just king high and he was back in the lead again. The crowd freaked out when they realized that Phil had made that call with nothing but air. Phil was so pumped up, I thought he would explode.

Hoyt had already battled back from a short stack a few times that day. At one point, he pushed all in preflop about a dozen times in a row to get himself back in contention. I especially liked the fact that when he was short-stacked, Hoyt constantly raised Phil's big blind. After that loss to Phil's king-high, however, Hoyt was short-stacked again and I didn't think he had another comeback in him.

Hoyt obviously didn't see it that way. Two hands later, he raised Phil's big blind again and Phil reraised all in with A-Q. Phil was obviously tired of Hoyt picking on him and was looking to shut him down. Hoyt, however, had a real hand this time. He flipped over pocket aces. They held and he doubled up.

Phil started complaining about his bad luck and I just jumped all over him. "Phil, if you would pay attention and stop whining all the time, you might know what's going on here." I was sticking him with the needle again, but Hoyt had given his tell on that hand, as big as could be. I absolutely knew that Hoyt had at least pocket queens and I would have bet he had aces or kings. But it's always about bad luck with Phil.

Phil grabbed a few small pots and then got into another hand with Hoyt. Phil called from the small blind with J-2 and Hoyt checked the big blind with 8-4. The flop rolled off Q-8-3, giving Hoyt middle pair. Both players checked. Phil checked the 5 on the turn, Hoyt bet out 20,000 and Phil check-raised it to 70,000. Hoyt thought for a while and called the extra 50,000. The river was a 7 and a third club and Phil bet out 65,000 without hesitation.

Hoyt went deep into the tank and finally said, "Boy, I don't see no way for me to have the best hand, but I'm not ready to turn it over, I'll tell you that."

After another couple of minutes he said, "I can't see no way I'm gonna win it, but I call."

With some ragged straight possibilities on the board and three clubs for the potential flush, Hoyt made the call. He won the hand with second pair and a weak-ass kicker—an incredible call! I really truly couldn't believe it. Naturally I said so, out loud, several times.

Phil was already steamed, but that totally set him off. He complained to his dad in the stands about Hoyt, about his bad luck, and all the bad plays the other players had made against him. It was just vintage Phil talk, but I was so happy to finally hear it. I had waited all day and all night for Phil to tilt and finally he had done it. I wasn't going to let him off, not now. Phil against Mike would be great television, but I wanted Mike against anyone. I just laid into Phil and kept telling Hoyt what a great, great play he'd made.

Was it a great call? Absolutely, yes it was. Was Phil's bet on the turn and again on the river a great play? Also yes. But Hoyt got the last move right, the one that paid—and the one that put Phil on tilt.

Just before midnight, I thought Hoyt and Phil were getting tired. It had been a long day and they had been mixing it up on some pretty big hands. I was thinking about all that when Hoyt limped in ahead of me. I raised with A-Q and Hoyt moved all in. I couldn't get a read on him. He just announced his bet, which he hadn't done before. He didn't have to move chips or cap his cards or do anything except say, "All In." In other words, he didn't give his tell, but then again, he didn't not give it either.

I looked at Hoyt from every angle. I knew he was tired and I suspected he was getting frustrated with all the back and forth play. I was sure he had made a mistake. I called. I was wrong: He turned over A-K.

The flop came 10 high with no queen and two diamonds, a bad one for me. I was now drawing to only three queens and Hoyt had the top diamond. For the first time all day, I thought it was over for me. I just couldn't believe I had pulled the trigger with an A-Q. Then a queen popped for me on the turn and the crowd went absolutely berserk. I went crazy too. But there was one problem; it was the queen of diamonds. I had hit, but Hoyt had just picked up a bunch of outs. He could hit a jack for the straight, a king for top pair, or any diamond for the flush. It wasn't over yet. We just stood there. Even when they finished setting up the camera shot after what seemed like a lifetime, no one sat down. Finally, the dealer turned over the river card.

A blank. I had won the hand of the tournament.

That near disaster was like a smack across the face. I should have been able to fold A-Q to Hoyt. That mistake nearly cost me the TOC. I wasn't going to let that happen again.

The blinds were pretty high and Phil was still short-stacked. He would have to play a hand almost immediately. He kept dancing around the table with his "I'll never give up" speech. Unfortunately, I doubled him up on a hand when his pocket jacks held against my K-J. After the hand, Phil became even more obnoxious. He announced that he was going to buy thirty bottles of Dom Perignon for the crowd if he won. But there would be no champagne. Soon after that, Hoyt busted Phil in third place.

Suddenly, we were heads-up and everyone was going to have to wait another day for the Matusow-Hellmuth million-dollar showdown. But I didn't care who I was playing—I was heads-up for $1 million and a real shot at redemption.

I had almost a 2.5 to 1 chip lead when we began heads-up play. I think they only showed a couple of our hands on television, but Hoyt and I actually played for over two hours.

Hoyt got the lead on me when he moved in with A-10 and I called with A-8 and his kicker played. I realized I had to go back to my strength, so I just started to chop away. I'd limp and then lead. I didn't play any big pots. I'd release a hand when he had something, but otherwise, I kept the pressure on. I didn't panic. I managed to take control of the pace of the match, even with a short stack. It took awhile, but I just stuck to my game plan and chopped my way back into the lead.

I raised 60,000 with K-9 on a K-J-4 flop. Hoyt thought for a moment and moved in. Certain that I had the best hand, I made an insta-call. I was hoping he had a jack or a weaker king. He turned over a Q-10. Even though he had the open ended straight draw, I was pretty happy. I had one of the nines, so he had four aces and three nines to win; or seven outs twice. I was over a 2 to 1 favorite. When he didn't hit on the turn, I knew I was going to win it. There are times when you know it's over, and times when you know you're going home long before the river comes. I knew this one was mine.

The river was a blank and I won the 2005 Tournament of Champions!

I'd only been out of jail a few months, but when that final card hit the river, I finally made it past all that. Emotionally, I'd not only come back, I'd moved on. The final table at the World Series had been great but it was still ninth place. This was a win. It was a big win. I did my "Vindication Baby!" dance. I shouted out those words over and over. I was shouting and crying. I'd played some of the best poker of my life against some of the greatest professionals in the world. I still have my Tournament of Champions trophy in my living room to remind me of the most spectacular tournament I ever had the privilege to play.

"This is the greatest moment of my life," I said in the post-tournament interview. "All the disappointments I've had. All the bad beats. All the bad decisions. This win meant everything to me."

By this time, everyone in poker knew what I was talking about. They all knew where I'd been and what I had gone through. They knew what this meant to me.

My 2005 Tournament of Champions proved to me that I could still play poker. It also erased any remaining doubts I had about needing street drugs to be a successful player.

Once I got home, I realized I had to get up in less than six hours to film the Poker Superstars Invitational. I was dead tired and ended up getting zero points in the first two tapings. I was also still a little buzzed coming off my TOC win. But I got my act together and went on to win the event for another half a million bucks. What an amazing week! Poker Superstars didn't air on TV until a year and a half later on Super Bowl weekend in 2007. I was asked to write an article about the hands from the tournament to promote the television show, but I could barely remember them after all that time.

But the hands from the Tournament of Champions—those I'll always remember.

Chapter Twenty-Five

Bipolar Poker

After my win at the Tournament of Champions I had a very diffi-cult year. It began with my decision to play less live poker and more online cash games. That decision was based on some changes that took place at my "home" poker room at the Bellagio.

During the previous two years, a couple of things happened that changed where I played. First, some huge cash games started up be-tween Andy Beal, the billionaire Texas banker, and a small group of professional poker players. If you don't know the story of those games, you can read Michael Craig's book, *The Professor, the Banker, and the Suicide King: Inside the Richest Poker Game of All Time*. I wasn't involved in those games, but a lot of the pros were. Most of them went on to start up the "Big Game" at the Bellagio. Actually it was their winnings from the Beal games that bankrolled the Bellagio Big Game.

I don't play in the Big Game, never have and never will. Stakes of $2,000/$4,000 and higher are beyond my bankroll and my com-fort zone. It's really a different game at those levels. Besides, why would I want to play a bunch of pros when there were plenty of fat fish swimming at more reasonable stakes? I wasn't the only pro with that view. While Doyle Brunson was a regular at the Big Game, his son Todd probably did just as well feeding off the tourists at the next lowest stakes.

I used to sit at more reasonable Bellagio high-limit games and taunt the Big Game players to come play me at my stakes, but I never got any takers. I guess there was no reason for them to bump down. For the most part, they were sitting on their Beal bankrolls and got to play in "Bobby's Room," named after Bobby Baldwin, the President at the Bellagio at that time and 1978 World Champion of Poker. The room opened in the spring of 2005 and was reserved for the highest limit games. Located inside the main poker room, it was separated by glass walls, giving the players a little more privacy and the Big Game an upscale, home-game feel.

Unfortunately, the Big Game and Bobby's Room changed the way Bellagio treated the rest of the players in the poker room. If you weren't playing mixed games for monster stakes, you were treated like the average $4/$8 game tourist. At that point, for me anyway, the poker room at the Bellagio, which had been a great place to play for many years, was no longer a special place. When the Bellagio poker room first opened, the staff bent over backwards to show their appreciation to the players. But by late 2004, early 2005, it was time to move on. I'd still play tournaments at the Bellagio because so many of the World Poker Tour events happened there, and I might take a seat in a game or two for cash game action during the World Series when the games can be good. But essentially, I was no longer a regular there.

To replace the live action at the Bellagio, I turned to playing much more on the Internet. Online poker had matured enough so that I could find big enough games whenever I wanted to play.

Nearly everyone puts the explosion of online poker sometime around the 2003 Chris Moneymaker World Series win. Chris won his seat into the WSOP online, causing a tremendous explosion in the number of people playing poker online. But in those growth years from 2002 to 2005, there weren't a lot of high stakes games online. Maybe you could find a $50/$100 no-limit game by 2005, and if you looked hard enough, you could find some smaller no-limit games where the all-in betting had gotten out of hand. But there really weren't a lot of online games that a professional high-stakes player would find tempting. The pros would wait in front of their computers for enough players to join higher limit games, similar to the early days at the Bellagio when we'd sit around the tables waiting for enough players to get even a $100/$200 game going. But times had changed, and I wound up doing a flip-flop in my cash games, playing more online rather than live.

My mother thinks I'm addicted to online poker. It's funny. She didn't see it that way when I was going to play live cash games at Binion's, the Commerce, or Bellagio seven days a week for twelve and fourteen hours a day. Maybe that seemed like I was going to work. But I guess lying in bed with a laptop looks more like an addiction than a job. I do play ridiculously long hours online, and yes, I do have food brought in so I can eat while I play. I've played long sessions, some lasting more than thirty hours. But it's not the hours or the location that make online play so different for me.

I'm not as focused in an online game as I am in a live game. Part of that has to do with the setting, but some of it has to do with my medications. I never like to take my ADHD medications when I'm at home. The drill down focus it gives me is great at the tables, but it doesn't really allow me to have a good conversation on the phone, enjoy dinner, or take in the fourth quarter of a football game. It's great for poker, but away from the table, it's like trying to live your life in a tunnel. So, it's always been a little harder for me to balance my meds and home life with online play. But I understand that and I generally find a way to work it out.

In late 2005 and all of 2006, however, nothing was working out. A one-two punch was going on in my life that I wasn't really aware of until after it was over. The first punch was online poker. The second was my medications.

After my Tournament of Champions and Poker Superstars wins, I had a decent amount of cash and tucked a lot of it into my Ultimate Bet account. I had run up Phil Hellmuth's $5,000 stake big-time on Ultimate Bet right after I got out of jail. After almost all of it had disappeared, I was probably crazy to put more money in that site, but I just couldn't accept the fact that I could be such a big net loser. I thought I could turn it around. I knew I could beat those players, I knew about bad runs and I knew about game selection. There was only one important thing I didn't know—and it wouldn't be until later that I found it out.

When I got out of jail, I had a huge tournament year in 2005, and every one in the poker world knew it. Russ Hamilton, the 1994

World Series of Poker Champion, would call me all the time to try to get me to play Omaha heads-up against him on UB. I didn't think he was that good a player, but he beat me time after time. Sometimes I told him I didn't have enough money in my UB account to play him. That was never a problem for Russ. He would instantly transfer money to my account and tell me to pay him back in cash. There were other times when his account was short, but I had cash in my account. Then I would send him money on UB. After he beat me, and he always did, he would just send back my original stake. Either way, he beat me time after time, session after session. I just couldn't seem to beat Russ. I don't even want to think about how long that went on.

Sitting at my mother's kitchen table one day in 2006, I went on and on about the $200,000 I'd lost the previous week on UB, a good portion of it to Russ Hamilton. I just couldn't believe my incredible losing streak. I remember it like it was yesterday because I actually told my mom, "Those guys play like they can see my hole cards."

Those words still haunt me today.

After the 2005 WSOP and TOC, I should have been riding high. I should have been the most confident player in the world. But my online losses had made me doubt my game. A professional player can't play with doubt. What they did to me was like kneecapping a professional basketball player. I kept wondering if I had really lost my game. Then I found out why I was losing so much money online, and it all began to make sense. Starting roughly in early 2004 and continuing through the beginning of 2008, there was a breach in Ultimate Bet's security software. Some insiders were using special accounts that actually allowed them to see all the players' hole cards. With that incredible advantage, they literally stole millions and millions of dollars off the high stakes tables.

I lost $1.2 million to the cheaters on Ultimate Bet. But the money wasn't the worst of it. Coming out of jail, I was at my most vulnerable and it affected every part of my game—my cash games as well as my tournament play. Confidence is so important in poker, and when you don't have it, you're playing at a huge disadvantage.

Every one of those cheating insiders is a criminal. But who knows if they'll ever pay for what they did? The legal jurisdiction for online cheating is a big rat hole. Those crooks sat in their houses in Costa Rica and Las Vegas, but their crime and fraud was laundered through the Internet. Not only did they cheat me out of my money, but every time I paid Russ back in cash, I was unknowingly laundering his money. The new owners who bought Ultimate Bet got stuck holding the bag. They have been trying to refund some of the stolen money, but players will never get back everything they lost. And I predict that the criminals will never serve a day in prison.

As for live tournament poker from the end of 2005 through 2006, my schedule included making the money at the Monte Carlo Millions in late 2005 and money finishes in 2006 at the British Poker Open, another Poker Superstars event, and both the Festa al Lago and the WPT Five Diamond at the Bellagio. I also played and cashed in two Full Tilt invitational television events, the Full Tilt Shootout at the end of 2005 and the Full Tilt Pro Showdown in June of '06. At the 2006 World Series that summer, I finished in the money three times, and made one final table in the $2,500 No-limit Hold'em tournament. I pushed with top pair early at that table and got snapped off by two small pair, finishing seventh for about ninety grand.

I was pretty unhappy with how the 2006 WSOP was run. When Harrah's bought the WSOP brand, there were a lot of things to work out with the new facility. They were running forty-five tournaments instead of the thirty-three they had at Binion's back in '04. On top of that, the sheer number of players had skyrocketed. For some reason, Harrah's also changed tournament directors every year, even though they initially had some of the best TDs in the business. I can't say that I liked what was happening to the Series under its new corporate owners. In 2005, I thought they'd changed too much, but I tried to cut them some slack. By 2006, however, Harrah's seemed to be continuing to take it in the wrong direction, so I made some of my concerns known to management. But how they ran the Series was probably the least of my worries.

After the WSOP I went back to playing online and getting stuck with more big losses. No matter how many live tournaments I played on the circuit and no matter where I traveled to play poker, I was having trouble separating what was happening to me online from my live play. While I had a plus year in tournaments, online was one big black hole of minuses, and I just couldn't understand why I was losing so bad. News of the cheating scams on Ultimate Bet had not been uncovered yet.

I was a member of Team Full Tilt, and had been since the site opened in 2004. Like most of the other new sites, Full Tilt built up its cash game limits slowly, increasing the limits as its player base increased. It probably wasn't until 2007 before Full Tilt had really high limit tables available. As a Team Full Tilt member, I have always played my hours on the site and interacted with the fans and other players. I try to take my Full Tilt team membership obligations seriously. One of the things I've always respected about Full Tilt is how cautiously they grew their business and how paranoid they've been about software security. Every site knew that nothing could bring them down faster than a cheating scandal. And if one site was "rigged" or crooked, it could bring down the entire industry. The tragedy of the scandals at Ultimate Bet and Absolute Poker, two major online sites, was that they made everyone doubt all poker sites, even the ones that were well regulated and policed.

My only regret about Full Tilt's caution was that it meant they were slow to bring in higher stakes games, which meant I played at Ultimate Bet more often than I otherwise would have. I think all the pros felt that way; most of us had accounts on multiple sites, always looking for a big game. So until Full Tilt offered high stakes games, I divided my online play between whatever I could find on Full Tilt and higher stakes games on Ultimate Bet. On Full Tilt, I usually played the big tournaments and the highest Omaha high-low games on the board. Sometimes I'd play lower stakes games just to hang out and talk with the fans. I like playing at Full Tilt. I only wish they had spread the higher limit tables sooner, so that I wouldn't have had so much money stolen from me at UB.

The major problem I had during 2006, besides my online play, was balancing my meds for live play. I was having a lot of "bad med" days. The side effects of these drugs can actually be just the opposite of what they are supposed to do. I would take my ADHD meds to help me focus and instead, I would be so out of it that I could barely see my cards. By the middle of 2006, I realized that I would basically be okay if I just took my bipolar medications. The Ritalin for my ADHD was the culprit, and any time I had problems, it was almost always on the second day of taking it. Most people prepare for a tournament by getting more rest or practicing in cash games. But most of my preparation revolved around trying to plan ahead far enough to get my bad Ritalin day behind me before the start of a tournament. Sometimes this meant being totally whacked out on a travel day. But in 2006, my girlfriend Jess traveled with me to most tournaments and she made sure that I didn't get lost in customs or baggage claim. Just having someone listen to me when I talked about my meds and remind me of my medication schedule made all the difference.

It's a bit sick to plan on a day of depression or a suicidal episode in order to play poker, right? But that was the med cycle I was on.

I was juggling my Ritalin pretty well until the WPT's Doyle Brunson North American Poker Classic at the Bellagio at the end of 2006. I restarted my Ritalin on December 13th, two days before Day One. I actually didn't have a tough day on the 14th and the next day everything seemed fine on my way to the casino. Then about forty-five minutes into the tournament, it hit me like a freight train. I was sick and shaky, barely able to sit upright in my chair.

The Bellagio uses the Fontana Lounge for the tournaments. They clear out all the cocktail tables to make room for the poker tables, but the room has built-in padded bench seats around the walls. I dragged myself over and curled up on a bench for about an hour. My eyes were rolled up in my head; I really had no idea where I was. This was a far different Ritalin reaction than I was used to. Meanwhile, the tournament played on just a few feet away. I came around after about an hour and managed to make it out of Day One with an average stack. I tripled my stack on Day Two of the tournament, which was my fourth day on Ritalin. But I just couldn't hold my focus on Day Three and I busted out.

I told my psychiatrist we had to find some other way to control my ADHD, so I could do my job. My bipolar disorder had been under control for nearly three years, but I still felt like I had to walk on eggshells every time I took Ritalin. I mean, it was just sick to be playing for millions of dollars and wondering whether or not a pill was going to work. You want to play your "A" game, but you have no idea what letter of the alphabet is going to show up. The incident at the Bellagio made me want to work harder at finding a balance that I could count on. Maybe it's selfish to want more. I've been playing poker for a living for most of my adult life and I am grateful for everything it has allowed me to do and have. After all, I could still be living in my trailer and dealing at Sam's Town. But still I wonder what kind of poker player I could be if I could maintain my concentration.

Once I was no longer being cheated on Ultimate Bet, my confidence started to return. The difference between 2006 and 2007 was like night and day. In 2006, I'd lost over a million dollars online. I thought my poker game was going to hell. I can't describe how much anxiety and sheer heartache that caused me. If I had only known that thieves were operating on Ultimate Bet. But I didn't. The only thing that kept me sane was that I was regularly cashing in live tournaments. Of course, no one could see my hole cards there.

But in 2007, the online tide started to turn. I had shifted all my online play to Full Tilt as more high-stakes tables became available. Suddenly, I became a winning player again. I wasn't killing the games on Full Tilt, but I was winning more than I was losing. And I didn't feel like I was playing under some evil, bad-beat curse. On the live circuit, I played fewer tournaments than I did in 2006, partly because I was getting road weary. Poker tournaments are held in casinos that look the same no matter where you are in the world. It all boils down to a plane trip, a hotel room, and a tournament room. The only real difference is how long the flight is.

I was very close to complete poker burnout for a whole lot of reasons—and then the 2007 World Series of Poker arrived.

Chapter Twenty-Six

My "Dark" Series

I made a final table at the Wynn Classic in Las Vegas in March of '07, but that was really the only hit I had under my belt before the 2007 World Series began. I had been so disappointed by the structures and schedules at the Series for two years that I wasn't sure I was going to play it in 2007. It just seemed that everything Harrah's did was about making a buck; it didn't really matter what the players thought or needed. Although I did end up playing, I was even more discouraged by the changes made in '07 Series.

To provide enough tables to accommodate the growing number of players, Harrah's set up an outside pavilion that was basically a tent. The big air conditioning units weren't able to keep the inside temperature below 90 most of the time. Windstorms are pretty common in the desert, especially on hot summer nights and the whole structure shook on windy days. There were a few times when players, including Doyle Brunson, just got up and quit a tournament because of real concerns about their safety. One guy got injured by part of the support structure that fell during a windstorm.

Then Harrah's allowed *Bluff* magazine to put about a dozen final tables into a big black tent in the middle of the Amazon room. Strange, huh? But that's exactly what they did. The idea was to show final tables with hole cards on a one-hour delay for a paid subscription service. Players were literally kept in isolation — locked away from their family, friends and fans — to prevent anyone from relaying any of the hole card information back to them. Otherwise they'd have an unfair advantage if they found out what their opponents were playing.

How would you like to finally make a final table at the WSOP and no one was there? The ultimate stupidity was when Phil Hellmuth won his record eleventh WSOP bracelet inside the tent — and no one got to see it. Even today, the tape of the event isn't available. I guess it was all about making money on the final tables by selling closed circuit subscriptions. But in the end, it was bad for the players and bad for their families who flew to Las Vegas on a red eye flight only to find out they couldn't actually watch their child or spouse play. It was just plain bad for poker, and they lost their ass on the subscription service.

By the time the main event rolled around, I was pretty turned off by the World Series. I felt that in the two years Harrah's had owned it, they had stripped the very heart out of the greatest poker tournament in the world. My mood didn't improve after I lost a $20,000 prop bet. I bet that during the main event no players would be seated in the stupid outside tent. I actually asked Jeffery Pollack, the commissioner of the WSOP, if they would use the tent if they got too many players. He assured me that they would open another indoor room if that happened. Under no circumstances would anyone be burdened with time in the tent because that would put them under a disadvantage to the players inside the air-conditioned Amazon room.

I was scheduled to play on the fourth Day One for the main event and when they got a bunch of late registrations, they put eight tables out in the tent. On top of that $20,000 lost bet, my medication had upset my stomach. I had zero chance of maintaining any kind of focus. The bottom line was that I really didn't want to be playing in the tournament and busted out late on my Day One.

Since 1999, I had made at least one final table at every World Series of Poker. In 2007, I broke that streak. But I just didn't care. I had made it into the money in three preliminary events. In fact, I made it down to the final two tables in all three of those events. I finished eleventh in a field of 1,013 in the $2,500 No-limit Hold'em tournament, fifteenth in the $5,000 Omaha high-low event, and sixteenth in the $50,000 H.O.R.S.E. tournament.

On June 3rd, I was sitting at the same table as Ted Forrest and he mentioned that I'd put on a lot of weight. He asked how much I weighed and I told him I was about 240. He offered a $100,000 prop bet that I couldn't lose sixty pounds in one year. I took the bet immediately. That night he weighed me in at 241 pounds. On June 3rd, 2008, I had to weigh 181 pounds or less to win the $100,000.

I spent the day after I busted out of the main event at home putting all the "Harrah's Hating" stuff aside and taking a long look at my play. I had all those excuses—I really wasn't feeling well, I was on tilt from the prop bet, and so on. But the truth was, as a professional poker player, I should have been able to get past those things. In the end, I'd just played poorly. No one from Harrah's had bet my hands for me, I was the one who had played like a donkey in main event. It didn't take very long before I got pissed at myself, which is where all the blame really belonged.

I decided that I either had to prove I could play better or punish myself for playing like a donkey. Maybe I needed to do both.

The next day I put up $10,000 for the World Poker Tour's Bellagio Cup III. A couple of years earlier the WPT had realized that it could attract a lot of the big players who were in Vegas for the World Series. They scheduled their event so they could grab all of the players who had busted out of the WSOP main event. The Bellagio Cup started immediately after the Day One flights of the World Series. Like many of the other main event bust outs, I put my money down.

The 2007 Bellagio Cup had three flights of Day Ones and I decided to play Day 1B. I couldn't believe how completely card dead I was for the entire day. The few times I did get a decent starting hand, I had to fold to a big reraise. I didn't have a hand to play all of the first day. But I remained patient. I gave myself a chance to survive by playing great laydown poker, which was pretty much the only kind of poker I could play with those cards. At some point, I got a twenty-minute penalty for using my cell phone at the table. I didn't realize the cell phone rule at the Bellagio was different from the one we'd been playing under at the Rio for the past five weeks. I raised a ruckus about that ruling but the floor kept saying it was "the rule at the Bellagio." Basically, it gave me something to bitch about other than my cards. Near the end of the day, I shoved in my last 5,400 chips against pocket aces. Luckily, I managed to make a flush on the river to survive.

I had the next day off while the last Day One flight played. I reviewed all my hands and my play. Any way I looked at it, I couldn't come up with any missed opportunities. I just had to accept that I'd been card dead and it would be better on Day Two. Though I knew I had my work cut out for me, I wasn't too discouraged.

For Day Two, the three flights of Day One players were combined. I started the day in 201st place out of the remaining 240 players. If I wanted to prove I could play my "A" game, I had the perfect proving ground. We knew it was going to be a really long day. The WPT had planned to get down to twenty-seven players on Day Two, but we knew that was never going to happen. They apparently had a backup plan to get to thirty-six, but even that proved impossible. By the end of our very long day, we still had fifty-six players. When they finally called play, it was 2:00 a.m. In a fourteen hour day, I had one of the best poker days of my career.

I hadn't seen many playable hands, but I knew that I couldn't afford to just sit on a short stack. With the blinds and antes constantly going up, I had to get chips. I went to work early, stealing blinds and pushing players off pots. I won more hands that day with bad cards than ever before in my tournament career. I'm sure that out of the twenty hands I won without a showdown, I was behind in at least fifteen of them when the other player folded. I read weakness so well that I thought I could take a shot at a pot with next to nothing in my hand. I played the players, not my cards.

Towards the end of the day, *Card Player* reported, "Mike Matusow has quietly built himself a chip stack. Usually the loudest guy in the room, Mike looks like he means business today."

He had that right. I finished the day with around 200,000 chips; every one of those chips was stolen property.

Day Three was going to be another very long day, as we were supposed to play down to the final table of six. Again, this seemed unlikely. Phil Hellmuth stopped by at the beginning of the day to wish me luck. Everyone had seemed so sure that Phil and I would get into a smackdown confrontation at the TOC. But the real truth is that after playing that amazing final table together, we became incredibly close friends.

At one point, it looked as though my appearance at the final table was in jeopardy. With about sixteen players to go, I was sitting with a stack barely over 100,000. The chip leader, Kevin Saul, was at my table with almost one million. I just gutted it out by taking a few pots off weak players, and was able to double up twice just before the dinner break. At one point, I played the 7♦ 4♦ against two players and caught a flush on the river to move up to over 800,000.

When we got down to the last table of ten players, we still had to eliminate four more players before the day was done. At this point in a tournament, the big stacks sometimes will shift into cruise control on their way to the final table. But that wasn't happening. Everyone was mixing it up, which left a lot of room to pick up chips. I was looking for chips wherever I could find them. I ended up taking out Nam Le in eighth place when he pushed with A-9 and I woke up with A-K. A few hands later, Shane Schleger took out Gordon Eng in seventh place and we had our final table. Here's what it looked like:

> Kevin Saul: 4,200,000
> Mike Matusow: 1,800,000
> Shane Schleger: 1,800,000
> Danny Wong: 1,000,000
> Konstantin Puchkoy: 1,000,000
> Eracles Panayiyou: 600,000

This was the first WPT final table I'd made since they fixed the blind structure. For years, players had complained that the WPT final table structure was nothing but a crapshoot. You practically had to move in on every hand. There wasn't a hell of a lot of real poker being played on those early WPT shows. But when we started this final table, the blinds were only 12,000/24,000 with a 3,000 ante. Even the shortest stack had plenty of time to play. We were going to be playing some deep-stack poker—at least, that's what I thought.

Instead, everyone was playing like they had somewhere else to go. With that structure, we had a lot of time, but people were making crazy calls for more than half their stacks. I had played with Kevin Saul most of Day Three, and I knew that he could be reckless. He started the final table with a commanding lead, but after the first two levels he'd lost most of his chips and was down to about 1 million. The other four players gave Kevin plenty of opportunities to get right back in it. I wasn't sure what they were thinking. At one point Shane Schleger doubled him up on a hand that still confuses me. Kevin pushed all in on a flop of 8-7-4 with two diamonds and "Shaniac" called. Kevin showed down the J-10 of diamonds, which gave him a flush draw and a gutshot straight draw. Shaniac flipped over an A-10 offsuit.

Huh?

Kevin made his draw and doubled through Schleger.

By 11 p.m., it was down to me and Kevin Saul's rebuilt stack. He had the chip lead but it wasn't even close to 2 to 1, so we both knew what one double-up would mean. We had played a dozen hands when I called a preflop raise with the 8♣ 7♣. When the flop came with the 10♥ 6♣ 5♣, I pushed in with my open-ended straight flush draw. Kevin called with pocket queens. The turn and river didn't deliver a club or fill my straight draw.

I finished in second place and won about $650,000. I was disappointed because I had really wanted to win it. But after putting in a terrible World Series performance, I was happy with my game. I'd played well for four days. I had to overcome crappy cards and a short stack for most of the tournament. I would rather have seen a 4♣ on the river in that final hand, but in the end, the cards were the cards.

By the middle of 2007, it was clear to me that my game hadn't really lost its edge. Even without understanding the truth behind my online losses, I had regained my confidence and had brought my "A" game to the table. In some ways, 2007 was probably more important to me than 2005, even with those two million-dollar paydays. 2005 had let me move past my legal problems, but 2007 had allowed me to move forward personally. By the end of the year, I was playing at the top of my game.

But more than that, my life had finally turned in a very positive direction, both inside and outside of poker. I was getting to a place where poker wasn't there every moment of my life. I was enjoying my time away from the tables and a whole new attitude was just around the corner.

Chapter Twenty-Seven

A Series of Changes

For fifteen years, my life had been completely wrapped up with poker. It was the driving force behind everything in my world. I had sat hopelessly glued in front of a video poker machine until a guy taught me how to play Texas hold'em. When the day to day grind of cash game poker became overwhelming, I moved into the dealer's box. Getting backed in higher stakes games eventually freed me. In 1997, I played in my first World Series of Poker tournament and never looked back. Each step I took along the way to becoming a professional poker player had brought a big and positive change.

Everything in my life was measured in chips. Happiness was a winning streak, a killer read, or a come-from-behind tournament day that led to a final table. Sometimes it felt like my whole life was falling apart when the cards weren't running good. Fifteen years is a long time to live inside a deck of cards.

Over a period of about a year, I began to realize that I needed one more change. I needed more out of my life than just poker. So in 2008, I started working on my other game—my life outside of poker. I started trying to find ways to become a better, more complete, person. I still wanted poker to be a big part of my life, of course, and I wanted to bring the best game I had to the table every time I played.

But could I play my "A" game and have a life outside of poker? I wasn't sure, but I was ready to try.

I won't say I've found a lock on how to live my life, but I credit having a great 2008 Series to all the changes I have made. I can't say it was my all-time best World Series, but I rocked it pretty hard and enjoyed almost every minute of it. But before I get into how I won my third WSOP bracelet and made it deep into the main event, I should probably explain what I did to improve my outlook on life.

Most of my friends and family have heard me say that I hate tournament poker. I don't really, but there were times when I hated being out on the tournament circuit. What everyone says about the road is true: all the hotels and the casinos look, sound, and feel the same. The only time you actually remember a tournament room is if you get stuck in a tent or end up seated near a noisy nightclub. And it always ends up in one of two ways. The best thing that can happen is that you play one long grueling poker tournament. The worst thing is that you bust out early and pray there's an open seat on the next flight out.

It's easy to get caught up in a cycle of going from one tournament to the next and the next. You talk to the guys at your table, and they're all going to Foxwoods, Barcelona, Tunica, or wherever the next one is. Before you think it through, you've booked a flight to some place you'd rather not be when you get there. It's like a hamster wheel, it seems normal to keep running in circles. My solution to the endless tournament trail has simply been to cut back. If it takes too long to get there, I'm generally a no-show. If I know ahead of time that the structure sucks, or that it was poorly run in the past, I don't go.

I don't think people realize how much it costs to play a full tournament schedule. You can spend $500,000 a year in buy-ins and travel expenses, easy. That's a big nut to cover every single year. Take a look at players' tournament records: How many players actually make that much money each year? Then look at how many players enter the average $10,000 tournament and you tell me how many players are actually breaking even.

I'll give you the answer—not many. Tournaments are tough.

It's hard to get up for each and every tournament on the seemingly endless circuit. Maybe it's easier for the hungry young kids just starting out in tournament poker. But after they've been at it awhile, the tedious schedule starts to take its toll. I've seen players get sloppy or stay out all night drinking before a tournament. They figure if they bomb out of one tournament, there's always another one right around the corner. I always have to work up my drive for a tournament. But when I have something to prove, I can bring it all to the table. That's exactly what I did at the Bellagio Cup right after I busted out of the 2007 WSOP main event. I was pissed at how I had played and needed to prove I still had my game. That was my way of getting psyched up for a tournament.

At first, it wasn't easy cutting back on my tournament schedule. On the plus side, I found that when I did play, it was because I really wanted to be there. I liked the city, I liked the tournament structure, and I liked how the event was run. But having more of a life away from poker meant that I had to work harder on my drive to win when I did play. When things were going well in my life and I was content, I wasn't as hungry for the win. Sometimes I had just shown up, bought in, and then played like shit. I basically didn't give a fuck and was just happy to get back home and jump online.

But in 2008, I slowly learned that with a little discipline, I could have it both ways. When I was committed to play, I learned to bring my passion for poker to the tournament table. When I wasn't ready to play, I stayed home. My life used to depend on poker. Now poker is just one part of my life.

Another thing that had to change was my health. Ted Forrest was right, I'd put on a lot of weight. Some of it was because of my meds, but a lot of it was because I was eating fast food and not exercising. I wasn't in my twenties anymore. I guess that was one of the main reasons I made that weight loss prop bet with Ted during the 2007 Series. That and the fact that I often make really stupid bets.

For the bet, I had to lose sixty pounds by the first week of the '08 Series. I had to weigh 181 pounds or less by then to win $100,000 from Ted. I didn't take things too seriously at the start and actually had put on a few pounds by the end of 2007. But when 2008 rolled around I got down to business. With about four months to go before the bet was up, I had lost almost thirty pounds. I stopped living on junk food and started exercising regularly.

Those first thirty pounds just flew off. I started to feel great. But then I had emergency gall bladder surgery, which slowed me down for about three weeks. And about two weeks before the World Series began, my girlfriend and I took a weeklong cruise. They throw food at you on those ships, but I only gained three pounds the whole week by eating right and running eight miles a day. Once I was back home, though, I still had twelve pounds to go and only nine days to lose it.

I would have to work every single day to hit the weight. That meant I would have to miss a few days of the WSOP and at least three events I could have played. Even if I did get to my weight, I knew I'd be pretty weak. I offered to settle with Ted for $50,000, but he wanted to let it ride. I buckled down and exercised constantly, fasting the last five days. I made it all the way down to 179. I won the prop bet, but I was damn tired and not really ready to play my best poker. It took nearly a week for me to get my strength back, but I felt great with all that weight gone.

Another part of my new health plan was to get my medications under control. Late in 2007, my psychiatrist switched my ADHD medicine from Ritalin to Adderall. While Ritalin had worked for about four years, it was never really the right medicine for me. The "bad med" days were coming more frequently and I just couldn't play a long tournament without losing time—and chips—to those off days. I needed to find another solution.

When I first switched to Adderall, it was fantastic. I had all the focus I needed without the Ritalin side effects. But balancing meds is a constant process and changes are just part of the game. Before too long, I started having some side effects with Adderall. They weren't as severe, but having a bad med day in the middle of a tournament was still a concern. It was progress, though. I'm still working really hard with my psychiatrist to try different ADHD medicines. The fact that I've lost so much weight has helped with all my meds, not just the ADHD meds. Because I weigh less, I can take lower doses of everything, even my anti-depressants, which seems to be helping on the med balancing act. I'm happier, seem to have better focus, and don't spend as much time worrying about crashing in the middle of a tournament. But this is a part of my life that will always be changing. Balancing meds is a process, not an end game.

I also had to work on improving my online game. A lot of times I used to play online poker more like a video game. I don't think I'm alone with this particular problem. It's too easy to just click, click, click, without focusing. With online poker, you should be playing as tight as you would in a live game, but it's not easy to develop that discipline online.

The biggest handicap for me is not being able to see the other players. You can't see the way they move their hands when they bet. You can't give them the once over when you think they're bluffing. I see all those things at the tables, and I think I can spot weakness in a live game better than any human alive. Online, I don't see any of that. It completely takes me out of my normal game of being able to bluff and picking off bluffs. You can pick off some bluffs online, but you have to really concentrate. I've been working harder at that. People who play multi-tables online are not playing poker. They're just playing the cards. When you multi-table online, you miss the small things that people do. When you miss the small things, you miss big opportunities to steal and pick off bluffs.

Because I can't see the players, I tend to play more H.O.R.S.E. or Omaha high-low online. In those games, you can play pretty tight and wait for the nuts. Because most people are still so bad at those games, you can get paid off with the nuts over and over again. I love it when guys put thousands of dollars in an Omaha game with just a pair of aces. All you have to do is wait for strong wraps and nut-flush draws. It's a game of small edges and a lot of it boils down to 55-45 advantages. But if that's what you're getting your money in with, it'll only take a few unlucky hands to bust you. You can lose all day long as a 55 percent favorite. The sweet spot is closer to 70-30 or 65-35.

Another reason why I don't play many no-limit games online is because it seems to me that the high stakes games have pretty much dried up. Back in 2005 and 2006, you could find a lot of clueless players at some pretty high limits. There was a lot of money to be made at those tables. Now, if you're lucky, you might fund a soft $5/$10 game. But you don't find many players putting their chips in stupid in a high-stakes game.

Most of the changes I've made to my online game in the past year are adjustments for playing against fewer and better players. You can get your ass handed to you playing a game plan that used to work against a lot of weak players. The online game has changed and I have had to change with it. I play fewer and shorter sessions each week.

I'll keep the rest of my changes to myself, just in case we meet at the tables.

I've had to change my tournament game a lot over the last few years too to adjust to the changing times. I used to play far more aggressively when that type of play used to pay off. But as every player became aggressive, I started playing more like a "nit." I folded more hands and often laid down when players came over the top. I'm not alone. If you study the games of Phil Hellmuth, Daniel Negreanu or Phil Ivey from just a few years ago, it wouldn't help you play against them today. Their games are nothing like what they were when they first came up. When things change, you have to change.

Another reason why someone's game changes is money. A lot of pros have made a lot of money, either from a few big tournament wins or from some of their business deals. When you're sitting on a few million, it's sometimes hard to keep that drive to win. Phil Ivey is one of the best players out there. He played year after year with an unstoppable hunger, no matter how much money he had. But over the last few years, even Ivey had his fair share of tournaments when he played as though he didn't care. Don't get me wrong, when he turns it on, no one can beat him. But when you start playing golf for six figures a hole or making prop and sports bets in that range, it's hard to work up the fight for a $2,000 buy-in tournament.

Even Phil Hellmuth doesn't have a consistent drive for all tournaments. He's got a thousand business deals going inside and outside of poker. But because of his lead in the WSOP bracelet race, Phil is always ready for a Series event.

I was always friendly with Phil, but more as an acquaintance. Maybe we'd grab dinner together once in awhile. We'd play Chinese poker, we'd talk, or maybe we'd go out for a drink. But we developed more of a bond after the Tournament of Champions in '05. He noticed a big change in my game and he respected that. He was impressed that I'd been able to change my game so much.

One day Phil and I were talking about the TOC and the upcoming 2006 WSOP. At the time, Phil wasn't that happy with his game. He felt like he was struggling. During our conversation, I invited him to hang out in the jacuzzi at my home and talk strategy. We spent over an hour picking his game apart. One problem we talked about in particular was that players were coming back over the top of his raises like crazy, forcing him to lay down a lot more often against a big reraise. I told him that players did that because they knew he didn't like to play big pots.

"You need to trap people and limp more often," I suggested. "And sometimes you need to reraise with nothing if you think they're just playing on weakness."

He started doing that more often, changing up his game a lot, and really taking control of the pots he played. In a *Bluff* magazine article, Phil actually gives me credit for his successful run in the '06 World Series. I can't tell you how good that made me feel. But I guess that's my point. If you aren't changing your game, you're falling behind. Hellmuth had won 10 WSOP bracelets including the championship before we talked. But even with that track record, he knew he needed to change. If you're playing against the world's best players, sooner or later they'll get a stone cold read on you. If you don't adjust, they will eat you for lunch.

The tournament in which I won my first bracelet in '99 had a $3,500 buy-in, one of the biggest tournaments in the world at the time. In that first big tournament, I played tight and attacked situations to pick up chips. I did well playing power poker for a number of years. But now, everybody has learned those skills: Everybody knows how to attack weakness. These days, you've got to attack the players who are attacking weakness.

It's like rock-paper-scissors. You can play rock all day long against scissors. But there's no edge in rock if that's what everyone else starts playing. So I moved away from power poker and started playing more "finesse" poker. Finesse poker actually takes balls because what you're really doing is counterattacking aggressive players. But I'd have to say that most of the top pros—certainly Ivey, Negreanu, Hellmuth and I—have shifted to that style of play. A few of the newer kids can still play a game of winning power poker, but some of that is because nobody knows who they are yet. They'll be able to get away with it until they build a name for themselves or get some TV time. But once enough decent pros get a read on them, they'll have to change their game.

The pros who started playing before the poker boom have had a lot of experience changing their games. To some extent, we had to. We wouldn't still be here if we didn't. It will be interesting to see how successful the post-boomers are at changing their games. Every year, about a dozen or so kids break through at big tournaments. A handful of them survive to play great poker for a few years. I'm sure some of them will be playing great poker in ten years. But by then, poker will have changed again. The survivors will be the players who adapt to the changes. The players that don't adapt will find themselves in the real world looking for a real job. Survival in poker is all about change.

Although I was playing a pretty good game at the end of 2007, I really picked my play apart. I wanted to go into the 2008 WSOP as a different player. I wanted to confuse anybody who thought they had a read on me. In the end, the adjustments I made may seem small. But I knew that even small changes could make a big difference for me in 2008.

Of course, no change was going to help me if I didn't also change my attitude.

Chapter Twenty-Eight

WSOP: A New View

My attitude toward the World Series of Poker in 2007 was terrible. I hated the way it was being run and I just couldn't get past it. Going to the Rio that entire summer was almost painful. A few times, I had a better outlook and played well, but for most events, I was annoyed and home by dinner. On many days, I didn't even bother playing. In '07, I only played twelve events out of fifty-five, probably the fewest number of events played by any pro. Without a good attitude, I knew I'd be pissing away the entry fee. I had been obsessed with what I saw as negative changes in the World Series. I knew it couldn't be like the old days downtown at Binion's. But I didn't like some of the decisions that had been made and how some things were being run. But in the end, I couldn't let those things be my problems. The only problems I needed to have were the ones I could handle, the ones at the poker table.

I was too caught up in all the side crap. There would always be some level of corporate crap; that wasn't going to change. I asked Jeffery Pollack, the WSOP commissioner, to meet with me. For one thing, I wanted to apologize for some of the things I had said publicly about how the Series was being run. I also wanted to let him know that I was coming back in '08 with a new attitude, and that I wanted to support him and the Series in any way I could to help it move forward. As it turned out, I ran into Jeffery at McCarran Airport in Las Vegas, and we talked while waiting at baggage claim. He acknowledged that some of the things they had tried hadn't worked and seemed genuinely concerned about several of the problems I brought up. While I really appreciated everything that Jeffery said, the thing that made me the happiest was that I finally felt that I had made my peace with the Series.

The perfect place to test all my changes was the 2008 WSOP.

With two events going on nearly every day at the Series, you can get deep into the schedule pretty quickly. In 2008, I missed nearly the entire first week concentrating on my weight loss bet. On the tenth day of the Series, I finally felt that I had recovered my strength and decided to play the $5,000 No-limit Deuce-to-Seven Lowball tournament with rebuys. If history repeated itself, this event would have a small field, filled with professional players who would make lots of rebuys.

In 2008, eighty-five players entered and made a total of 272 rebuys. That's an average of three rebuys by each player, for a total average cost of $20,000 per player. I felt great playing those first two days. I was calm, focused, and I enjoyed being there. Since the tournament was loaded with top pros, no one was surprised to see a final table line-up like this: David Benyamine, Barry Greenstein, Erick Lindgren, Tony G, Jeff Lisandro, Tom Schneider and me.

Erick was chip leader when we started the final table with about a 2 to 1 chip lead over Barry, who was second in chips. I was just behind Barry in third place. It was a pretty fast-paced table and we were down to just four players in less than three hours. By that time, Erick still had a slim lead with about 1,300,000, but Barry and I were right on his heels with about 1 million each. Jeff was hanging tough as the short stack at about 330,000.

The action was brutal once it got down to four-handed. Chips were flying. The lead changed on almost every hand, and the play became even more aggressive. However, it would still take almost three hours for Erick Lindgren to go out in fourth place. In the toughest hand I played against Erick, I opened for 90,000 and he called. I stood pat and he drew one card. I checked and Erick bet out 140,000. I only had jack-low, but I really thought I had him beat.

As soon as I made the call, he rapped the table and said, "Good call" without showing his cards. I won another pot from Erick a few hands later.

In the last hand we played together, Jeff raised to 85,000 and I flat called. Erick pushed all in. Jeff got out of the way, and I thought long and hard. I was feeling a little tired at this point and was starting to lose my focus. I had thought about taking a pill, but it's always a mistake to take one on an empty stomach. Besides it was only another half an hour until the dinner break. I finally called. Erick had 7-6-3-2 and drew one card. I drew two cards with 8-7-4. I wasn't loving the hand at this point, but I felt a lot better once I flipped over 6-3. Erick slowly turned over another 2 to pair his hand. He went out in fourth place.

During the half hour before dinner, I struggled. On the last hand before the break, I bluffed away a quarter of a million chips to Jeff, giving him the lead with about 2 million chips. Barry had 1 million. I fell down to just 400,000. The dinner break saved me. When we got back, I was completely refocused. I was the short stack, but I was ready to play. Within about four hands, I had crawled back into second place.

Barry Greenstein is one of the best deuce-to-seven players in the world, so the good news for me was that Jeff and Barry got tied up in a couple hands where Jeff caught perfect. Barry busted out in third place, leaving Jeff and me to play heads-up for the bracelet. With the chips he lifted off Barry, Jeff had a pretty good lead on me. But even with the shorter stack, my strategy was to be the player applying all the pressure.

To start things off, I open shoved, pushed all-in on the very first hand and I was a little surprised when Jeff called. We both drew one card. I had a 9-6 low to his 10-8 low, but we both still needed a live card.

"Don't let me double up, baby," I said, half teasing. "It's all over if I double up."

I peeled off a 10 for my last card. While Jeff had an edge, he still needed to make a hand with his final card. He flipped over an 8 to pair his hand and double me up. I put the pedal to the metal and took down the next ten hands in a row. I had about a 6 to 1 chip advantage when I open shoved again on a hand and Jeff called. I debated a long time and finally decided to stay pat with only a queen-low. Jeff showed a 9-6-5-3 with one card to come. He almost squeezed blood from his last card—and finally exposed a queen. I edged out his Q-9 low with my Q-8 low.

I had won my third bracelet and $537,862!

It was such a great win for me, a complete win all the way around. I was feeling great physically, and for the first time in a couple of years, I was really happy about being at the World Series. I was completely overwhelmed when Jeffrey Pollack personally conducted my post-bracelet interview. For the last three hours of the final table, Jeffery had sat in the media row and watched us play. He later told me that he wasn't going to miss the chance to give me a bracelet, which really made me feel good.

Okay, change definitely didn't suck.

Just a week and a half later, I made my second final table, this time in the $10,000 Omaha high-low event, one of the tournaments I aim for at every Series. It's one of my best games and I was ready for it. The final table was loaded: David Benyamine, Toto Leonidas, Ram Vaswani, David Chiu, Eugene Katchalov. And me.

This was a three-day tournament, but the second day was so long, play had been stopped at 18 players. On the final day, we were going to have to play it out from eighteen instead of just nine. When it got down to ten players, we took a break while they reseated us all at the same table. While they did that, I grabbed the microphone and introduced all the players to the audience. I was just joking around, but I also wanted to make a point. I wanted all the players to realize that I knew them, which also probably meant that I had a good read on them. You have to use whatever you have to win these things!

Berry Johnston went out in tenth place, which gave us our official final table. Ram Vaswani and I were short-stacked with under 200,000 chips each and David Benyamine was the chip leader with over 1 million. I had a lot of work to do.

In the first hour of final-table play, I played some great Omaha high-low. I kept warning everyone not to let me double up. But did they listen?

I hit three big hands, pulling my stack up to 600,000 chips. Just before the dinner break, we lost Tony Ma in ninth place. Right after the dinner break, it looked like I might join him. First, Eugene nailed me with a bigger boat than mine. Then I got quartered in a three-way hand. That knocked my stack down to under 200,000, just about where I had started the day, but I was able to build back to over 400,000 at the expense of David Benyamine.

We had been playing eight-handed for three hours when we suddenly lost David Chiu, Ram Vaswani and Eugene Katchalov, all within half an hour. Unfortunately, I wasn't responsible for any of those bust outs, so I was the short stack when we got down to five players. I took a couple of quick hits and was down to 150,000.

Then I got all my chips in on a hand with two other players when the board delivered two queens. Benyamine showed a queen for trips and I was just about to muck my hand. I'm lucky I didn't, because I took one final look and realized I had rivered the nut flush with the K♦ 3♦ in my hand. I had found the winning hand. But almost mucking the winner knocked me off my game. I played the next hand badly, losing all my chips against Toto, who scooped the pot and sent me to the rail in fifth place.

Actually, I wasn't too disappointed. I'd been short-stacked all day long and had come back at least four or five times, winning $138,000 for my troubles. A little more than a week later, I had another minor cash, in the $1,500 H.O.R.S.E event. Again, I wasn't too disappointed with my performance. I never really had any traction and considered myself lucky to make it through to the money.

Each year when the main event rolls around at the World Series, every professional poker player thinks one of two things: "This is my year!" or "There's no chance in hell I'm gonna win this thing." I'm usually in the second group. With fields of six or seven thousand players, you have to be an idiot to think you have a shot at making it to the final nine, much less winning it.

I had made three good runs in the last seven main events, making the final table in both 2001 and 2005. And if I had gotten past Greg Raymer in 2004, I had a shot at that one too. But I'm pretty realistic about the big tournaments. Making it to one main event final table is phenomenal; I've made it twice and I realize I might not see another one in my lifetime. I may never get to play a day four or five again, the tournament is that big and that hard.

On Day One in 2008, I was assigned to a table that wasn't going to break until very late in the day. Over 1,800 players started on my Day One; over 1,200 of them busted out by day's end. In all that time, only three players busted out at our table. It was probably one of the tightest tables I've ever played. With only three fresh stacks coming in to replace the broke players, everyone at our table was hurting for chips. The unbelievably strange thing was that it only got worse over the next few days. Not only were my tables tight, each day I was facing better and better players wherever I sat. No one was giving their chips away. The few times someone tilted off their chips at my table, I was out of the hand. All around me I could hear dealers calling out "All in and call!" to alert the ESPN camera crews of a potential bust-out. But my dealers barely made a sound. My table was locked down tight.

I can't say it was the best poker I've ever played but it was the most patient I'd ever been. I had to be patient: There were just no spots to steal chips and no weak players to get them from. While it was torture at some points, I just kept playing the game I had to play. Of the 6,844 players who entered the main event, only 474 remained by the end of Day Three. And I was in ninety-fifth place with 438,500 chips. On Day Four we lost another 300 players, but I got zero action the whole day. My stack had barely inched up to 458,000. But I just kept doing what I knew had to be done. My attitude was good. Even ESPN kept commenting on my "new power of positive thinking."

Not until Day Five did I get any action. I played at the ESPN feature table that entire day and managed to more than double my stack to 1.1 million. The good news was that I made it into Day Six with only seventy-nine players left. The bad news was that all of those incredibly tight tables had given me so few spots to play that my 1.1 million put me in fiftieth place.

But still, I was there with a shot at another main event final table.

ESPN and Harrah's always hope that the championship final table will have at least one big poker name. When Day Six started, they were happy to see that Phil Hellmuth and I were still in the hunt. Their hope for us didn't last too long, however, as Phil busted out in forty-fifth place. I played the best I could, trying to survive the day. I may have made one bad read when my pocket jacks got run down by a set of eights, but I didn't lose my whole stack. I was ready to double up later on a hand when I had A-J on a flop of A-A-5. My opponent and I both checked. I put him on a weaker ace. All my money went in on the turn when a 9 hit. Only then did I discover that his weak ace was an A-9. He made a boat, beating my set and ending my 2008 run in thirtieth place.

I know it's sort of crazy to be disappointed in beating out 6,814 players in a 6,844 player tournament. But as Doyle Brunson has said, "The worst day of the year is the day you get knocked out of the main event."

I had made my fourth deep run in the main event in eight years. That's a record few people can boast. Still it's been very hard on me to keep coming up short so close to the end. It was painful to play six long patient days, only to get taken out by a three-outer. I was happy to win the $193,000 I got for finishing in thirtieth place, but for poker players, the main event is never really about the money.

Chapter Twenty-Nine

Now I Know

Way back at the beginning when I was living in my trailer and working in my parents' store, there were a lot of things about myself I didn't know. I had no idea what bipolar disorder was or that I might be in the earlier stages of it. And I didn't know that people played poker in casinos and some actually made a living at it. Of course, no one had any idea that tournament poker would explode like it has. I didn't know why I was such a loner or why I got so depressed for what seemed like no reason at all. I knew nothing about how street drugs could change the dark way I looked at life and I had no clue that there were prescription medications to help me with my problems.

Today, I know a lot more about myself, both the good and the bad. I also know that a lot of people aren't going to believe or pay any attention to my story. There are also some people, my fans, who don't care what I have done wrong. They care about me because of who I am. I hope I can live up to that kind of forgiveness. I also hope that I have given those other people some evidence that I really am not the bad guy they thought I was.

I feel it is important to talk about my problems because I know there are millions of people who have struggled with the same problems themselves or with family members.

For everyone who thinks I'm still on drugs, I am. I take four or five medications prescribed by my psychiatrist to control my bipolar disorder and ADHD. What I take and the amounts I take have changed over the years. Finding the right combinations of drugs that control my symptoms and don't drive me crazy with side effects has been challenging. Some of these medications have serious life threatening side effects, which I've been lucky to avoid so far. And almost all of them have some other really annoying little daily side effects that I have just learned to live with.

There have been times over the years when I've played a major tournament in sheer terror, not knowing whether I could find a way to survive, let alone play poker. Unfortunately, depression is a side effect of the medications that help with ADHD, making my depression a much bigger problem and more difficult to control with meds. So, I take some of my drugs just to counteract the side effects of other drugs.

It's a tough balancing act, which doesn't always work.

Balance is especially hard to find because of what I do for a living. It's tough to play poker, probably tough to do any job, when you're unhappy and tired all the time. The meds have helped with my chronic depression, the long periods of debilitating sadness I used to have. And while the meds have made my bouts of extreme suicidal depression fewer and shorter, they haven't made them go away entirely.

I also have trouble sleeping, a less extreme problem, but one that's hard to deal with during longer tournaments. The World Series of Poker main event lasts two weeks; each day of play can be twelve hours long. In 2008, I played five days straight and had to take a sleeping pill every night. I was drowsy in the morning and needed to take even more drugs when I woke up to find my focus for the tournament. I work especially closely with my doctor during long tournaments, but it's still a little like trying to keep the drug rollercoaster from flying off the tracks. It's ugly sometimes, but that's what it takes.

Another place where my poker and bipolar symptoms don't mix well is regulating my emotions. Poker has a lot of ups and downs, but you can't let yourself get emotional whiplash with each hand you win or lose. Unfortunately, sometimes the bipolar chemicals in my brain kick in and I lose my control—or at the least, controlling my emotions becomes very difficult. The media has come to call these moments, "Matusow Meltdowns." I am a naturally emotional guy, which accounts for some of those incidents, but there are other times when I simply have no control over what comes out of my mouth. And sometimes the cameras are there to catch every little detail.

I've come to accept that my bipolar symptoms will always be with me, in one form or another. The meds aren't perfect, but they help. Just having a better understanding of how the disorder affects me helps me cope better on and off the tables. Knowing what is going on, even if I can't control it, makes the confusion and depression a little easier to deal with.

It's really not the bipolar symptoms, but the ADHD that can kill me at the poker table. If there is a funny side to my ADHD, it's that one of the most common symptoms is excessive talking. I mean, how could you even fucking tell in my case?

Well, actually you can tell. Or at least I can. I know that I can talk some nonsense, but sometimes totally unrelated shit comes out of my mouth and I barely know what I'm saying. And that goes double for what I type during online poker games. Of course, some of that is because I can't type for shit, but a lot of it is because my head is in too many places at once. It's like my brain is hitting random play and my mouth doesn't know what's coming out next. If you've ever been a victim of my brain running wild, I apologize.

I also can tick people off because they think I'm ignoring them or not listening to them. I'm just easily distracted, that's all. When I began dealing, I could listen to three or four conversations at the table, participate in all of them, and still keep the game moving. These days, it's hard for me to follow a conversation with more than one person. Either I get totally derailed and forget what I was going to say, or I block out all the other voices and keep talking. If a player comes by my table and talks to me, I completely forget anything I was saying before he or she got there.

Most of my close friends have adjusted to these quirks and know not to get offended by them. They understand that I have a fairly damaged brain. But at the tables, it sometimes makes me seem like an ass. I know, I've seen the televisions tapes. Believe me, I'm really not trying to be rude. I'm just working with the best signals I get from my brain, and they don't always come through as clearly as they do for most other people.

But ADHD causes me bigger problems than just spewing verbal crap or not being able to follow a conversation. It's hard to focus or pay attention with ADHD, which probably are the most important skills for a successful poker player to possess. You have to watch the action and remember how your opponents play. Making correct reads is critical in high-level poker, and I have a disorder that interferes with doing that. Also, my short-term memory is shot. ADHD is probably one of the worst diseases a poker player can suffer from. It's my biggest nightmare.

The meds help, but not consistently. I have good days and bad. I've learned to do a few things to help me get through the bad days, but sometimes nothing works. Some days I just can't play poker at the level required to compete in a major poker tournament. I sometimes become really frustrated, which can trigger one of my famous meltdowns.

I have to wear warm socks when I play online poker because one of the meds makes my feet cold and clammy. One drug made my skin itch all the time. And another drug makes me bark like a dog. I'm not kidding. I have a mild form of Tourette's Syndrome caused by the meds. When I get tired, I start to yip like a fucking dog. I barely know I'm doing it, but it totally freaks out the people around me. Still, most of the side effects are nothing compared to the symptoms I would have if I didn't take the meds. Believe me, the tradeoffs are worth it.

There are several kinds of bipolar disorder; the kind I have is mostly about depression with some periods of manic outbursts. Manic, for those who don't know, is happy, loud, over-the-top behavior. I know that's the side of me that television loves to capture, but my version of bipolar is more about the depression. Thankfully, the depression mostly happens in private, at home and away from the cameras. Most of my manic swings are pretty well controlled by my meds. The manic effects I usually get come in the form of short bursts of energy like the kind you sometimes see at the tables. I talk even more or sing loudly to the fans on the rail. Or I might do something like try to tackle Mr. Peanut, the Planters mascot, like I did during the 2007 World Series of Poker. For the record, if I had been in the shape I'm in now, I could have taken that oversized nut.

But if you're playing against me when I'm in my manic phase, don't think for a minute that it's a good time to take advantage of me. As a professional player, I've learned to use even my mania to my benefit. When I'm singing at the table, I'm aware of the effect that behavior might be having on other players. Sometimes I'm having manic rushes and other times I'm calculating exactly what some over-the-top behavior might do to a player who is just about to tilt off all his chips. You gotta go with what you naturally have at the poker table and I have bipolar disorder. I guess the bottom line is that the "up" side of bipolar has never been a big problem for me; it can work for me at the poker table.

I genuinely like people and I enjoy talking with them. Of course, some of that talking and joking around is just good poker strategy. If I talk and joke with a player, he might eventually let down his guard. Or I can totally annoy the shit out of a player with my singing and taunting until he goes on tilt and makes a bad play. Talking either makes players comfortable or uncomfortable—both ways work to my advantage. It's not just me and the other nut jobs in poker that talk at the table. Daniel Negreanu talks a lot more than I do. He mostly does it to get a better read on his opponents. He'll guess at someone's hand or make a comment about their play just to get a reaction. He'll joke and smile and sooner or later, he gets exactly what he wants.

Some players are less friendly about it. They glare or just get downright nasty. They're looking for information too, but they're also trying to push their opponents into making a mistake. They know that some players will play too weak when faced with a bully while others will get all riled up and play back at them too aggressively. There are lots of ways to use odd behavior to get what you want at the poker table. I happen to be a talker, that's who I am. At the table, I talk and other players listen and some talk back. I'm just being me, but it's also about playing a complete game of poker and using all my skills. So I am not going to change a lot at the poker table. Actually, I am getting better and better at using my problems to my benefit when I am playing.

Away from the poker tournaments is where my life has really changed. When you have a positive outlook, you really appreciate it when good things happen. When bad things happen, you handle them better and you recover faster. I worked on eliminating all the bad things in my life: losing weight, getting over my negative attitude about the Series, reducing the side effects from my medications, and working on the weaknesses in my game. The power of positive thinking is just such a simple idea but it works for me. You know, though, maybe it's not so much about the power of positive thinking. Maybe it's always been about how I allowed negative thinking to fuck up my life. When you think bad shit is going to happen to you, it does. When you're negative and dark about everything, you focus on every bad thing that comes along and miss out on some really cool things in life. I've learned that to find happiness, I need to expect happiness.

I spent a lot of my life believing that a great run of cards or a spectacular tournament win was all that I needed to keep my life on track. I didn't realize that if I worked on my life outside of poker, poker wouldn't have to be the only place I could turn to for happiness. Poker actually could be just a part of my life, not my entire life. I see that now, and my life is totally different as the result.

Today, I am a new Mike, a better Mike, a changing Mike. Things are going well for me. I'm happy. I enjoy my life away from the tables. I'm also playing some great poker. Maybe I'll even get back to another World Series of Poker final table before I stop playing poker—a game that has been very, very good to me.

Glossary

Attention Deficit Hyperactivity Disorder: ADHD stands for Attention Deficit Hyperactivity Disorder. ADHD is a medical condition that is characterized by hyperactivity, an inability to concentrate and focus, and poor short-term memory. People with ADHD have chemical and/or physiological differences in the portions of their brains that control attention and activity levels. This often means that they may have trouble focusing on certain tasks, or they may seem hyper, wired or manic. Some of the common symptoms of ADHD are:

- difficulty paying attention or staying focused on a task or activity

- excessive talking and trouble engaging in activities quietly

- inability to pay attention to details or a tendency to make careless errors

- fidgeting, squirming, or a difficulty staying seated

- restlessness, nervous energy

- blurting out rude or insulting remarks, or speaking without thinking.

- difficulty sustaining effort over long periods of time

- low tolerance for frustration and stress

- trouble remembering things, even for a short time

- acting impulsively without regard for consequences

Benny's Bullpen: The famous Binion's Horseshoe has a separate tournament area on the second floor, which was used exclusively for big tournaments, including the World Series of Poker. It was named after the casino's founder, Benny Binion.

Binion's Horseshoe: In 1970, the World Series of Poker began at Binion's Horseshoe Gambling Hall & Hotel in downtown Las Vegas. Binion's was owned by the legendary Benny Binion who, inspired by Tom Moore's poker tournaments in Reno, gave vision to the World Series of Poker. For many years in the 70s, 80s and early 90s, the biggest cash games in Las Vegas were played at the Horseshoe. When Benny passed away in 1989, Binion's was taken over by his son Jack, who later sold his stake in the casino to his sister Becky Behnen in 1998. The famous poker room remains an icon to many poker players who still play there when they are in Las Vegas. The World Series of Poker trademark was purchased by Harrah's Entertainment in 2004; the last WSOP final table was played at Binion's in 2005.

Bipolar Disorder: Formerly called manic depression, bipolar disorder is a category of mood disorders. It is a psychiatric illness that causes major disruptions in lifestyle and health. While everyone has occasional emotional highs and lows within a somewhat normal range, people with bipolar disorder have extreme mood swings. They can go from feeling very sad, despairing, helpless, worthless, and hopeless (depression), to feeling as if they are on top of the world, hyperactive, creative, and grandiose (mania). This disorder is called bipolar because a sufferer's mood alternates between two completely opposite poles—euphoric happiness and extreme sadness.

When a person is in the grip of this disease, chaos can occur. Bipolar disorder can cause major disruption of family and finances, loss of job, and marital problems and is also associated with a high risk of suicide. Many people with bipolar disorder turn to drugs and alcohol to "self-treat" their emotional disorder, resulting in substance abuse and dependence.

Bipolar disorder may not be properly diagnosed until the sufferer is 25-40 years old, at which time the pattern of symptoms may become clearer. There are a number of sub-categories within the bipolar disorder diagnosis that differ according to specific symptoms and the degree or manifestation of those symptoms. About six million people in the United States have the disorder. Bipolar disorder is a long-term illness that will require proper management for the duration of a person's life.

Bluff: To bet aggressively with an inferior hand, one unlikely to win if called, to cause opponents to fold better hands, thus making the bluffer a winner by default.

Box: The "Box" refers to the area where the dealer sits, and includes the bank, cards and other implements a dealer uses to run the game. Dealers refer to their shifts as "being in the box."

Broadway Straight: An ace-high straight of mixed suits: A-K-Q-J-10

Chip Reese: David "Chip" Reese was universally acknowledged as one of the best cash game players in the world. He was also known within the poker community for being one of the truly "good" guys. Chip bailed many players out of a variety of scraps. His untimely death in 2007 at fifty-six stunned the poker world. The $50,000 H.O.R.S.E. Championship at the World Series of Poker now awards the Chip Reese Trophy. Chip won the inaugural event in 2007, just a few months before this death.

Collusion: Any attempt by players to cooperate in a hand to gain an advantage or cheat the other players.

Come Over the Top: To raise and, in particular, to reraise a player.

Cooler: A hand that not only costs you the win, but has such long odds that your entire "hot streak" is ended. You are "cooled off."

Crystal Meth: Methamphetamine is an addictive stimulant, which initially can enhance alertness, pleasure, sex and the ability to concentrate. As with many street drugs, over time, the effects decrease and users find that they need to take higher doses to get the same results.

Deals: Agreements between final-table participants are common in poker, driven by the steepness of the payout structure and the uncertainty associated with the final result. The large disparity between the money awarded to the first place and subsequent finishers serves to motivate players to lock up a more equitable distribution prior to the event's conclusion. Few daily tournaments held in local cardrooms are played out until the end; most are suspended after the last few players make a deal to split up the prize pool. Major tournaments that allow deal making have the stipulation that, regardless of the deal, players still must play out the tournament for the bracelet or trophy. Today a number of major tournaments have banned deal making at final tables, believing that deals may affect final table play.

Deuce-to-Seven Lowball: A poker variation in which the lowest and best card is a deuce, and the highest, and therefore worst, is an ace. Flushes and straights count against the player, so the best hand is 2-3-4-5-7 of mixed suits.

Doubling Up: To double one's bankroll on a single hand, by being all-in against another player and winning the showdown.

Ecstasy: Also called MDMA (3,4-methylenedioxy-N-methamphetamine)—though most commonly called Ecstasy—this street drug's effects are often described as producing euphoria and a sense of intimacy with others.

Fish: A weak player who tends to lose to the stronger players and is therefore always welcome at a poker table.

Flop: In hold'em and Omaha, the three community cards that are simultaneously dealt face up upon completion of the first round of betting and can be used by all active players.

Fold: Get rid of one's cards, thereby becoming inactive in the current hand and ineligible to play for the pot.

Freeroll: A tournament where players do not pay an entry fee and the prize money is put up by the house or host. Players generally qualify for a freeroll by playing a certain number of hours in a casino cardroom or as a reward for winning other smaller tournaments.

Gutshot Straight Draw: A straight draw consisting of four cards with one "hole," such that only one rank can complete the hand; for example, 2-4-5-6, in which only a 3 can complete the straight.

H.O.R.S.E.: A game with rounds rotating among five variations: limit hold'em, Omaha 8-or-better, razz, seven-card stud high, and seven-card stud 8-or-better. Typically each variation lasts for one round of cards; sometimes, for a specified time limit.

Laydown: The act of folding, often implying folding a good hand in the face of pressure.

Leak: A weakness or "hole" in a player's game. Often an activity away from the poker tables that drains one's bankroll, such as craps or sports betting.

Limit: The terms "limit" refers to the amount a player may bet during each round in a game of poker. The various games referred to in this book ($1/$4/$8/$8, $20/$40 etc.) are betting limits. In Texas hold'em there are four rounds of betting: 1) after the players' cards are dealt; 2) after the three card flop; 3) after the turn card; and 4) after the final river card. In a $20/$40 game, the betting in the first two rounds would be limited to $20 per bet or raise, and in the final two rounds, $40 per bet or raise. In most limit games the total number of bets and raises in each round is also limited. The standard rule is a bet and four raises per round. So in a $20 round, there could be an initial bet of $20 and four raises of $20 each, to make the betting limit per player for that round $100. Today, since the poker boom, the biggest games are no-limit games—there is no maximum limit to the amount of chips a player can bet during any of the betting rounds and a player can bet any or all of his or her chips.

Muck: To fold. Also, the place on the table where discarded cards are placed.

No-Limit: Betting structure in which the maximum bet allowed is limited only by the amount of chips the bettor has on the table.

Nuts: The best possible hand given the cards on board.

Omaha: A high poker game featuring four starting downcards, a flop of three shared community cards, a fourth community card called the turn, and then a fifth or river card, with four betting rounds. At the showdown, the final hand must consist of two cards from the player's hand—no more, no less—and three cards from the board (as opposed to hold'em in which any five cards can be used). The best five-card hand wins the pot.

Omaha High-low: A variation of Omaha played with a requirement that the best low hand must have five unpaired cards of 8 or lower to win the low half of the pot or else the best high hand will win the entire pot.

Outkicked: Where a higher unpaired card determines the winning hand. Player A with K-K-Q-Q-9 loses to Player B who holds K-K-Q-Q-A. Each player has two pair kings and queens but the ace outkicks the 9.

Pocket Pair: When a player's two hole cards are the same value, making a "pocket" pair, such as pocket aces or pocket sevens.

Position: A player's relative order of acting compared to opponents, particularly with respect to the number of players acting after his turn. Specifically, good position, that is later and better than opponents.

Pot Odds: The amount of money in the pot compared to the cost of a bet. For example if $50 is in the pot, and a player needs to call a bet of $10 to play, he is getting pot odds of 5 to 1.

Prop Bet: A wager made by poker players on a particular event occurring during a game, one that has no relation to poker skills. For example, in hold'em, players may make a proposition bet that three suited cards come on the flop. Also, any side bet whether it has to do with the poker game or not.

River: In hold'em and Omaha, the fifth and last community card dealt or its betting round (or both considered together). Also, fifth street.

Serotonin Receptors: In the central nervous system, serotonin plays an important role as a neurotransmitter in the modulation of body temperature, mood, sleep, sexuality and metabolism. In the human brain, a serotonin receptor regulates the intake of serotonin. When a person has fewer or damaged receptors, he may have trouble regulating these various functions.

Set: When a player's hole cards are a pair and another card of the same value falls on the board to give him a three-of-a-kind hand.

Single-Table Satellites: Mini-tournaments that are held at most large tournaments. Players play what amounts to a one-table tournament with the buy-in being a fraction of a bigger tournament and designed such that a player can win an amount sufficient to enter into that event. Satellites at most major tournaments do not pay out in cash, but instead give the winner a "lammer" or token chip. These chips can be used to buy into any of the tournament events. Chips are generic;

chips won in an Omaha satellite can be used for any tournament event, not just an Omaha event.

Small Ball: A tournament strategy where a player attempts to keep the pots small with drawing hands, while avoiding big pots unless playing the nuts or near-nut hands. A powerful strategy when executed by a skilled player.

Split Games: Another term for high-low games, where the pot is split between the highest and the lowest hands.

Stud: A poker variation in which some of the cards in each player's hand are dealt face up and some face down. For example, seven-card stud (three downcards, four upcards) and five-card stud (one downcard, four upcards).

Tell: An inadvertent mannerism or reaction that reveals information about the strength of a player's hand.

Texas Hold'em: A high poker game featuring two starting down or hole cards, a flop of three shared community cards, a fourth community card called the turn, and then a fifth or river card, with four betting rounds. At the showdown, any combination of the best five out of the seven available cards wins the pot.

Tilt: A player who has lost control of his emotions due to a bad loss or succession of losses and is playing recklessly; that player is considered to be "on tilt." The term is borrowed from what happens to a pinball machine when it is shaken too violently and no longer operates properly.

Turn: The fourth community card in Omaha and Texas hold'em. Also fourth street. Also, the point at which it is a player's turn to act, deal, or receive cards in a game.pots unless playing the nuts or near-nut hands. A powerful strategy when executed by a skilled player.

About Amy Calistri

Amy Calistri is a writer and editor, living in Austin, Texas. She has covered poker and the gambling industry since 2004 and has been a contributing writer for a number of poker media outlets including *Bluff* magazine and PokerNews.com. Amy is also published in the areas of investment and economics and is the author of the popular blog, AimlesslyChasing.com.

About Tim Lavalli

Dr. Tim Lavalli holds a Ph.D. in Psychology and is the author of the popular column, "The Poker Shrink." He lives in Las Vegas and writes on a wide range of poker topics—including major tournaments, news, and poker room reviews—for a number of print and online clients. He appeared in the 2006 WSOP documentary *House of Cards* in his role as the Poker Shrink.

About Mike Matusow

Mike "The Mouth" Matusow, one of the top professional poker players in the world—and the most compelling—is a favorite among the millions of television viewers who have come to count on his outrageously candid comments, emotional outbursts, and constant taunts that affirm the aptness of his nickname and make for great television theatre. He has over $7 million in tournament earnings, made an amazing 13 final tables at the World Series of Poker (WSOP), including two final tables in the main championship event. He has also won three coveted gold bracelets at the WSOP and the prestigious 2005 Tournament of Champions.

Mike readily admits to having both bipolar disorder and attention deficit hyperactivity disorder. He went through several years of street drug use in the vain attempt to self medicate these problems and eventually landed in jail when he was caught-up in an undercover narcotics sting.